The Market-Driven Supply Chain

The Market-Driven Supply Chain

A Revolutionary Model for Sales and Operations
Planning in the New On-Demand Economy

Robert P. Burrows III

AMACOM

American Management Association

New York • Atlanta • Brussels • Buenos Aires • Chicago • London • Mexico City
San Francisco • Shanghai • Tokyo • Toronto • Washington, D.C.

Bulk discounts available. For details visit:
www.amacombooks.org/go/specialsales
Or contact special sales:
Phone: 800-250-5308
E-mail: specialsls@amanet.org
View all the AMACOM titles at www.amacombooks.org

This publication is designed to provide accurate and authoritative information in regard to the subject matter covered. It is sold with the understanding that the publisher is not engaged in rendering legal, accounting, or other professional service. If legal advice or other expert assistance is required, the services of a competent professional person should be sought.

Library of Congress Cataloging-in-Publication Data

Burrows, Robert P. (Robert Penn)
   The market-driven supply chain : a revolutionary model for sales and operations planning in the new on-demand economy / Robert P. Burrows III.
      p.   cm.
   Includes index.
   ISBN 978-0-8144-3163-4 — ISBN 0-8144-3163-1   1. Business logistics.
2. Production planning.   3. Customer relations.   I. Title.

   HD38.5.B87   2012
   658.5—dc23

                                                              2012021291

About AMA

American Management Association (www.amanet.org) is a world leader in talent development, advancing the skills of individuals to drive business success. Our mission is to support the goals of individuals and organizations through a complete range of products and services, including classroom and virtual seminars, webcasts, webinars, podcasts, conferences, corporate and government solutions, business books and research. AMA's approach to improving performance combines experiential learning—learning through doing—with opportunities for ongoing professional growth at every step of one's career journey.

Printing number
10 9 8 7 6 5 4 3 2 1

Contents

PART II: CHANGING BEHAVIOR

Chapter 3: Managing by Analytics   91

Chapter 4: Establishing a Customer-Centric Culture   127

PART III: DESIGNING NEW PROCESSES

Chapter 5: Designing and Implementing Collaborative Planning (Segment-Level S&OP)   165

Foreword

Gregory P. Hackett

I HAVE KNOWN Bob Burrows for more than 30 years, from when we both were consultants in the Cleveland-based operations practice of Booz Allen & Hamilton, now known as Booz & Co. I was the junior guy on many manufacturing operations teams that he led. When I first met Bob, he was working closely with Keith Oliver, a senior partner, and their project team coined the phrase *supply chain management*. At that point, supply chain management was very much operations-focused, employing new technologies and tools to manage and reduce inventory.

The big problem with supply chain management is that while it produced results, it never fully achieved its promise. The fact is we could never properly forecast demand. I remember many conversations with Bob in the mid-1980s about how the new technologies of manufacturing were only as good as the forecasts. The projections of customers and of the customers' customers were needed.

While others went on to refine supply chain management tools and approaches, Bob shifted gears and began to work on the front end of the supply chain, which really starts with the customers' customers, as you will discover in this book. Over the years at Booz Allen, I saw Bob's work evolve from being manufacturing-centric to being customer-centric. As he worked with more and more clients, he built and constructed new ideas on how to change a company's behavior toward the customer by employing different analytical tools, value segmentation, simulation models, and customer-centric behavior. Bob broke the code: He figured out how to get the missing pieces to forecast demand.

Then Bob moved on from consulting into leadership roles at Figgie International Inc., where he became president of a very customer-demanding division, Rawlings Sporting Goods. As we continued to work together, I got the chance to see him putting customer centricity fully into play. While competitors were bringing supply chain approaches to widely fluctuating demand, Bob worked really closely with customers to understand what the customers' customers needed. Bob's new ideas came to fruition as he restructured the organization to get in tune with customers as well as changing management approaches, the culture, attitudes, and behavior. His concepts of customer-centric sales and operations planning were really put into practice. It was a live test bed; he could implement his whole thinking and was responsible for the results. He was doubly incentivized to get it to work—and it did, remarkably well, as you will learn through reading this book.

When Bob returned to the consulting world with The On-Point Group, he took those experiences, successes, and bruises and refined, rebuilt, and retooled his approach to market-savvy sales and operations planning (S&OP). He believes that the root of supply chain management sits at the front end and that the organization's approach can be modified to create competitive advantage in product and service strategy.

During the past ten years, I've seen Bob take this approach to myriad industries to help companies generate competitive advantage by enhancing their market share, better serving their customers, lowering costs to operate, decreasing inventories, and liberating cash flow. All of these are required of a successful company in the new demand economy. Read on!

Gregory P. Hackett is the founder of The Hackett Group, the premier business benchmarking company.

Foreword

Lora Cecere

SALES AND OPERATIONS PLANNING PROCESSES are 30 years old, yet no two processes are alike. The processes are individualized by company and have often not kept up with current process thinking. In this book, Robert Burrows shares his insights through work with companies on how to make the S&OP processes "market-savvy." By following Bob's approach, companies can design an S&OP process that moves to the drumbeat of the market in a way that can deliver superior balance sheet results.

The results that Bob talks about in this book do not come easily. They require leadership and significant change management efforts. His case studies are excellent examples of leadership in action.

One of the elements of Bob's techniques to implement a market-savvy S&OP approach for our joint clients that has been particularly successful is the use of an experiential game called S&OPOLY. Through this experiential activity, companies learn the value firsthand of forecast bias and error, the principles of supply chain strategy, the requirements of financial integration, and the fallacies of a *one-number plan*.

While many practitioners talk about S&OP excellence, Bob brings it to life in his writing. If only all companies could be market-savvy in their S&OP processes.

Lora Cecere is the founder of Supply Chain Insights LLC and formerly lead S&OP analyst with AMR Research.

Acknowledgments

KENNETH FLETCHER of Goodyear has been a great sounding board as we have traveled around the world doing audits and helping each profit center become Class A S&OP process leaders.

Beth Brumbaugh of bbrumbaugh@mergershop.com was the detail person. Beth edited each page down to the word prior to my sending chapters to the publisher for their review and edit. Beth's considerable experience in business and in consulting gave her the content insights necessary for a full edit of ideas as well as grammar and spelling.

My wife, Susan, is the most important of all. She helped with each chapter outline, listened to my countless struggles with content alternatives, and patiently pulled me back on track when the discouragements set in. All those 5 AM work sessions, vacation days spent writing, and weekends away from our horses were made easier when she provided coffee and toast. We have been married 44 years, and I would certainly pray for another 44, at least here, and then we can be together for eternity.

The Market-Driven
Supply Chain

Introduction

WE ARE IN THE MIDST of a profound shift in the ways of commerce: The economic engines of supply and demand have traded places. The business of buying is shifting from a centuries-old supply-driven model and moving rapidly to a market-driven, customer-centric one. Customers are dictating what they purchase, insisting upon specialized products for unique situations and tastes. Product-line complexity is getting broader, and demand variability per product is growing higher by orders of magnitude. Seemingly excessive service levels and response times are becoming the norm.

While sales and operations planning (S&OP) traditionally has been an important operations management process, its design has remained essentially unchanged for more than 40 years. It customarily has been internally focused, with a one-size-fits-all-customers mindset. Today, however, S&OP is being whipped by strong, unrecognized market forces that are increasing inventory and lowering manufacturing and distribution productivity. The forces that drive our economic engines are rapidly changing in the United States and

Europe and will spread to all other markets as those markets mature. In today's on-demand economy, demand has come to dominate supply as the driving force. This new circumstance is why the traditional, 40-year-old approach is failing.

We have implemented the new market-driven supply chain processes using advanced S&OP in many good companies. In most cases, the share price increases by three to nine times over the course of the few years required for full implementation and realization of benefits. The company's value increases because of the process and increased cash flow, not because of some information technology (IT) system. The market-driven supply chain delivers customer value, defines and delivers competitive advantage, and generates free cash flow. All three of these deliverables are not even considered in operations-driven S&OP or demand-driven supply chains.

Studies done by AMR Research, now part of Gartner Group, have found that more than 70 percent of companies are stuck in entry-level S&OP processes, reacting or responding to the winds of change in the market. Traditional approaches are operating two or more steps removed from the market. In order to not only survive but thrive in the new on-demand economy, you must learn how to implement an S&OP process built on market savvy and operating "at the market." *The Market-Driven Supply Chain* will show you how your business can accomplish this.

A revolutionary transformation in business management processes is required to deal with the profound changes emerging and expanding in the world economies. Today, the economy of business has a whole new set of dimensions, as shown in Figure I-1. The figure outlines how an enterprise views the overall planning process, given a supply versus a demand view of the economy.

The supply chains of the future must become *market-driven* rather than operations-driven or even demand-driven. As we describe in Chapter 1, the market-driven supply chain uses a Level IV, or advanced, S&OP. In the market-driven supply chain, the customer's definition of value is the paramount concern. In contrast, in demand-

	Supply Economy	Demand Economy
Market segments	Homogeneous	Specialized
Change rate	Supply-constrained	Exponential
Products	Rationalized on cost	Complexity-enabled
Segmentation	By demographic	By customer values
Demand	Linear, normal	Volatile, random

FIGURE I-1. THE EMERGING ON-DEMAND ECONOMY.
In the on-demand economy, the necessity to implement an advanced S&OP becomes a requirement for your basic survival.

driven or operations-driven supply chains, internal economics and inventory are the drivers.

From a supply view, markets are seen as homogeneous; we manufacture a hammer, and everything looks like a nail. Conversely, from a demand perspective, markets are specialized by consumer/customer groups, with different solutions and products required for each group. Prior to the 1970s, in a supply economy, the rate of change was very slow; a product's life cycle was measured in decades. Today, in a demand economy, a product life cycle of even a few years is considered long. In the 1990s, product rationalization was the mantra. Now, an S&OP process tuned to the demand economy enables complexity when it is necessary to address specific customer needs in specialized markets. Segmentation now needs to be done on customer values. In the old supply view, decision making was driven by customers rather than sales or marketing efficiency. In the old economy, with vastly less product complexity and high concentration in distribution, planning models were developed using the assumption that the underlying demand patterns were normally distributed. Today, demand at the product stock-keeping unit (SKU) level is significantly more volatile. Analysis finds most SKUs have random demand patterns. This factor alone necessitates a very profound change in approach.

A significantly more dynamic, customer-focused, and forward-thinking S&OP model is needed to achieve success. The market-driven supply chain needs to be managed by an S&OP process with lots of market savvy. To distinguish between the market-driven supply chain and the process managed by it, we refer in this book to market-savvy S&OP as the most advanced and Level IV S&OP process. In the market-driven supply chain, the market—not the manufacturer—leads, and even dictates, the ways of commerce. A new "market-in" approach to business planning and product production and deployment is essential if a company is to be successful in today's challenging business environment.

To win, the enterprise must manage to "at market" demand and manage the customer's demand for valuable services. If your present S&OP has an uncommitted top management, is mired in detail, or lacks strong marketing and sales leadership, you must change the culture starting here and now. If your process does not have strategic vision or consists of interdepartmental rifts and disconnects, your move to a new S&OP process is critical.

This book will help you create a market-savvy S&OP that is built on strong cross-functional collaboration and market insights. A market-savvy S&OP becomes a competitive weapon, designed to achieve market share growth and positive cash flow. The robust process empowers and multiplies the strengths of individual executives in a collegial culture.

In this book, you will learn how to make a successful transformation, both in management process to operate "at market" and in the company's culture, to move to a customer-centric approach that generates remarkable business results. You will not only see how your business can compete but how it can dominate in its markets. The major benefits your company accrues from implementing market-savvy S&OP will be free cash-flow generation and market share gains. These are the serious objectives most boards of directors require of senior management. Achieving these benefits will have direct impact on the company's stock price and will create value for shareholders.

You will also learn about a powerful new management process that will bring about full organizational collaboration and be highly effective in implementing your company's strategy. The need for full cross-functional collaboration in planning and execution has never been greater, and the need is growing. The issues are far more complex than can be effectively handled by individual functional areas operating independently.

You will learn as well how being market-driven is practical and mirrors reality, despite initially seeming to be counterintuitive. Becoming market-driven may appear to be a daunting task, but in the end, it is not difficult to achieve with the tools described in this book—tools for the transformation of the culture, tools for the design of new processes, and tools for the accomplishment of the transition to the new S&OP.

Many in business have long desired and even attempted to have cross-functional collaborative management, to develop processes that drive market-share growth, and to generate free cash flow. Only a few have succeeded. This is often because of two factors: the lack of a compelling reason for change, particularly when people are operating inside individual functional areas, and a less-than-rigorous change management process.

Individuals who have studied, labored, and stressed over achieving change in enterprise culture in many different arenas—from public to private, in both social and industrial organizations—know that change comes only when the whole organization desires it. Change cannot be forced or dictated, nor can it be accomplished by IT installations. The CEO must be a role model for change, envisioning increased cash flow and market share, then cultivating the desire to change through communication and education. The CEO must recognize change has three distinct aspects: vision, behavior, and process. A transition to the new vision, with new behavior and new processes, is required. A change in culture is implemented through a disciplined change management process articulating the vision, accentuating the behavior, and adopting the process.

This book is structured to demonstrate how to apply these three aspects of change to create a winning market-savvy S&OP process. We will show you, step by step, how to make the supply chain a strong and successful competitive weapon. The overarching framework for the book is shown in Figure I-2, with the associated relevant chapters.

Part I, "Creating Vision," focuses on the first management change required to implement a market-savvy S&OP process. Vision in this context means to correctly define customer values and needs and to determine what strategies you will use to satisfy these needs.

Part I has two chapters. Chapter 1, "Seeing Anew from a Market-Savvy Perspective," establishes what it means to be market-driven and market-savvy. It describes market-savvy S&OP and explains how to conduct this type of planning in a way that is fundamentally different from what you are now doing. The chapter also examines value segmentation and describes in detail how to perform it, leading to the development of a go-to-market strategy, which is the statement of how each functional area within the organization will accomplish the goal or strategy of the business.

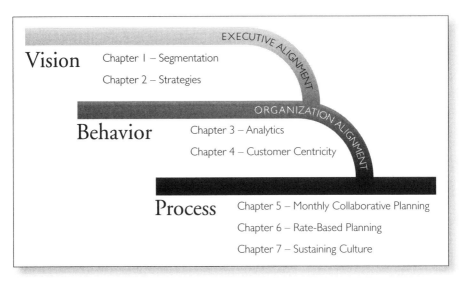

FIGURE I-2. THE THREE-PART STRUCTURE OF THIS BOOK.
Changing from a traditional Level I S&OP to an advanced Level IV S&OP with market clout is accomplished in three major parts.

Chapter 2, "Competing on Time and Customer Connectivity," describes the time advantage and customer connectivity strategies that hold the potential for desirable performance improvement when a market-savvy S&OP is implemented.

Part II, "Changing Behavior," looks at the second aspect of change management. The two chapters in this part explore the driving aspects of changed behavior in an S&OP context: robust analytics and a customer-centric culture.

Chapter 3, "Managing by Analytics," discusses the critical requirement of replacing conventional wisdom based on past behavior with facts and market-savvy, which look into the future.

Chapter 4, "Establishing a Customer-Centric Culture, " covers the drivers of collegiality and a foundation for open and productive collaboration across, up, and down the organization, all of which are vital for achieving a customer-centric culture. Chapters 1 through 4 set the stage by creating and communicating the need for change and outlining the behavior needed to accomplish the change to a market-savvy S&OP.

Part III, "Designing New Processes," is the third and final phase of the change management process. The processes fall into three major areas: (1) the monthly collaborative planning processes, (2) the rate-based planning processes in operations, and (3) the sustaining culture processes of audits and continuous improvement. Each area is discussed in its own chapter. Together, they reach the overarching goals of gaining and sustaining competitive advantage and free cash flow.

Chapter 5, "Designing and Implementing Collaborative Planning (Segment-Level S&OP)," describes the monthly planning processes for managing demand and becoming customer-centric that are led by senior management, with ownership and significant participation by the organization's business units.

Chapter 6, "Designing a Rate-Based Planning Process," covers weekly execution of the rate-based planning processes for demand fulfillment at the operational level. These processes enable the organization to become market-driven in inventory replenishment, procurement, and production. You will learn that rate-based processes replace MRP (material requirements planning) and work hand in glove with lean manufacturing initiatives.

And, finally, Chapter 7, "Transitioning to a New Culture of Market-Driven Supply Chain," discusses sustaining processes for continuing and increasing competitive advantage, including the establishment of process clubs.

Using the principles you will learn in this book, you will be able to successfully implement a new and highly productive S&OP in your company. The new processes will have a profound impact on the business and on your career. The companies that have implemented market-savvy S&OP now dominate their industries, some by further strengthening and most by revolutionizing their impact on the industry.

Seven Guiding Principles of the Design of Market-Savvy S&OP

Seven *guiding principles* or design principles are described in the book, one for each chapter. The seven principles provide a useful overview of what you will be learning:

1. Market In
2. Segment Level
3. Management by Analytics
4. Organize Around Customers
5. Process Heavy, People Light
6. Rate-Based
7. Change Culture

The journey begins with creating a vision. You will learn about this exciting new approach in Chapter 1.

PART I

Creating Vision

VISION IS THE STARTING POINT in implementing the seven guiding principles for the design of market-savvy S&OP. The first two principles are described in Chapters 1 and 2: "market in" and "segment level." Vision is a comprehensive understanding of the market segments in the business and the strategy for each segment. With vision developed, the S&OP team members will be able to more fully appreciate the uniqueness of the markets they serve and the requirements for success. A truly collaborative planning process will more naturally flow from a proper vision.

Only at the market segment level is there enough clarity and relevance for you to be able to define a complete and unique vision definition. In turn, value delivery can be defined only by segment, and value delivery is the only way to create competitive advantage, leading to share gains and increased free cash flow. Chapter 1 explains how to create the vision through a new market segmentation process leading to the go-to-market strategy, defining how to create competitive advantage and an action plan for all functional areas for each segment.

Chapter 2 describes the framework for the generic strategies from which you can choose, including the revolutionary new strategies of time advantage and customer connectivity.

Throughout the book, we will refer to the diagram shown in Figure PI-1 as a conceptual roadmap. The critical management change step of visioning is accomplished by the group of processes in the upper left, the round objects depicted in the diagram.

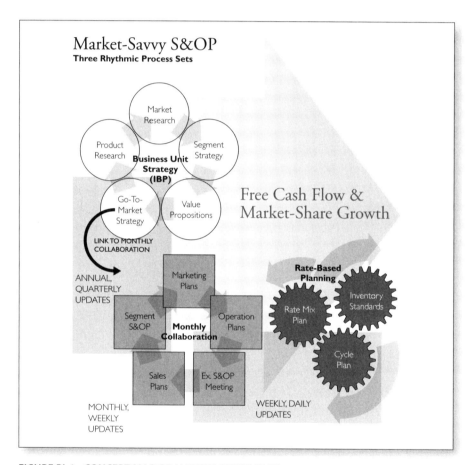

FIGURE PI-1. CONCEPT MAP OF MARKET-SAVVY S&OP.
Market-savvy S&OP adds two new process sets to the traditional S&OP: annual segment-level value chain strategies and weekly rate-based planning.

CHAPTER 1

Seeing Anew from a Market-Savvy Perspective

IN THE NEW DEMAND ECONOMY, a significant competitive differentiator is market savviness, which is another way of saying mastery of the marketplace. Companies prevailing competitively possess remarkable comprehension of their markets. They lead in understanding customers, demand, and competitors and in articulating a distinctive go-to-market strategy.

The marketplace actually distills this strategy, so the executive team no longer needs to rely on historical data for strategic planning. Plans come from observing signals about future trends, rather than seeking insights from the plans of predecessors or historical data about the past. This new approach is known as *predetermined planning*. Most companies currently rely on either a presumptive or a projection approach to planning: They *presume* their market position will remain unchallenged, or they *project* a modest, easy-to-achieve improvement. In predetermined planning, in contrast, the essence of planning is transformed from looking at history and internally developed strategies to discovering what has been determined about your products and segments by customers in the marketplace. The first guiding principle for designing market-savvy S&OP—market in—begins with this approach to planning. (See Figure 1-1.)

This predetermined planning perspective is the key to understanding the market-savvy approach to supply chain management. In the on-demand world, opportunities exist for those willing to discover market realities, gain marketplace mastery, and determine how to gain competitive advantage.

Planning is done best when there is clarity of both customers and competitors. When planning is done at a high level of aggregation such as for a whole profit center or, worse, for a group of profit centers at say a corporate level, different groups of customers are mixed together and a broad array of competitors are involved. The planning done in the market-savvy approach requires disaggregation down to

Presumptive Planning	Projection Planning	Predetermined Planning
"Everything will remain the same."	"History shows a 5% increase."	"I know the markets and the customers well."
Removed from the market	Two to three steps removed from the market	At the market **and consumer**-driven

FIGURE 1-1. PLANNING APPROACHES.
Predetermined planning is the essence of the "market-in" principle for market-savvy S&OP.

the market segment level. We have found a *value segmentation* of the market works best.

Value segmentation is a departure from traditional segmentation, describing markets in the providers' terms, such as how much of your product they buy or where they are located. It determines how customers are grouped according to the values they hold most dear as well as how they generate cash. Value segmentation is achieved by research done by a cross-functional team of savvy professionals. The team approach seeks answers to the question, "How can we be of value to you?" Traditionally, the fieldwork is done by sales reps asking, "How much do you need, and how much will you pay?" This research seeks to broaden depth of knowledge about customers.

Value segmentation leads to the articulation of a *go-to-market strategy*. The go-to-market strategy by segment educates everyone in the organization about your overarching goal in each segment.

Market-Savvy S&OP Defined

Market-savvy S&OP is fundamentally different from traditional S&OP in profound ways. Most important is its customer focus and its impact on the performance of the enterprise. In market-savvy S&OP, the overarching goals are increasing market share and generating free cash flow (FCF). Both are goals of prime importance to senior management. In market-savvy S&OP, multiple teams are focused on achieving the goals for which the CEO is held accountable by the board of directors.

Four Levels of Maturity in S&OP

Market-savvy S&OP is the highest level of maturity in S&OP, as described in Figure 1-2. The market-savvy S&OP is the process used inside a market-driven supply chain.

In traditional S&OP, the goal is operational excellence, with a cross-functional culture in the internal organization. Traditional S&OP determines sales volume and identifies product mix requirements. The idea is to efficiently use manufacturing capacity.

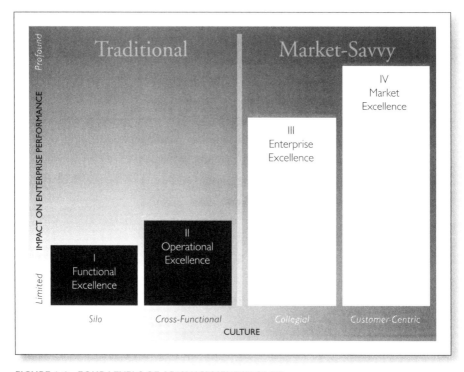

FIGURE 1-2. FOUR LEVELS OF ADVANCEMENT IN S&OP.
The more advanced applications of S&OP generate far greater benefits than the entry levels.

Today, however, markets do not react to manufacturing efficiency alone; they require much more. Market-savvy S&OP changes the entire focus of the organization to the outside—to an "at-market" level—and brings those market insights in to start the planning processes. Specifically, it:

♦ Strives for market excellence with a collegial and customer-centric culture transcending the internal organization to include customers and suppliers in the most intimate levels of planning and decision making, including product selection decisions and inventory strategies.

♦ Is run at the major market segment level within a business unit—not one-size-fits-all, but tailored to customer needs.

♦ Requires forecasting demand two steps closer to actual demand. Traditional S&OP forecasts demand at the manufacturer level and may plan inventory at the customer level (vendor-managed inventory, or VMI). Market-savvy S&OP forecasts consumer take-away from the customer.

♦ Manages capacity to demand and manages production to demand through rate-based planning and flexible inventory standards, the replacement for material requirements planning (MRP), and safety stocks.

♦ Closely aligns performance measures to senior management's objectives: free cash-flow generation and market share capture.

The demand-economy requirement is to move to a market-savvy S&OP process. It should not be confused with the well-known operationally focused S&OP process, shown at Level I of Figure 1-2, used by most companies for the past 20 to 25 years. Market-savvy S&OP is practiced in part by fewer than 5 percent of the most successful companies in the United States and by an even smaller percentage of the world's manufacturers. Precious few—in fact, we have not found any—practice the full complement of market-savvy S&OP processes.

The *P* in Market-Savvy S&OP

The *P* in S&OP, planning, is the predetermined approach to planning as illustrated in Figure 1-1. This type of planning requires a more rigorous investigation of how your products are being accepted or rejected and how your selected competitive approach stacks up in the real market. Predetermined means the market will have provided signals about what will be successful. For sure, some aspects of your plans may be more difficult to prove than others. In the predetermined approach, the cross-functional team must find leading indicators of the success or failure of planning alternatives. Leading indicators may be very knowledgeable individuals or leading indicator stores. Often, the best approach is to structure your go-to-market strategy with well-defined trigger points at which a disciplined assessment of your plans is completed before just forging ahead. At the beginning of each business cycle, normally once per year or season, decisions can be made based on how the market reacts to your offerings and your competitor's. The key is to be in the market and finding the signals.

It is essential to adopt a predetermined planning approach. Most planning processes have been built on the concept, historical data regarding the manufacturer's shipments well defines the future, and all one needs is a little care given to new products and possibly marketing programs and promotions. However, in the new demand economy, product and demand patterns change so rapidly, and market forces are so specialized and volatile, historical data at the manufacturer's level become stale very quickly. Predictive information—gathered two or more steps further down the demand network of manufacturers, wholesalers, retailers, and consumers—is required.

In the future, planning must be done very close to the consumer/customer to understand what is changing and by how much. Certainly, the basic demand driver of price points, combined with consumer/customer perceptions of quality, still applies, and product applications remain somewhat constant. But what changes are competitor offerings; the availability of products from different sources, including the Internet; the customer's desire to sell; and network inventory. Predetermined planning relies on a high level of interaction between cross-functional market-focused teams and consumers/customers, using knowledge to anticipate changes in demand.

IBP Provides the Strategy

As shown in our seminal diagram, Figure PI-1, business unit strategy is within market-savvy S&OP. The process is commonly known as integrated business planning, or IBP. There is a fair amount of confusion around the definition of IBP today, so it seems appropriate to offer some explanation and clarification regarding our viewpoint about it. We see IBP as a formal process in and of itself; it should not be mistaken for a more advanced form of the common monthly S&OP

process, as some authorities suggest. IBP provides the business strategy for the overall market-savvy S&OP process.

Some professionals may think of IBP as a financial planning process and not necessarily part of S&OP. IT professionals would like to see IBP as a very mature process within S&OP, with all data fully integrated by one mega-software solution. Neither view is correct. Financial planning cannot be done apart from market-savvy S&OP. Every piece of information financial planners require must come from it. In our client experience, financial and operations planning systems do not need to be integrated. However, they do need to be developed collaboratively.

IBP is in part a financial planning process, but it is more correctly defined as the annual business strategy redevelopment process. Financial projections and plans properly flow from the information and strategies developed through IBP. What is important is the process, not the IT solution. The analytics rely heavily on a database of information, but not at all upon having operations and financial data fully integrated in one mega-system.

IBP focuses on the supply chain—the network of customers, manufacturers, and suppliers. As A. G. Lafley, the highly successful former CEO of Procter & Gamble, said, "At P&G, supply chain is the business." In IBP, we want to understand the market dynamics leading us to a specific set of actions so we can determine whether or not they have potency and relevance in the real world.

IBP addresses a critical need arising because of the on-demand economy. The on-demand economy moves quickly; the rate of change is exponential in all aspects, including product technology, but also in terms of customer characteristics, competitive offerings, and sourcing opportunities. A strategy planning rhythm matching these dynamics is a requirement. An enterprise can no longer set a strategy once to last for many decades. In addition, the complexities of the on-demand marketplace are so extensive a separate strategy unit outside the business unit or including only one or two strategists is not going to be successful. The management team of the business unit must apply its considerable market savvy to properly develop an effective strategy.

Figure 1-3 depicts the process steps in IBP. It is a yearly thinking process of revitalization for the business unit. While done annually, it is updated quarterly through status meetings with customer groups. IBP normally has a three- to five-year time horizon. (Note that while product research is part of IBP, this is not product life-cycle management, or PLM. The output of IBP is the essential market view feeding into the PLM process.)

The output of IBP, the go-to-market strategy, is the IBP or market-in link into the monthly collaboration processes. Once the IBP steps have been completed, the output will provide the written and agreed-to statement of strategy and key metrics, namely, how much cash

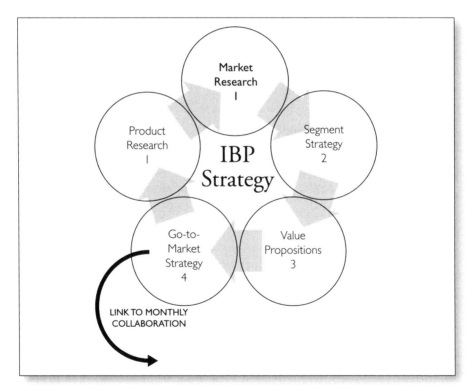

FIGURE 1-3. SEGMENT-LEVEL STRATEGY.
IBP links the market to the monthly planning by setting a segment-level strategy for market-savvy S&OP to implement.

should be generated, how much market share should be gained, and how the company is to create competitive advantage.

Defining Market Segmentation

There are five steps, the first two numbered "1" because they are done simultaneously, in our model of IBP, as outlined in Figure 1-3. In this approach, individual market segments are defined. This is the second guiding principle of market-savvy S&OP design, segment level. When operating at the segment level within a market, stark clarity of competitive position is found. The customers by definition have homogeneity, and competitor strategies are more easily determined. The reason so many companies have difficulty setting strategies is they try to do it at too high a level of aggregation; find exception after exception; and, thus, end up generalizing. The result is a strategic direction providing no meaningful information for functional executives, so metrics become muddled and action plans uncoordinated. The key to success is to properly segment the market and then set a strategy for each segment.

Segments are aggregations of like consumers/customers within the business unit's overall market, with each member having essentially common characteristics of product preferences, buying habits, service requirements, and so forth. Sometimes, a segment is one very large customer, such as Wal-Mart, which can amount to 35 percent of business for consumer products companies providing tires, or beauty aids, or the like. Normally, we find only three to five segments of significance in a business. We had one client who believed it had one segment equal to 97 percent of its business, plus two smaller segments. However, we found the organization's thinking was incomplete. The large segment was actually three segments, and the two smaller ones were actually subsets of the three properly defined segments.

Segments tend to be large portions of the market. They may be as large as 40 percent or as small as 10 percent, but rarely larger or smaller. We had a client who had 3,000 different items in the product portfolio. Some 300 of them accounted for more than 95 percent of the overall market and 96 percent of the company's unit sales. A sales representative or a marketing professional inside the company could list a reason why each of the 2,700 items, accounting for less than 5 percent of the company's total market, was absolutely required. Focusing on market segments, we were able to pinpoint the duplication of items. When customer aggregates were interviewed, they said they were confused by all the extra items beyond the top 300, wanted direction from the manufacturer about how to cut back on the number of items offered, and did not want to inventory even the top 300 items, but only about 70 or so. After months of discussion and heavy application of analytics, more than 2,000 items were dropped from the portfolio. The team determined the other 700 items in the 5 percent group were emerging new products and could replace one or two of the products in the top 300 group. Some of the lower-volume items actually had an exclusive niche of 1 percent of the overall market.

We are talking market segments, not segments of your business only. A business traditionally serving only one part of a market should look at market segmentation for the broader market to find whether opportunities are available. The business may not be in some of the segments of the market, or it may have the segment defined in its terms, not in market terms. The business may chose to stay out of certain segments. The segmentation is useful, then, in determining those products and services not required.

For example, some years ago, I worked with a manufacturer of electric motors, nonfractional or one horsepower (HP) and up. Fractional motors represented a totally different technology and market so were not considered in my evaluation of opportunities. The client saw itself as a full-line manufacturer competing with GE, also a large electrical products manufacturer and full-line. Our client had one large assembly line in an older plant in the upper northeastern United States. Revenues and profits had been declining for a few years, and corporate management envisioned a turnaround.

We did the research to determine the market segments and the competitive positioning. From internal research, we developed a list of major motor buyers, including many multibillion-dollar electrical distributors and the rotating engineers in big A&E (architectural and engineering) firms. We found there actually were four significant market segments. There were, for example, groups of customers, accounting for 60 percent of the market, who treated motors as commodities and purchased only on price in the smaller sizes of one- and two-HP motors. Another segment existed for motors to be installed in Greenfield sites on longer lead times with a high variety of different sizes and configurations required; this was a nice fit for a full-line manufacturer. An additional segment existed for three-HP and up motors in the replacement market. The four segments were:

1. One-HP motors, sold on price only, primarily through distributors

2. Two-HP motors, sold on price only, primarily through distributors

3. Three-HP and up motors sold to A&E firms, original equipment manufacturers (OEMs), and large industrial companies

4. Replacement motors sold to maintenance managers for immediate use

The competition had already sorted out the segments. In segment one, Baldor Electric Company of Fort Smith, Arkansas, made almost all of the one-HP motors in a highly specialized factory, with nothing to sell but the lowest price. There is only one low-price competitor in a market, and when the segment value is almost exclusively low price, that competitor owns the market segment. Baldor, in fact, did. In segment two, a Japanese company, a manufacturer of robotics, took on the two-HP motor segment with a fully automated factory and very limited complexity. GE had decided the three-HP and up motors in segment three was where it could then play, and it took a very large share of that market. In segment four, a large number of distributors and service companies dominated.

The result of this segmentation? Our client had done the segmentation too late. The company struggled for a year or so longer and finally closed shop.

Within each segment, we are looking for a strategy—an approach to create competitive advantage. A competitive advantage produces more than five points of market share greater than the competition. A strategy is not just a simple goal. It describes how you can strongly differentiate your company from competitors and how you can sustain the differentiation over time. Whether you call this a strategy, a goal, or a tactic is not important; the terms mean essentially the same thing. We prefer to call the IBP process output a strategy to imply an overarching directive. Goals tend to be things like "We will reduce inventory 20 percent." Tactics tend to be something done for one customer.

In the segment strategy development process, demand generation is the objective. You may have some segments in which you are number one, with a high share inside the segment. You should be trying to find ways to increase the share. However, if it is not possible or imprudent to raise the market share, then higher margins should be sought. For example, GE Lighting enjoyed a 65 percent share of the incandescent lamp business in each of four segments. To avoid an antitrust lawsuit, the company did not want to raise its share. So, it priced up to keep share down to 65 percent. GE had a 30 percent price premium over its competition. Not too many companies enjoy such a position. Companies should be looking for increasing market share or at least beating down an emerging competitor.

Research, Research, Research

The only way to properly define market segments is to do primary research and to keep the research fresh with quarterly probes into key customers and a formal annual research project done afresh.

The ideal research pattern is shown in Figure 1-4. Research starts internally with the data. The research you undertake first should be dominated by how the business works now and what is good and not so good about it. It is very important to spend most of the research

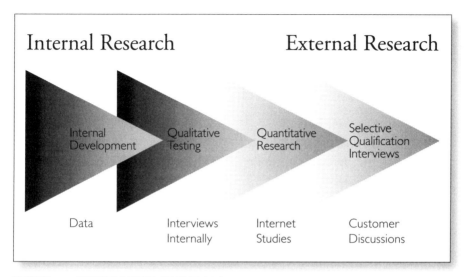

FIGURE 1-4. MARKET RESEARCH APPROACH.
The success of the IBP process depends on research done by cross-functional teams, not just marketing.

time on how the current business works before you start thinking about how it can be improved. The clearly defined metrics of the current business are a constant analytical touch point for future thinking.

Let's look closely at the four types of market research shown in Figure 1-4.

Internal Development. The data need to be analyzed initially to outline how your markets currently work, at least as far as your customers currently see you. The analytical team is looking for groupings of customers and products and manufacturing resources. Most often, you find that a few customers dominate the demand for a group of similar products. The product and customer groupings are unique to the individual company. The groupings are always logical: high quality to lower quality, high-complexity customers to low-complexity, new versus reworked. It is often helpful to rank the products, then the customers who buy them.

Heavy use of the 80-20 rule is the link to sanity: 80 percent of revenue will be purchased by 20 percent of customers. Eighty percent of unit sales will be in 20 percent the products. Please note: I only use two categories, 80 and 20. I want to distinguish between big as important and small as miscellaneous. Adding all the other gradients normally used in a full Pareto analysis the analysts will be distracted from the main purpose of the research and make it so time consuming as to perhaps stop progress altogether. By doing the analysis of volumes and mixes using the 80-20 rule, some facts come out that must be reconciled. Why are these products and customers linked? Care must be taken to sort out decision makers from ship-to locations. If the basic buying decisions are made by a corporate entity with many distribution points, do not make each distribution point a customer. For example, Wal-Mart is a single customer with many ship-to locations; Sysco is a single customer for some decisions but may also be multiple customers because of its strong decentralized decision making. Having every ship-to as a customer is an old enterprise resource planning (ERP) approach, one only adding confusion. Sort out where the major decisions are made, not where the orders come from.

Qualitative Testing. Qualitative testing is done by asking internally of the customer-facing people to provide insight as to why certain customers tend to buy products or why sales are concentrated in certain areas. The competitive situation often starts to emerge in these discussions. The analytical team is looking for insights on how customers are making buying decisions. We had a client whose major customers were the scientists who helped develop products. The scientists owned part of the intellectual property rights. In any competitive situation where our customer was not a rights-holding scientist, we did very poorly and, in reality, sold only test samples, with very little ongoing business. The research led to a hard look at how product development actually worked. A great deal more customer input from scientists and buyers who did not own rights was required.

Quantitative Research. The research must move outside the company once you have gained a solid analytical footing. The quantitative research phase seeks market share information. Often, you must rely upon quantitative research done by a third party. However, the numbers must be placed in perspective. Internet research can yield key market size information and can verify or even modify the third-party research. Papers presented at industry symposiums can also be helpful. Product announcements from competitors should be researched and understood in terms of market trends, competitive threats, "what do they know we don't?" and the like. The analytical team members must individually look for information from different sources. I find engineers can talk with other engineers to find out key information that sales and marketing people would never discuss. Another source of information can come from industry groups of customers, who often hold conferences where their frustrations are vented.

Selective Qualification Interviews. Now the team must take its collective findings to the customer. Key customers may allow individual interviews by the team. Customer groups can be very effective in identifying how products perform now and what new products are required. To illustrate, a group of Goodyear Tire & Rubber Company representatives had fleet managers from major long-haul trucking companies in for a panel discussion. The fleet people asked, "Why don't you put the new consumer tire technology into the commercial market?" Goodyear's experts answered that trucks had no need for the new blowout technology since they have much stronger tires and better maintenance. The fleet managers explained, trailer tires are just like consumer tires with regard to road hazards and travel down into loading dock wells, having all sorts of debris and sharp objects present, could destroy a tire. The truck is just as broken down with a flat trailer tire as with a flat tractor tire. So, a new market for new-technology consumer tires was born, and Goodyear dominates the trailer tire market, a not insignificant new market segment.

Value Segmentation: The Preferred Method

The point of the research is to define value segments in the market. As mentioned earlier, value segmentation is distinctly different from traditional segmentation, as shown in Figure 1-5.

The whole approach here is to find out what the customer's requirements are. Instead of asking, "How much do you buy?" or "How are we doing today?" you want to know "How do you generate cash?" and "How do you interact with your customers?" and "How do you use new technology, if at all?"

Value Segmentation Defined

The value segmentation approach is so dramatically different from the traditional approach that the cross-functional team of researchers should expect to find radically new ways of helping customers. In my experience, the team approach has been highly successful in finding new market opportunities. Individual marketing people doing the research tend not to be successful in finding new

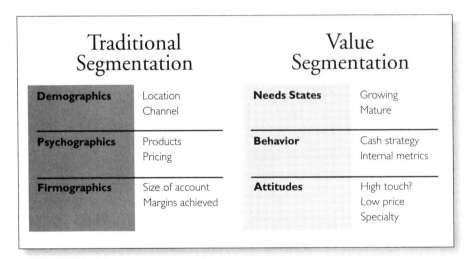

FIGURE 1-5. TRADITIONAL VERSUS VALUE SEGMENTATION.
Value segmentation looks at customer values rather than your salespeople's values.

approaches. The team members, working together, will combine their experiences in many different disciplines to discover customer needs in logistics, in products, in inventory support, in commercial terms, and in combinations of all of these.

This approach may take an extended period of time to achieve. As president of Rawlings Sporting Goods from 1983 through 1988, I had to listen to, then do, what the customers wanted, then build credibility, and then listen some more. After two years of working the value segmentation approach, we gained a trust relationship with our customers and started to have very rich dialogues. I can see our sales vice president, Stan Morrison, standing in front of a group of dealers saying, "This is what you told us at the last meeting. We did it! Now what more can you tell us about how we can better serve you?" They learned to love Stan. We learned to be good listeners.

In Figure 1-5, each of the three groups of characteristics on the right represents areas of research the analysts need to address.

Needs States. How are the customers grouped in terms of the level of maturity in business: well established or looking for something new? What are customer attitudes toward new products, techniques, and approaches? A series of different questions could be offered to probe their thinking. For example:

♦ An established set of customers with comfortable market positions will likely not want to "shake up" the market. Disruptive marketing—that is, changing the status quo—is not going to be of interest to these customers.

♦ Other groups of customers may be looking for ways to challenge the established market leaders.

♦ There may be a group of customers who need full support in product positioning, technology application, and the like, and want to use your products as a competitive weapon. These companies will have a whole set of needs way beyond the norm.

Continuing the Rawlings example, we sold to institutional dealers—the people who work from warehouses, not retail stores, and service large sports team complexes and college and professional teams. Some dealers were very well established, had excellent sales-people, and needed only good shipment of our standard products. We also found a group of struggling dealers who were fighting for position against our competitors in an area. These organizations needed tech-nical support from our research and development and manufacturing experts. The companies also were keenly interested in new technology (like new protective equipment designs, new uniform designs, and more). These were high-growth prospects with high-value-added potential.

Behavior. The questions in this area have to do with how the cus-tomer makes money, both the customer itself and the customer's people. The area is sensitive and should likely not be the first one you probe. It's an excellent idea to use observation here. What is the customer's approach to inventory management: high stocking levels or minimum, even too little, inventory? How does it pay its bills: always using long terms or taking discounts? Does the customer have good businesspeople, or are they clueless?

A generally important area of concern is determining how the people making the buying decisions are incentivized. If inventory shrink (or the dollars deducted from net worth on the balance sheet when inventory is lost, stolen, or just not there due to error) will get them fired, then find out how to make sure your shipping and invoic-ing information to them is 100 percent accurate, and make sure they know you are working on it with them. Have the customer rate your performance. If having a high gross margin per square foot in a retail store is key, work with the customer to position the product mix. Working with the customer to show you are able to help make them successful will build trust and identify ways of increasing both revenue and margins.

Attitudes. The way the customer treats its customers is revealing. There is a definite tradeoff between service and price. Wal-Mart's everyday lowest price strategy comes at the cost of customer service. Sam Walton used to say, "The local hardware store should not feel threatened by us. They can provide the advice and the specialty products required. We only offer the basic items and no advice." The customer groups who are "high touch" offer the quality manufacturer a whole range of market-share improvement options. High-touch customers are those who have a high service component to their business and not so much a lowest price idea. They tend to buy a much broader range of items. A specialty set of customers will be full-line buyers and may also be high touch, but not necessarily. Examples of high-touch, top-line grocery chains are Albertsons, Kroger, and Wegmans, as well as many smaller chains. They have a "hyper-local" merchandising strategy. They cater to the specific needs of customers in the vicinity of the individual stores. Manufacturers can prosper if, for example, they support these chains' strategy by providing specialty pallets and cross-docking to achieve high mix at a store without excessive handling and costs.

The whole point of the research is to find out what the customer wants you to know about them. It is not what you want the customer to know about you.

The research must address several generic areas to be complete. These are shown in Figure 1-6. They include competitive scenarios, or how competitors will likely move in the future; potential responses; and future market dynamics, or new competitive threats.

In the final stages of the research, the analysis should generate some hypotheses about gaps in the current segment definitions. The gap hypotheses must be qualified with the customers—no marketing myopia allowed. Make sure your definition of underserved needs gaps and unprotected opportunities matches with the customer's thinking. Some consumer research may be required for consumer and commercial products. The underserved and unprotected areas will lead to a

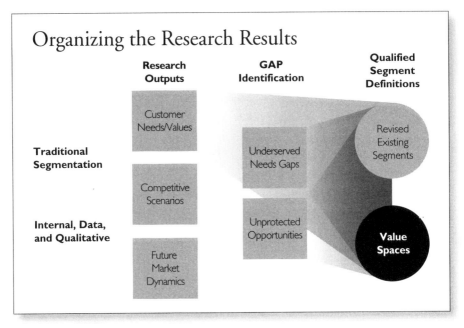

FIGURE 1-6. MARKET RESEARCH RESULTS.
IBP links the market to the monthly planning by setting a segment level strategy for market-savvy S&OP to implement.

redefinition of the existing segments and identification of *value spaces*, the holy grail of market-savvy S&OP. The working hypotheses of gaps and revised segment definitions should be resolved into specifics through the qualification interviews with the customers.

Normally, value spaces are found if the research is done properly. In fact, the dynamic nature of the on-demand economy almost requires new value spaces be formed often. Value spaces are the areas where customer needs are not being serviced. They are opportunities for extraordinary market share improvement.

Cross-Functional Teams Do the Work

For best results, cross-functional teams should be formed to actually work through the work steps of the value segmentation research. The teams will gain a richer and more in-depth appreciation for customer values than a marketing group or third-party research group can gain. If you were simply doing a demographic segmentation, the cross-functional teams would not be as important. Making sure you have a thorough understanding of the customers' ideas is critical to everything else you do in market-savvy S&OP.

Discover Common Values. A word about the research team: The essential element of this value segmentation approach is a cross-functional team doing the work. The sales representative is always going to be responsible for the relationship, but the team does the discovery. Normally, a salesperson is the only customer contact, and he or she protects the relationship fervently. The team approach is to support the salesperson. Sensitivity and groundwork will be required to convince sales representatives they need the assistance.

The cross-functional team approach is so important you should not go forward without it. If the sales force pleads with the CEO revenue will drop if these "team bozos" irritate the customer, the CEO may ask the team to perform a pilot run with a customer to prove the worth of the team approach. Perhaps a review of benchmark data is required or visits to companies who have successfully implemented this team approach. Salespeople must be on board, but they cannot stop the team from meeting with the customers.

Sales personnel are trained and incentivized to make the sale, do it efficiently, and stay within the territory. So, they naturally look only at demographics and psychographics. They think about what the customer has purchased before. (We call this *firmographics*.) A cross-functional team conducts the research in a much more expansive way. The manufacturing group, for instance, asks, "What can we do in manufacturing to serve the needs of the customer?" The answers are likely to be change lead time, add special features, and so forth. Each functional area seeks to know how it can contribute to the value the customer is receiving.

New S&OP and supply chain staff will likely be required: people who are able to understand the perspective of other functions and, most important, understand how to work with senior management at major customers. You need some strategic thinkers inside the supply chain organization. Increasingly, the supply chain organization is the one that must compile and communicate the S&OP process, its requirements, its findings, its performance, and its outputs. The master-scheduler model of a clerk working inside the factory is probably not going to work.

Describe and Name Segments. The research to define market segments must come to a timely conclusion. Subsets of the full cross-functional team may begin the internal research a few months before the annual review is to be published. Then, the team must complete the fieldwork and draw conclusions.

You are looking for a list of three to six segments, each accounting for a significant portion of the overall market. Figure 1-7 describes the summary information required for each segment.

Segment Research Summary

	Working Name for the Segment	Market Size	Our Share	Key Products	Major Customers	Value Definition
1		$	%			
2						
3				**Examples:** **Main Line**	**Top 2 or 3** **and % to**	
4				**New Tech** **Full Line**	**total**	
5						
6						
Total		$	%			

FIGURE 1-7. ELEMENTS OF THE SEGMENT DEFINITION.
From the research, the team defines each segment with a name and key information.

The value spaces should be highlighted in the "working name for the segment." Comments about competitive scenarios and future market dynamics might be essential and should be added under the value definition section. It is important to keep the words to a bare minimum; a big picture approach is what is desired. Simple one- or two-word descriptions can be memorable and, more importantly, will capture the distinctive, not the minutiae.

Figure 1-8 shows comparisons of traditional segments and value segments in a technology company.

The technology company represented in Figure 1-8 had been organized exclusively around industry verticals and firmographics—a fairly common segmentation approach in the technology industry. As a result, there were vice presidents for the banking industry vertical, the manufacturing industry vertical, the insurance industry vertical,

Traditional Segments		Value Segments	
Industry Verticals	Common industries	**Resistant to Change**	Investment
Firmographic	Size of customers	**Customer Focus**	e-Services
Use Segmentation	Retail stores Erratic peaks	**Vendor Dependent**	IT safety net
Product	Types of energy Types of hardware	**Do-It-Yourselfers**	IT tool kit
		Achievers	On-demand
		Expansionists	Global, virtual

FIGURE 1-8. COMPARISON OF SEGMENTATION APPROACHES.
The traditional segmentation did not identify customer value differences critical to understanding the competitive situation.

and so on. The vice presidents were further ranked into small-, medium-, and large-size accounts. Vice presidents were everywhere.

However, the value segments here are completely different from the traditionally used segments. The value segments focus on customer needs and differences. Inside each of the industry verticals were those who used the company's servers as a competitive weapon—the achievers—as well as those who were resistant to change, some who were vendor-dependent, and so on. The entire value chain was found to be different based upon the value segment, not the industry vertical. The industry vertical segmentation, plus firmographics, did not provide any insight on how to differentiate or how to gain competitive advantage at all. The new value segments provided a rich understanding of key customer differentiators. As a result, the "on-demand" computing segment became a very important and high-growth segment for the company.

Figure 1-9 provides another example of comparing traditional segments with value segments, this time in a manufacturer of jalapeño poppers.

Traditional Segments		Value Segments		Needs
Product	Poppers Moz Sticks Fancy	**High-Mix Food Service**	Sysco	100% 2 weeks
Firmographics	Regions Size of customers	**High-Touch Retail**	Kroger	4 items service
		Promotional Retail	Wal-Mart	Collaboration

FIGURE 1-9. SEGMENTATION IN A FOOD MANUFACTURER.
Customers differed sharply inside the traditional segments.

The jalapeño popper company in Figure 1-9 was totally product-focused in manufacturing and in sales. Sales reps were assigned by region and size of customer. All reporting and data came by product line by region. The company's entire go-to-market strategy was build-to-stock and ship-same-day-from-stock, with everyone expediting like mad to correct inventory shortages. Twice a day, the company held production line master scheduling change meetings.

Through value segmentation, the company found three separate businesses having no affiliation with either product line or regional location. The high-mix food service business was a national business centered on Sysco, U.S. Foods, and a few other large distributors. The key need was not ship-from-stock, as the one-size-fits-all strategy suggested. Large food service warehouses gave the company more than ten days' notice to marshal the many line items on an order. The second business, high-touch retail, was a hidden segment. Almost no attention had been paid to the key individuals in the segment. Lots of effort was focused by the commercial people on the big box stores—the third separate business—due to the high volume potential. VMI was done by salespeople who had zero inventory management experience and zero knowledge of manufacturing capabilities. Inventory investments made to service this highly erratic, seasonal business were so large as to run the company out of cash. The new segment definition allowed the entire organization to understand the collaborative needs. The company focused on the high-mix food service segment. It was highly successful.

Test for Analytical Completeness. The research is not complete until the full market has been divided into a logical and balanced set of segments. There must be:

♦   Three to six segments
♦   Specific differentiators and key customers

- Balance (a segment equal to more than 35 or 40 percent of the total market is probably in need of subdividing)
- Completeness (all products and competitors fit without being squeezed in)
- Full view

The full view requirement is essential. A common practice of some organizations is to exclude the market portions in which they have traditionally not competed. The cross-functional team needs to make sure all aspects of the market are considered. We had a client who made a common piece of rotating equipment. The product was used by steel mills, chemical plants, water purification plants, textile mills, paper mills, and similar facilities. The client defined the customers as A&E companies designing new facilities and owners building new facilities. The client excluded replacement equipment because, traditionally, it was provided by local distributors that supplied replaced parts and rebuilds, but did not handle new pieces of equipment.

The team's research found new replacement equipment was actually equal to new original equipment in total market size. Initially, the interviewing teams at the major customers asked about new projects, plant expansions, and capital expenditure plans. The customers actually offered data on replacement purchases. As the team investigated more, they were able to determine who was providing the replacement equipment. They found two companies, and from the research data, they determined the approximate unit volume of each. The team found distributors were the first responders for a replacement, which naturally usually occurred during an emergency and at night. The distributor generally dispatched a local truck, rigged something to keep the mill going, and then purchased and installed a replacement item a few days or a week later. Since our client made it nearly impossible for distributors to purchase the product, the distributors had found another "pirate" source. When told of all this, the CEO was elated at the news there existed a new market opportunity requiring nearly zero capital investment. A project team was established to create the new value stream and a new business within the business was born.

Segmentation Put to Work

Once the segments are determined, work needs to be done to rank and prioritize them. The analysis continues, and more research may be required. From the segment research summary table (shown in Figure 1-7), a competitive assessment must be completed and a disciplined scientific process undertaken to determine whether or not you have market opportunity or can create competitive advantage. It is not enough to just know you have different segments and are positioned with certain market share. The whole idea of this research is to find ways to generate demand improvements by finding new competitive advantages.

The competitive assessment may be done using several sources of information. Your own sales force knows the competitors. Former employees of competitors are a good source of information as well. In addition, we have found newspapers from towns where competitor plants are located have a wealth of information about new products, plant openings and closings, new process equipment (with pictures), and so forth. For this reason, it is not surprising to find numerous large companies are keen on keeping reporters and cameras totally out. Fortunately, we also have the Internet, an amazing source of competitive information.

The competitive advantage discovery process proceeds from here. The team is looking for three types of segments:

1. Segments where the company already dominates
2. Underserved segments
3. Value spaces, or unserved segments

We have developed a methodology, very effective in finding competitive advantage, in the IBP process. We call it the DHSSD process, defined in the following dot points:

♦ Discover the segments.

♦ Hypothesize alternatives for closing the needs gaps.

♦ Simulate the results of applying each hypothetical solution.

♦ Select the best alternative.

♦ Deploy the metrics and quantify the costs, benefits, and cash flow.

Discover. The discover element should be done as a result of the research you have just completed. No more than a one-or two-page definition of the customer needs, competitive positioning, and voids or gaps is necessary. The cross-functional team and perhaps the CEO should study the definitions of the market segments and offer their insights.

Hypothesize. This is the creative element. The team needs to brainstorm various ways to satisfy the market needs and to fill the gaps. Root cause analysis techniques are normally applied in developing the hypotheses. It is helpful to come up with three or four different hypotheses of competitive advantage approaches.

Application of the "five whys" to causal analysis is very helpful here. The five whys are asked of the team and, most important, of the customers:

1. Why is the needs gap a problem? Quantify the issues.

2. Why does it occur?

3. Why is the first answer a hard rule?

4. Why is the second answer a hard rule? (Continue question four until a root cause is found.)

5. Why can't an alternative approach be considered? (Continue question five until a feasible alternative can be found.)

Another root cause analysis technique we use is to define each of six sources or manifestations of the gap between the customers' needs and the current segment offerings. Look at the six individually and sort out which one has the most profound impact:

1. Machines	Physical distribution
2. Methods	Services
3. Manpower	Sales/channel support
4. Mother nature	Seasonality
5. Materials	Products
6. Measures	Customer metrics

Keep in mind the magnitude of market share gains you would need to justify for a perceived advantage to become an actual advantage. We are looking for advantages to gain five points of share when most often, companies have trouble gaining half a point—an order of magnitude gain. A rule we often apply was given to me by Tom Jones, a partner at Booz & Co., in my tender years: "For a difference to be a difference, it must make a difference."

Merely defining a hypothesis of how you would be different is not nearly enough. The approach must provide at least five points of market share gain over the near term. The hypothetical competitive advantage must be significant and required in the depth of the soul of the customer's culture. You need to think of great ways to satisfy the customer's base needs, to make free cash flow much better in a demonstrable way.

We had a medical technology client whose leading sales representative had significant success increasing sales in a market segment of particular interest due to the segments' international growth potential. The salesperson had demonstrated an appreciation for the customer needs in the segment. The company jumped on the suggestion of a new selling approach using referral sales methods and ran with it. Unfortunately, the hypothesis for improvement was not well defined using all six factors in the root-cause analysis (presented above). The new selling approach for gaining share did not work in any other sales territory. The reasons why the sales rep had been successful in the past were not well defined. The real root cause of past success was in sales channel support, training, and technical assistance. In addition, the segment definition was much too broad. Only a few of the customers in the market were interested in the products offered, not everyone. So, the share gain estimates made for replicating the selling approach were greatly inflated.

Simulate. The team needs to estimate the resources required, how the organization may change, and all other aspects of the business. Confirming the approach may involve role play of the interaction between the customer and the team. We have even visited friendly customers to discuss the details of the plan. Using the whole cross-functional team in this area provides a full set of inputs as to what is required.

The simulation must be done at market. The customers or at least the sales reps must be thoroughly involved. The objective is to find how each functional area in the company will participate in developing the full competitive advantage and realizing the capture of market share. The financial experts need to apply themselves to calculating margins and capital investment requirements and to preparing *pro forma* financial statements. A critical part of the simulation is to calculate free cash flow over time. Each of the five parts of free cash flow—inventory, capital utilization, receivables, payables, and margins—needs to be calculated and vetted.

It is not fair to merely say "no" at this stage. Try to say "yes, we can" meet the customer's needs and find a way.

Select. Once the simulations are complete, the best approach should be selected. You probably will not find two approaches have the support of the team. In fact, you should continue the simulation for a few days to make sure you have a clear best option. The segments where you can create clear competitive advantage and gain share while generating free cash flow are the ones where you should commit. You should exit or significantly revamp segments having negative cash flow.

Deploy. A deployment plan needs to be developed for those new segments. At this point, the DHSSD process should yield key metric information. Some of the items to be quantified in developing the metrics include how much market share, how much cash flow, how much capital investment, and how the organization will change. These answers should be used as key factors in the go-to-market strategy, discussed below.

Look for *bombs*, factors that would kill the implementation. A bomb could be a major objection raised by an executive or by a customer during the simulation. Bombs do not kill a strategic approach, but they must be specifically addressed in the go-to-market strategy.

Go-to-Market Strategy Completed

Development of your go-to-market strategy requires the forming of a value proposition and a value-chain description. The *value proposition* states the particulars around the competitive advantage defined in the DHSSD modeling. The *value chain* is composed of the physical elements—the network of suppliers, manufacturers, distribution, customers, and users.

Value Proposition. Companies struggle with value propositions because they do not have a formula. The value proposition has five distinct parts. In the initial stages, these five parts may be considered individually. Then, ask your team to make all five fit into a lucid paragraph. Ask these five questions:

1. For whom?
2. What values will be provided?

3. By what means?

4. To what end?

5. How will results be measured?

For whom is a statement of the value segment target group and the key characteristic taken directly from the summary description.

What values will be provided is answered by the research in conjunction with the DHSSD analysis of alternatives. Six areas of value should be included here:

1. Value differentiation	How will we be distinctly different?
2. Value delivery	How will our supply chain generate benefits?
3. Value packaging	How will services be bundled and pricing handled?
4. Value creation	How will customer appreciation be achieved?
5. Value targeting	Who will be key contacts in customers?
6. Value defense	How will competitive advantage be sustained?

While all six of these areas are very important, I cannot emphasize number four enough. How will the customers know you are providing valuable benefits to them? The best way is for the customer to actually measure performance for you and give you feedback. We discuss this phenomenon more thoroughly in Chapter 5, covering the monthly collaboration process, where we advise having customer management actually in the monthly collaboration meetings.

By what means is partially answered in the value delivery statement. This part is the cross-functional statement: What is each functional area going to do to support value provision?

To what end is normally about the quantitative factors such as cash-flow improvement and market share gains.

How will results be measured is a statement of how the customer will know you have provided a significant set of values.

For example, The On-Point Group's value proposition is:

> Within the confines of our ethics statement, On-Point will rec-
> ommend and provide proven manufacturing services and strate-
> gies to middle-market-sized clients seeking a market-driven
> competitive advantage. We will have positive cash flow each
> quarter and maintain a debt-free business. We will know we are
> winning when our clients' customers are satisfied their busi-
> nesses have realized economic benefit.

Value Chain. Each functional area and the whole network for suppliers to end users are identified in the value chain. The specific
contribution of each function and each part of the network is
described. The value-chain description may include many of the following elements:

- Channel objectives
- Distribution strategy
- Sales coverage and organization
- Marketing initiatives
- Supplier configuration, complexity, and collaboration
- Manufacturing requirements
- Marketing program support
- Communication plans
- Handling bombs defined in the simulation part of DHSSD

The go-to-market strategy is presented to senior management.
This strategy is then the starting point for the monthly S&OP planning cycle. However, we must cover some additional elements of the
cultural change prior to moving to monthly S&OP in Chapter 5. On
the way to Chapter 5, we need to discuss the strategies to be applied,

including the new ones, time advantage and customer connectivity, which are covered in Chapter 2—as well as the behavioral changes required for implementation, covered in Chapters 3 and 4.

Looking Back

♦ The new on-demand economy requires revolutionary changes in the way you plan your business. The intensity of the customer's demand for performance and products is the driving factor requiring changes.

♦ Cross-functional teams are the norm in successful companies. The customer issues are too complex for any one functional area to fully comprehend.

♦ The predetermined planning principle underpins the new planning techniques. Predetermined planning requires the enterprise to plan at market, not steps removed at distribution or at production. The standard predictive planning approach embedded in all ERP systems needs to be replaced. However, new IT approaches are not required. Process, not IT systems, is the key to success.

♦ Market-savvy S&OP is the mature S&OP process; addressing the new economic realities and building on an at-market approach to planning. Three rhythmic processes make up market-savvy S&OP. (See Figure PI-1.)

♦ The first process is integrated business planning, or IBP, which is accomplished through value segmentation, a comprehensive market research and strategy development cycle done annually. Cross-functional teams perform the research steps and discover the strategy for each defined market segment. The end result of IBP is a go-to-market strategy made up of two parts: a value proposition and a value-chain definition.

The go-to-market strategy by segment is the starting point of the monthly collaboration cycle, discussed in Chapter 5.

Case Study: Sports Uniform Manufacturer

I learned a great deal about the sports uniform manufacturing business when I became president of Rawlings Sporting Goods Company in 1984. The following case reflects my experience in the market.

A sports uniform manufacturer, like most of its competitors, was losing money and losing market share to low-cost Asian manufacturers. Monthly losses of more than $1 million were typical. The company was burning cash, drawn from the conglomerate parent. The parent wanted the bleeding to stop ASAP, and the company was given six months to stop the cash drain or be dissolved. The overall business was about $500 million in three sports (baseball, football, and basketball), with a total of 13 product groups. These groups included baseball and softball gloves; baseballs; protective equipment for baseball and football; uniforms for all three sports, in special order and stock types; and inflatables for football and basketball. Each of these product groups had items specifically designed for use at the pro, college, and youth league levels. To complicate the business further, the company was selling to retailers, mass merchants, team dealers, sports parks, and pro sports teams through three different sales teams.

The company had substantial operations in Asia, with a major strategic partnership with a key sports equipment manufacturer in Japan. The company had five factories domestically, with two dedicated to uniforms. Typical of sports equipment manufacturers, the company also had a factory in the Caribbean.

Situation. The uniform business was generating major losses, which had to be stopped. The company had a strong position with professional sports teams, which did a great deal to build brand equity, with pictures on the cover of *Sports Illustrated* and logos on pro players. Once the uniform business was addressed (as discussed below), a major turnaround of the core business had been accomplished. Inventory was reduced, cash flow of some $100 million was realized, and the company was operating at three times the industry average in margins.

The two factories in the Midwestern United States were major employers in their regional areas, both of which were characterized as areas of high unemployment and high poverty levels. The company was headquartered in the Midwest and felt some responsibility to keep from adding to the economic problems of the region.

Actions. *Current Segmentation and Competitive Position Were Assessed.* The basic IBP process, a value segmentation analysis, was undertaken. The product design had excellent competitive advantages because of the company's connection with pro teams. The company had baseball uniform designs to fit the baseball player physique for serious players in all age ranges: youth, college, and pro. Prior to the value segmentation, the company looked at its business as having the traditional channel and firmographics makeup.

A comparison of the traditional segmentation and the segments found through research of value needs and states is shown in Figure 1-10.

The segments were assessed, with significant competitive advantage opportunity found in each of the three value segments defined.

Traditional Segmentation		Value Segmentation		*Needs*
Channel	Retail Pro Teams Institutional Dealers	**Price Buyers**	Retailers Youth Leagues	Commodity
Firmographics	Channel Sales Forces Size of Customer	**Highly Customized**	Pro Teams Some Dealers	Special Order
		Specialty Teams	High-Touch Dealers	No Offering

FIGURE 1-10. SEGMENTATION IN THE SPORTS UNIFORM BUSINESS.
The value segmentation found a new, untouched segment of specialty teams served by *high-touch* dealers.

For each of the value segments, we outlined the gap closure alternative the teams had developed:

♦ *Price Buyers.* This segment had to have a uniform at less than $20, with immediate delivery and some styling. These could not be provided from the Midwestern U.S. factories; they had to move to the cost-advantaged Caribbean plant.

♦ *Highly Customized.* Support from a design specialist was required and four- to six-week delivery. Unfortunately, the company quoted 13 weeks and often never delivered at all. Our salespeople dubbed the shipping policy "13 weeks to never." Also, a style and fabric selection guide for our very high complexity of fabric types and colors was required.

♦ *Specialty Teams.* This was an unserved segment. They were willing to pay up to $80 per uniform. They needed to have reasonably fast delivery of less than four weeks, probably two weeks, and accuracy was a big requirement.

The value segments and each segment's value proposition were then outlined, as shown in Figure 1-11.

Priority Order	New Offering	Competitive Edge Objective	Competitive Edge Approach
Special Design	Manual "picture book" design guides	Fast response Attractive pricing	Web interface Easily calculated Designs and price
Highly Custom	Online configuration Tech support	Flexible service Value pricing	High list price Deducts for feature removal
Price/Commodity	Some style features add annually	Meet competition	Simple price book List pricing

FIGURE 1-11. VALUE-SEGMENT DEFINITIONS.
Each segment was outlined by stating the critical value issues in each.

The value proposition statement was as follows for the new segment, Special Design:

The Special Design space serves minor leagues, major colleges, and schools, as well as youth traveling teams seeking a unique look through institutional dealers and sports parks. Uniforms with unique features including trim in the consumer's colors, fabric alternatives, and in-vogue designs would be offered. Fast response is vital, since teams are formed and start playing within weeks. Dealers increase profit by having a no-hassle higher margin offering. The key value metric is providing finished product less than three weeks from order. A $100-million revenue volume within three years is reasonable to expect, with above-normal margins of 60 percent.

A bomb was dealt with: Customers interviewed about the new segment strategy were skeptical. They could not believe we would transform from our past practice of delivering in "13 weeks to never," which had been the actual practice in the special order business for years. So, we had to offer a big incentive using the most powerful word in marketing: *free*. We guaranteed delivery in two weeks or the uniforms were free.

The value chain for the Special Design segment was defined as follows:

♦ The product would be six special uniform designs, developed from our professional team experience.

♦ Each uniform would be available in 12 colors, six fabrics, and two major trim types; 144 combinations were possible, so uniqueness could be accomplished for a league.

♦ A supplier for each of the fabrics was found to provide reliable one- or two-week delivery of the greige (undyed) goods in bolts.

- A dye house was found to process the greige goods to a rate of manufacturing, updated monthly and monitored weekly.
- Factory personnel were trained using a special program through the state of Missouri, so we had a ready complement of sewers.
- A rate-based manufacturing approach was defined for uniform production.

The overall financial goals for the segment were also defined:

- Inventory: Finished Goods = 0; raw material, eight days maximum
- Accounts receivable in Days Sales Outstanding, 30 days
- Margins over 60 percent
- High-growth business

Organizational requirements were also outlined:

- A cross-functional organization was established.
  - ◇ Order entry was relocated from headquarters to the uniform factory.
  - ◇ Central purchasing dispatched a fabric supplier coordinator to the factory with a telephone hotline to the supplier's planner.
  - ◇ Human resources set up a sewing training room, hired to rates.
  - ◇ Engineering developed custom processes to make the six designs as efficiently as commodity uniform designs.

- The growth objective and two-week guarantee clearly were embraced by the cross-functional Special Design value space team.
- A special training program was defined for key sales personnel, and a dealer salesperson training and incentive program was developed.

♦ Marketing created the communication plan and selected key customers for ongoing feedback and evaluation. Advertising at sports parks was initiated. Trade show contacts with institutional dealers, including testimonials of leading dealer successes, were organized.

Business Results Achieved. The business grew at a remarkable rate in the first two years. We actually increased employment in the Missouri plants. The two-week guarantee was the key to gaining initial orders. As far as anyone could tell, the company never failed to deliver on time. Profit, inventory, and A/R goals were achieved and revenue targets were exceeded.

The dealers who were most skeptical were stunned when we delivered the initial orders. One said, "Wait, I only guessed at the players' names. I never thought you would actually deliver the apparel."

CHAPTER 2

Competing on Time and Customer Connectivity

IN CHAPTER 2, we remain focused on demand generation, the vision portion of the change management process for implementing market-savvy S&OP. The guiding principle of market-savvy S&OP design covered in this chapter is: Demand is most effectively generated at the *segment level* by leveraging a *market-segment-specific* strategy securing competitive advantage.

This chapter begins by describing the five fundamentals of a value-segment strategy: *Segment Level*, *Market-Driven*, *Advantaged*, *Collaborative*, and *Delivers Value*. The chapter describes a short history of strategy development since the 1970s to distinguish between a portfolio strategy that helps determine what businesses should be kept and a segment strategy, which is our main concern—the strategy for growing demand in a business that is being kept.

The segment strategy alternatives are described starting with the four traditional strategies and then moving to the new strategies made viable by the on-demand economy. We discuss how the new strategies—*Competing on Time* and *Customer Connectivity*—can be used in established markets to generate remarkable business results against entrenched competition who has dominated using one of the four traditional segment strategies.

I rarely see the segment strategy principle applied even in well-managed companies. When it is applied, the companies thrive. But during the past 30 years, we as business leaders and students have been harried by "strategists" who are actually portfolio analysts and not developers of true competitive advantage. These strategists work at the overall business level, not the segment level. They cannot develop strategy for competitive advantage because they have a mixed group of customers and competitors, not a set of homogeneous groups of customers with common values, so they cannot distinguish between competitors who are meeting customer needs and competitors who are serving their own or other customer groups. The portfolio strategists actually operate to the total distraction of running businesses in an advantaged and highly profitable way. As a result of the distraction, a process for developing and more importantly for implementing a strategic approach for each market segment is not in place in most companies. Jack Welch had it right when he fired all the strategic planners at the General Electric Company soon after becoming CEO. Strategists typically teach portfolio analysis or methods to determine which businesses should be kept or divested. When Welch sorted out GE's businesses, he did it with savvy business managers, not starry-eyed strategists fresh out of business school.

The value segmentation described in Chapter 1 provides the clarity required to start the strategy development process. Chapter 2 clarifies the difference between portfolio and segment-level strategy development, with the latter being the approach leading to a competitively advantaged market-savvy S&OP implementation. (Please note that the segments in market-savvy S&OP are the value segments defined in Chapter 1.)

The Five Fundamentals of a Value-Segment Strategy

To provide an overall perspective on strategy content, the five fundamentals of strategy as applied in market-savvy S&OP are briefly described in the sections that follow. The strategy must be specific at the segment level, market-driven, advantaged, collaborative, and sure to deliver value.

Segment Level: Specific to a Customer Type and thus Implementable

Customer needs and values can be clearly matched with a strategy only at the segment level. Segment-level specifics allow for clarity and depth in the strategy and greatly enhance implementation prospects. At higher levels of aggregation, strategy specifics are often compromised to fit aggregated customer groups when the customers should be in a separate segments. At the segment level, competitors are clearly identified and their specific approach to the segment, if in fact they have one, can be seen. In many cases, the competitors have used a one-size-fits-all approach to a combination of segments and thus have likely provided an opening for you to develop a competitive advantage. Developing strategy at the segment level is in concert with the economic drivers of the new on-demand economy and builds upon the guiding principle of "market in" discussed in Chapter 1.

Market-Driven: Desires Coveted by Customers

To be competitive means customers want what you offer. Thus, the proper starting point is the value space definitions and value segmentation from Chapter 1. You will find most competitors offer what they have and largely ignore the customer's value definition. This provides you with opportunity. One of the most important aspects of segment strategy definition is to suggest ideas and listen to customers, letting them tell you what will work and what is off the mark.

Advantaged: Creating New Values Not Easily Duplicated by the Competition

Your strategy must be better at meeting customer values than the competition's. Advantaged is not *same as*, but creates value for the customer by increasing the customer's cash flow or enhancing his/her profitability. To be advantaged, the strategy must be sustainable, not easily copied. The best way to determine whether or not your strategy options are advantaged is to ask your customers. I have seen cross-functional teams of people gain remarkable insights by jointly interviewing and listening to customers.

Collaborative: Multiplying Strengths of All Functions

The best strategies are ones well coordinated across the value chain to provide maximum overall coordinated implementation. Collaboration across all functional areas and with suppliers and customers provides the multiplicative effect. In a collaborative process, cross-functional organization friction is removed and replaced by a collegial customer-centric model of the culture.

Delivers Value: Meeting the Critical Needs of the Customer Group

Value chains are different from supply chains and value segments. Supply chains describe the physical movement of product. Value chains describe how customer values are delivered from each section of the supply chain. Each value segment has a value chain. Value segments have commonality of customer types based on what they value or covet most. Demographic segments have commonality of metrics important only internally; these are size, geography, products used, and level of exclusivity (psychographics). Market-savvy S&OP is the collaborative process accomplishing strategic implementation. The value chain as used in market-savvy S&OP is described in Figure 2-1.

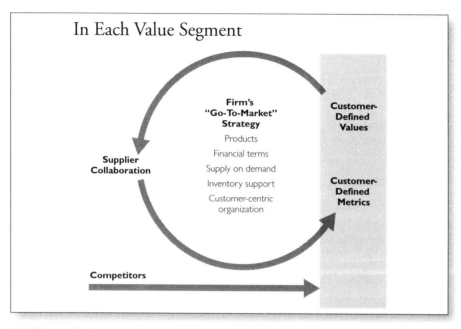

FIGURE 2-1. THE VALUE CHAIN IN MARKET-SAVVY S&OP.
In market-savvy S&OP, value chains start and end with the customer's values and metrics.

Portfolio Versus Segment Strategies

It seems as if business strategy has been around since the beginning of time. The merchants in the Casbah no doubt knew location was of paramount strategic importance, and they probably fought over booth location. Wal-Mart implemented a strategy similar to the Casbah approach, with everything in one destination. Certainly McDonald's, Wendy's, and the other fast-food chains all strive to be like the Casbah merchants, located close to each other.

While there is nothing new under the sun, the economy today is much more complex than ever before. Thus, the common approach to portfolio strategy development as depicted by leading thinkers in even recent history is of limited value in today's economy. While some of the basic principles such as location, location, location are still applicable, they must be applied correctly.

Traditional portfolio strategy approaches are still being taught in most major business schools. While these approaches are very different from the segment strategy approach covered in this book, it might be helpful to discuss several of the most popular to provide a historical perspective. First, I cover *a three-part generic portfolio strategy approach.* Then, I discuss two portfolio strategy approaches emerging in the late 1970s and still representing the core principles taught by leading business school professors—those of the Boston Consulting Group and of Michael E. Porter of Harvard Business School. Both of these approaches were built upon the generic portfolio strategy approach.

Three-Part Generic Portfolio Strategy

The generic strategy definition is simplistic and highly generalized. Figure 2-2 describes the approach.

The three strategies are:

1. Overall low-cost provider in the industry (the upper left quadrant)
2. Broad differentiation in the industry (the upper right quadrant)
3. Focused or niche player (the lower left and right quadrants)

According to this approach, the overall cost leader must be the absolute low-cost provider and must have parity with competitors in the other basic aspects of doing business: service and quality. The lowest cost position can be held by only one competitor per industry.

A good example exists in the Baldor Electric Company, the motor manufacturer mentioned in Chapter 1. Baldor came into a market dominated by industrial giants GE and Westinghouse Electric Corp. Both competitors offered a full line of electric motors from one HP up to 300 HP. Both made all their motors in single factories, GE in Fort

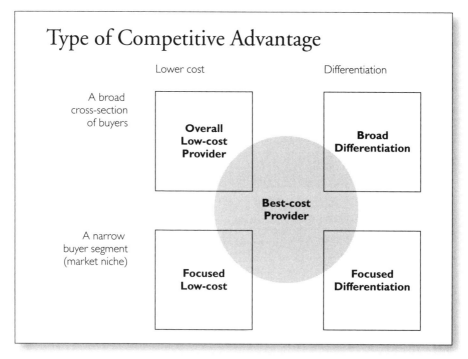

FIGURE 2-2. GENERIC STRATEGIES.
The generic strategy approach is primarily an industry-level strategy orniche strategy, not a market-segment-level strategic approach.

Wayne, Indiana, and Westinghouse in Buffalo, New York. In the mid-1970s, Baldor determined that 50 percent of the market was in one-HP motors used by a plethora of buyers in myriad applications. One-HP motors were as common as an industrial product could be, similar to the lightbulb or the water pump and found everywhere. Baldor decided to manufacture this motor in a low-cost factory in Fort Smith, Arkansas. Baldor had high quality and superb service and was hands down the lowest-cost provider. It enjoyed high profitability as the nearly exclusive supplier of one-HP motors to the broad market. The stock price doubled in the 1980s and doubled again before ABB bought the company.

The broad differentiation strategy requires defining a uniqueness widely accepted in the market across most segments. The differentiator must command a higher price than the cost of differentiation. General Electric for decades provided inventory of lightbulbs on consignment to retailers and set the retail price to maximize retailers' margins. The strategy was applied for everyone and was very successful, gaining GE a 65 percent share of the market overall. GE was forced to drop the strategy when the Department of Justice repeatedly sued the company for price maintenance under the antitrust laws. The cost of defense became excessive for GE. In addition, mass merchants developed merchandising strategies around "everyday low prices" or "lowest prices," both counter to GE's strategy.

The focused strategy is to become the cost leader or unique competitor in a market niche. This niche is not a value segment as described in Chapter 1, but a demographic segment defining how the producer gains value, rather than how customers derive value. Michelin used the radial tire technology to differentiate itself among premium consumer tire customers. The company entered the highly competitive U.S. consumer tire market 50 years after industry leaders but gained share rapidly with the radial technology. It grew enough to build manufacturing plants in South Carolina in the 1970s, after convincing Ford to go radial on its luxury cars and convincing Sears to offer radial replacement tires. The tire industry ignored the Michelin push, sticking with bias ply tires, until Michelin expanded to additional market niches and took away double-digit share points. Today, Goodyear is the only one of the big four tire manufacturers to have survived Michelin's onslaught: Firestone is now Japanese; Goodrich and Uniroyal were absorbed by French, German, and Italian companies.

In application, these strategies are very difficult to maintain. All three are highly vulnerable to changes in the underlying industry or niche assumptions. In today's economy, industry changes occur rapidly and specific niches readily vaporize, so a continuous review and refresh element must exist in every strategy development process. The generic strategy approach is useful, but because it is too simplistic and generalized, a more robust process-oriented strategy development approach is required.

The Four-Quadrant Chart of the Boston Consulting Group

Bruce Henderson of the Boston Consulting Group (BCG) developed the growth-share matrix, or four-quadrant chart of the cash cow, to describe strategy development. BCG's approach is primarily focused on which businesses a company should have in its portfolio, as opposed to how to improve profitability in a given business. The approach was popular in the 1970s, which was the beginning of the era of the conglomerate. Many CEOs then began to believe the only way to sustain profitability was to have many complementary businesses, so the question became which ones.

The growth-share matrix is shown in Figure 2-3.

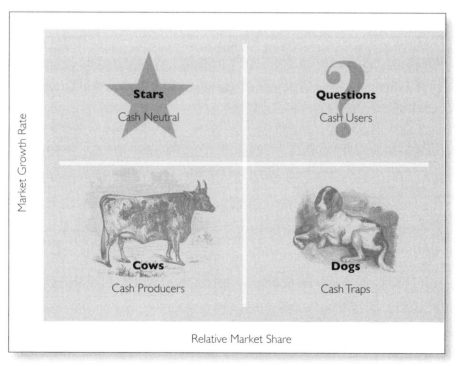

FIGURE 2-3. BRUCE HENDERSON'S GROWTH-SHARE MATRIX.
The analysis emphasizes keeping businesses with share leadership in high-growth markets.

The most important point to observe is that the vertical center line denotes one. This means there is only one business in each industry to the left of the center line, since to have a relative market share of greater than one means you are the market-share leader. All other companies in an industry are either dogs or questions. So, according to this matrix, only one company in each industry can be a star or cash cow—a somewhat limiting guiding conclusion, I believe.

The growth aspect is on the Y axis, with the horizontal center line being the annual growth rate of the specific industry or industry in general. Most industries grow with the population, so a growth rate of greater than three or four is unusual. Stars are those companies in an industry growing faster than 3 percent or more per year, and they are the market share leaders.

In practice, BCG advised a great many companies to exit businesses using this matrix. The practical value is limited primarily to portfolio analysis. If your business is a dog, you should go further into the strategy development process discussed earlier in this chapter to discover how to become a star in specific market segments within your industry. Certainly, if you participate in several different businesses, then perhaps this initial approach to strategic analysis would be helpful.

As BCG further developed the application of Bruce Henderson's principles, the company became aware of the need to focus more on analysis of segments within industries. Otherwise, taken to the extreme, BCG's model would have advocated each industry having only one competitor, which is illogical. There are more ways to make a remarkable profit than just to have high overall market share in a high-growth industry.

The Five Competitive Forces Approach of Michael E. Porter

Michael E. Porter, leader of the Institute for Strategy and Competitiveness at Harvard Business School, is considered the leading expert on competitive strategy. Porter's core principles of competitive strategy are described in the first section of his book *Competitive Advantage*.

Although he refers to the generic strategy approach we discussed earlier, it is used in combination with his five forces approach, a framework to determine industry profitability. The five competitive forces are shown in Figure 2-4.

Porter's approach is useful in framing the specific challenges a management team faces in a particular industry. However, his approach does not in itself or in conjunction with the generic strategies lead to a specific strategy selection. In practice, many companies

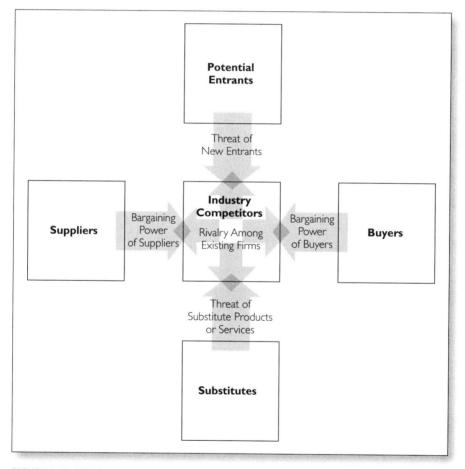

FIGURE 2-4. MICHAEL PORTER'S FIVE COMPETITIVE FORCES APPROACH.
Using Porter's approach, the generalized profit potential of an industry is assessed, but not a segment strategy or a strategy's profitability.

are highly profitable in industries where the five forces work against their prospects for profitability. In fact, the majority of companies today have high threats in all five areas outlined by Porter. If the CEOs of all the industries facing four or five highly adverse forces decided to exit their industries, we would have total chaos and a disaster. On the other hand, we would have lots of opportunities for new entrants.

Segment-Level Strategies for Value Chains

In today's on-demand economy, the adverse conditions Porter describes are the new normal. Management teams must find profitable paths regardless of industry conditions. The alternative—exiting the current business—is simply not acceptable in most cases and unnecessary if segment-level strategy development is perfected.

In the 1980s, I was on a project team working for Republic Steel in Cleveland. Our challenge was to find a way to speed up the modernization of the steel mills. Interestingly, we followed McKinsey & Company into the engagement. The CEO decided to hire us after the brain trust at McKinsey told him to exit steel because of low industry profitability and instead to enter the insurance business, a high-profit industry. This tells us that some very smart people have totally abused Porter's concepts.

Porter does use the value chain in his approach. In his book *Competitive Advantage*, he writes:

> *The book describes the way a firm can choose and implement a generic strategy to achieve and sustain competitive advantage. It addresses the interplay between types of competitive advantage—cost and differentiation—and the scope of a firm's activities. The basic tool for diagnosing competitive advantage and finding ways to enhance it is the value chain, which divides a firm into discrete activities it performs.*

Porter's definition of value chain emphasizes the company's discrete activities and leaves out the market or customer drivers of value.

This approach was very appropriate for the old supply economy, in which strategies were primarily internally focused on cost and product with the assumption "if we build it, they will come." Today, customers have too many alternatives to allow this internally focused approach to work.

The definition of value chain used in our approach is very different. We start with customer values and end with customer-defined metrics measuring success of implementation. Value chains describe how value is delivered. Porter's value chain is much more like a supply chain. Supply chains were defined by Booz & Co. in the late 1970s in a fashion very similar to the depiction of value chains in Porter's books. Supply chains and Porter's value chains describe how to deliver products, not value. The value chain as I define it, inside a specific market segment, is a major diagnostic tool used to discover competitive advantage and to find ways to enhance competitive advantage.

The traditional, widely taught and used portfolio approaches to business strategy are helpful. Certainly, the consultants who have applied these approaches have been successful, and many companies have benefited greatly from their use. However, today's on-demand economy necessitates a more effective approach. Market segments defined by the customer—not by our own interpretation of demographics and psychographics—are the beginning, and developing the value-chain definition and a competitive plan within each segment will provide the strategic answers.

The generic strategies and portfolio analysis approaches all have a major fatal flaw: clarity in understanding customers. They all rely upon a general definition of the industry and the competitive players within it. Even the focus or niche strategies fail to define key differences between competitors and customers because the approach is internally focused. The niche strategy and Porter's definition of value chain deal with how companies will deliver product, rather than how they can identify and serve the customer's value. These approaches all *tell* what companies will do for customers. In contrast, the segment-level value chain, and segment strategy approach of market-savvy S&OP *asks and listens* to discover the values customers desire.

In the highly competitive arena of selling to Wal-Mart, the most frequent discussions I hear are sales representatives telling Wal-Mart buyers the pricing and volume expectations of their companies. The buyers are highly motivated to have the lowest-cost items in their mix, so this selling approach is common. A generic strategy of being the low-cost provider or perhaps some differentiation strategy would be consistent with this scenario of the business, and, in fact, some companies look at Wal-Mart as a niche in itself and provide specific products just for Wal-Mart. In my experience, this strategic approach does not lead to a profitable business, just a high-volume giveaway. The market-savvy S&OP approach would have a team of people from each of our functions meeting with more senior Wal-Mart executives. In fact, as president of Rawlings, I met with Sam Walton on many occasions and addressed and listened to his senior staff; as a result, we had a profitable and productive relationship.

The key to success is *market in* at a segment level. Listen to what the customers in a value segment deem most valuable to them. A strategic approach that looks at the generic industry factors or focuses on internal capabilities and products will be overwhelmed by a segment-specific approach built on an external focus, our guiding principle of *market in*.

Four Traditional Value-Segment Strategy Options

In terms of value-segment strategy alternatives, there are four traditional options still of significant value: (1) lowest cost, (2) highest market share, (3) location advantaged, and (4) innovation leadership. (See Figure 2-5.) In market-savvy S&OP, these are applied at the value-segment level where they can be sustained. There are also two new options: (5) competing on time and (6) customer connectivity. The new options, discussed later in this chapter, are made possible by the dynamics of the new on-demand economy, where the customer is the driving force. The

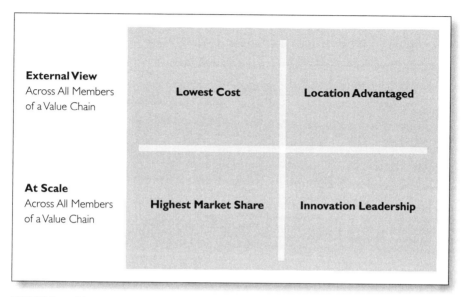

FIGURE 2-5. FOUR TRADITIONAL VALUE-SEGMENT STRATEGIES.
The four strategies are viable in market-savvy S&OP if two guiding principles are correctly applied: market in and value-chain-wide.

four traditional options can be combined with the two new options of time advantaged and customer-connectivity advantaged.

Lowest Cost

Cost leadership means you are the absolute low-cost provider within a segment. The cost leadership strategy is perhaps the most misunderstood and applied of all the strategies. If you looked at a business using either the generic strategy or the five forces approaches, you would exit all businesses that have China Inc. as a competitor. Unfortunately, many CEOs have given in to the supposedly insurmountable cost leadership of the low-cost manufacturing in China. But in our value-segment approach, China is very likely a highly vulnerable competitor. Even more so now as the yuan is finally being forced into proper alignment with other world currencies and thus eliminating the artificial exchange rate advantage China has enjoyed for several decades. When the yuan reaches the correct level against the dollar many U.S. businesses will find themselves cost advantaged; as they should be given the far superior manufacturing productivity found in well-managed U.S. factories. I have long said the yuan should be 3 or less to the dollar, not 8 or 9 as has been the case.

Let's look at some basic facts about cost in a manufacturing industry or in a service industry like a call center. Labor and materials together are the large variable costs. To the cost accountant, the sales, marketing, and administrative costs are "fixed," and costs outside the company are completely ignored. Cost inside a value segment requires looking at all the costs in the whole value chain, as described in the introduction to this chapter: the customer's costs, our costs, and our suppliers' costs. In this view, your labor and material costs are a fraction of the total cost in the value chain. China Inc. has the big cost of ocean freight, which is more than labor plus materials in many, many cases. The cost of missing peak promotional volumes as a result of long ocean freight time is enormous to the customer, if we can only demonstrate this.

In an example with one of my clients, we asked Wal-Mart to calculate the benefit of having product available in days or hours, not weeks, during promotions. Wal-Mart said it would be willing to pay a full 5 percent price premium to have short lead time availability of the exact mix actually selling through. Five percent is greater than the total labor cost for most manufactured products. So where is the advantage of China Inc.? It is vulnerable to those U.S.-based firms willing to confront total costs, but the fact is few companies actually do, so you have an opportunity. I would be quick to point out that combining a cost-leadership strategy with a time-advantaged strategy using in-country production is a potent approach and one that is rarely found. Where the combination is found, you have a company that dominates its industry.

Consider cost leadership in a service industry. The cost of the phone operators is likely the only cost most companies consider when choosing whether to locate a call center in-country, with the same culture and local knowledge, or in a different country with a low-cost structure, such as India. In many cases, low-cost centers—particularly in India—do provide excellent service. These centers have employees with sufficient English-language skills, and the employees have scripts to guide them successfully through calls. If these were the only factors involved in the service center's cost within its value chains, then the discussion would be over. Of course, though, you must also ignore the hours the consumer spends on the phone trying to communicate with people in such a call center. We are increasingly finding that the lowest operator cost option is a poor one when considering an expanded view of cost reflecting total cost to the customer. Bundling services and providing creative solutions are two of the more significant value considerations of the strategy assessment.

Zappos.com has built its business on the principle of finding creative solutions, not just taking orders for shoes. Its core value is "embrace and drive change." The Zappos family of employees is highly motivated to be creative. The phone representatives can discuss fashion options, stockout alternatives (rarely needed), delivery options, and even solutions to tangential concerns such as ordering a pizza to go with shoes as a gift for a special occasion. An operator in India would not be able to perform any of these extra services. It's a culture thing.

Commercial tire maker Goodyear has a 24/7 service-call center in Akron, Ohio, for fleets. The goal is guaranteeing the driver will be back on the road making money within two hours of a blowout. To do this, close coordination of repair trucks and night cages (storage locations accessible at night) at independent dealers throughout the country is required. In addition, operators must have available an up-to-the-minute, highly accurate computer record of what tire was on the truck when the tire blew, shredded (think highway alligators), and is now nowhere to be found by the driver. The level of coordination and accuracy required could not be achieved by people in a different culture who first ask for the serial number on the tire.

Highest Market Share

We saw in the generic and portfolio approaches that only one competitor has highest market share. This is particularly evident in BCG's matrix approach. In the value-segment strategy approach, highest share means highest share within a value segment. In the value-segment strategy approach, share is measured inside a segment for the specific value chain.

Many market-share leaders in an industry cannot compete profitably because their overall operating complexity increases costs higher than the benefits of size. The need to support a "full spectrum" product line requires investing in low-return products and services. To maintain share leadership, a company must serve the small customers as well as the big ones. A hypothetical example, but one I believe you will agree is representative of many industries, follows.

Consider an industry with three major competitors plus some small competitors in which there are a total of 100 customers. The major three competitors nearly equally split up the 20 largest customers, which account for 80 percent of the market. (The 80-20 rule always proves to be true.) So each company has about seven customers and about 25 percent share, which means that no clear market-share leader exists here. To gain real share leadership, the company pursuing industry share advantage must service the 80 small customers to gain clear leadership of 45 percent share. To win these small customers, the sales force complexity grows, product complexity grows, and a more complex distribution network is put in place. The small customers then complain that their pricing is not fair because the bigger customers receive volume discounts (perfectly legal and logical) and can sell at lower retail prices than the small customers pay at wholesale. The standard cost systems do not capture the cost of complexity, nor do they capture the total cost to serve the small customers. Overhead costs and selling costs are spread equally based on volume alone. Distribution costs are equalized geographically to match competition, so supposedly the cost to sell one at less-than-truckload (LTL) rates to one customer in Idaho is not significantly different than the cost to sell 1,000 at LTL to the customer in a state adjoining the state in which the plant is located. The cost-party rule of the differentiation strategy in the generic approach is satisfied. In final analysis of our hypothetical example, the market-share leader probably cannot make a profit because of the excessive overall complexity of operations.

In the value-segment approach, you can have less-than-dominant share overall in the industry but pick segments to dominate in share and have a very profitable business. International Harvester (IH) manufactured trucks; its successor company, Navistar, still does with roughly the same strategy and results. IH boasted the highest market share in the truck industry. It ignored Ford, which sold more pickup trucks than IH sold trucks in total. This aside, IH was the share leader.

When IH ran into major financial problems in the 1980s, it asked Booz & Co. for assistance, and I was on the team. Our firm's marketing experts found that in the large-truck business, there were (and still are) nine market segments of significance. IH did have overall share leadership. However, it was no better than third in any one segment and a poor fourth or worse in some. At the IH plant in Fort Wayne, Indiana (now closed), we found there were more than 100 different fuel tanks on offer—all kinds of sizes and shapes to fit the requirements of local haulers, regional haulers, long haulers using fleet trucks, individual sleeper trucks, economy models, and so on. In the large and lucrative (for some) individual owner-operator segment for long haulers, IH offered 35 different fuel tanks. Its competitor, PACCAR—which builds trucks under the Kenworth and Peterbuilt names—offered 50 fuel tanks in just this one segment. The highly discerning buyers of individual owner-operator long haul trucks were naturally more likely to buy from PACCAR. This complexity problem was not limited to fuel tanks but infected every other fashion and performance feature of the truck. IH had much greater complexity overall, but poor segment market share and major financial problems.

Using a market-share leadership strategy in the value-segment approach actually enables greater complexity among competitors in the segment, but lower overall complexity in the industry. The cost of complexity inside a segment is much easier to measure and manage. For the industry generalist, almost any example of one customer requirement for product or service is justified and provided. For the segment specialist, the customer's true needs are clear and discernment is easier.

Location Advantaged

The location advantage is normally thought of as applied to retailing, but it is also a very potent strategy for commercial and industrial providers. In the value-segment strategy approach, a location advantage can be well understood. In the generic strategy approach, differentiation by location is much more difficult to accomplish, but is often assumed.

In any make-to-stock (MTS) industry, from paint to pumps, consumer durables, and even medical devices, the competitors all have warehouses and presumably use sophisticated mathematical models to locate distribution centers in precisely the right locations to minimize costs and maximize service. They then all assume they have service advantages because of superior location. From the perspective of a consultant who has done way too many distribution modeling studies, there is no real difference possible. If you were to choose a West Coast distribution center such as Sparks, Nevada; a Midwest distribution center in Chicago; an East Coast center in King of Prussia, Pennsylvania; a Southwest center in Dallas; and a southern center in Atlanta, you would have the same service and cost structure any potential competitor could possibly develop. Once you have five distribution centers spread out across the country, you have optimized cost to a level of 98 percent or better.

Location advantage can be had if you can truly provide a clear value advantage to the customer in a value segment. My firm, The On-Point Group, worked with Specialty Minerals Corporation, a spin-off from Pfizer Inc. The client described its business as putting dirt in a bag—very nice dirt from limestone quarries in Adams, Massachusetts, and other places in the United States. The limestone is used in many different products, including TUMS heartburn remedies and Soft Scrub home cleaners. Several solid competitors existed. The company had been making a precipitated calcium carbonate (PCC) product since the turn of the twentieth century. Looking for competitive advantage in this commodity business, Specialty Minerals determined it could provide PCC to paper mills to use as a whitener, replacing wood pulp. PCC is a base with a high pH, as opposed to wood pulp, which is acidic and has a low pH. PCC makes paper environmentally friendly by eliminating most of the acid.

The problem was that all its competitors could quickly follow Specialty Minerals's lead in applying PCC to paper mill processing because the conversion process is very simple. The company decided upon a location strategy of placing a limestone processing operation next to the customer's paper mill and running the product directly into the mill in a pipe, rather than transporting it by truck from a large centralized plant. The cost trade-offs were minimal because transportation costs were a major factor and process scale could be achieved at very low levels, such as one paper mill's requirements. Specialty Minerals quickly built small satellite PCC plants next to more than 60 percent of the appropriate paper mill capacity in the United States and then expanded into Europe. The location advantage was nearly impossible for competitors to circumvent. In the value segment of paper mills, the needs of the customer were very different from the needs of other customer groups, and a tailored value chain using satellite plants was developed because there was clarity in the value proposition.

Innovation Leadership

The innovative leader must have a continual flow of new products well ahead of the competition. Differentiation as an innovative leader for the broad marketplace is difficult to achieve. We have all seen examples of this strategy working for Apple Inc. in a portion of the consumer electronics industry. Apple continues to innovate, from graphical user interfaces to devices. In the iPhone and iPad ventures, the value chain includes thousands of outside application developers as well as hardware suppliers. Apple is routinely ranked as a top performer in supply chain excellence studies done by Gartner Group and the former AMR Research. I would argue Apple serves a value segment of customers who like to "play" online, as opposed to customers who use online access devices for actual work. In reality, BlackBerry smartphones and personal computers are work devices, and the iPhone and iPad are toys. (Try to prepare a report or even a long memo on an iPad; this is not a productive exercise.)

Rawlings Sporting Goods successfully executed an innovation strategy in performance baseball gloves for many decades. It dominated the segment until the company was acquired by an inexperienced group of investors, who dropped the strategy and promptly lost the leadership position. For 80 years from 1910, Rawlings was the only baseball glove manufacturer researching baseball glove design and generating patents. The goal was to come up with three patentable ideas annually, a formidable goal given the product is simply a glove used to catch a ball.

The value chain was reasonably complex for a relatively small business. The method Rawlings used to develop the patents was a key part of the value chain. The glove designers traveled to spring training each year to work directly with professional baseball players. The designers had a large truck housing workshops. The players received free glove repair and were able to order custom-made gloves.

Over time, each of the nine baseball fielding positions came to have distinctively different glove designs. The needs of catchers and first basemen are obvious. But middle infielders wanted very small, flat gloves that simply tipped the ball to the throwing hand, rather than catching the ball, which required digging it out of the pocket—a time-consuming, unneeded step. The shortstop glove was the most extreme in flatness; meanwhile, a little more pocket was designed for second basemen and a normal pocket was designed for third basemen. Pitchers wanted a deep glove to hide the ball inside while taking the signs from the catcher. Outfielders, particularly in center field, needed a glove that had internal cantilevers to snap around the ball, clamping it in as it hit somewhere near the inside of the glove. Rawlings also made special gloves for specific players. For example, designers created a special palm pad for Cincinnati Reds catcher Johnny Bench that protected his thumb against the constant pounding that could cause internal bleeding. The pad and plastic insert did not interfere with his job of catching, so the design was not insignificant. The pad and protector are credited with extending his baseball career. Many of the innovations that Rawlings developed for the pro players ended up in the high-end retail gloves designed for Little League, high school, and college players.

Another key aspect of the Rawlings baseball glove value chain was having the professional players actually endorse the gloves. Since the endorsement contracts did not carry very much financial compensation, the primary way to secure the endorsements was through product performance. Of course, the players loved recognition, so Rawlings invented the Rawlings Gold Glove Awards, which are presented by Sporting News (another excellent St. Louis, Missouri, company). The honor is of particular importance to the players because it is awarded based upon the votes of their peers. Rawlings's goal was to have more than 75 percent of the 18 Gold Gloves bestowed annually (nine each from the American and National Leagues) awarded to Rawlings glove users. It was an unusual year when this goal was not achieved. As a result, Rawlings had a continuous and broad supply of endorsee names to print on the retail gloves. Rawlings was able to provide geographically significant names on gloves—for example, Dave Winfield in New York or "Mr. Shortstop," the Chicago Cub's Ernie Banks. Not many people know the Gold Glove Award as really the Rawlings Gold Glove Award, but the proof is on the award itself.

Manufacturing was also a key part of the Rawlings value chain. The professional gloves and the highest-quality "Heart of the Hide" branded gloves were always made in Ava, Missouri. The U.S.-based operation allowed Rawlings to protect its intellectual property rights and provide fast response to the custom-design requirements of the professional players. In addition, the manufacturing knowledge of material yields, labor content, and quality control requirements was useful for managing contractor factories in other parts of the world. A significant aspect of the overall value-chain design is the excellent supply chain control Rawlings was able to maintain for its retail business. The subsequent rate-based manufacturing strategy used by Rawlings for the long lead-time baseball gloves in a highly seasonal market is discussed in Chapter 6. Without the U.S.-based high-quality factory, the rate-based manufacturing would not have been as successful and perhaps not even possible.

The Rawlings innovation strategy was highly successful. The company was able to defend its powerful market position from the Japanese sporting goods giant Mizuno Corporation when it made a strong bid for a share of the U.S. market in the 1980s. Mizuno was responding to Rawlings's successful entry into the Japanese market, which is the second-largest market for baseball equipment in the world. Rawlings had captured a remarkable and very close number two position to Mizuno overall and number one in high-end equipment. Rawlings also defended its position successfully against Nike Inc., which literally bought its logo onto pitcher's hands. In the end, the performance players stayed with Rawlings, the performance leader. Pitchers play only every fourth day and are not known for fielding prowess, so their endorsement in baseball gloves did not mean much.

Unfortunately, Rawlings was divested and the strategy was curtailed. An innovation strategy stops providing benefits shortly after innovation stops.

The Apple and Rawlings examples illustrate how the innovation strategy must be undergirded by a robust group of support activities from each cross-functional area. Manufacturing, third-party producers, the sales force, designers, the marketing staff, and many others have key roles in an innovation strategy.

Market-savvy S&OP uses the segment strategies to define the role of all functional areas. Without the segment strategy and value chain definition, it is difficult to execute a collaborative organizational design.

New Segment Strategies

Two new strategic advantages are made possible by the on-demand economy: competing on time and customer connectivity. These two strategies build on the collaboration principle described elsewhere in this chapter. The two are not just tacked onto the four-square chart as subsets of traditional strategies. Instead, they are all-new strategies, chosen instead of one of the traditional four.

In the real world, creating competitive advantage is hard work. If your company depends upon only marketing or sales to come up with the strategy, it will be of limited value to the customer. The best strategies come from cross-functional teams working together to maximize the combined strength of all functions in the company. The traditional strategies of lowest cost, highest market share, location advantaged, and innovation leadership require near-zero collaboration across functions. They can be effective. But a competitor using a collaborative approach will come up with a much more potent strategy that is far easier to defend because of its implementation complexity.

Time and customer connectivity are just such complex strategies. They are different, but in ways they are the same. Time advantage is having the fastest possible response to changes in customer demand. Customer connectivity is being close to your customer and, in turn, its customers. Variation in demand is manageable with limited inventory, and value factors other than time become primary. In both of the new segment strategies, service is very high, near 100 percent, but more important, customer cash and your cash are both conserved.

Competing on Time

Time advantage becomes primary when your customer's demand patterns are highly variable and product complexity is high (from 50 to thousands of items). Time advantages by your company generate tangible benefits to your customer: near-zero inventories, high realization of sales due to availability, and high cash flow.

Some readers may be thinking I am talking about just-in-time

(JIT) production. Time advantaged does not mean JIT, which is not a strategy at all; it is a manufacturing management practice. JIT means the enterprise uses excess capacity, rather than inventory, to handle demand variability. It does not involve any engagement with the customer; it simply says that no matter what the customer wants, we will make it now, because we have enough excess capacity to make everything every day. JIT is affordable only for very simple manufacturing processes, including light assembly or limited complexity fabrication. More complex manufacturing operations—the vast majority of manufacturing operations—should use a rate-based manufacturing practice, as described in Chapter 6. Many complex manufacturing operations use material requirements planning, the time-phased technique built into all enterprise resource planning (ERP) systems. JIT can be compatible with a time-advantaged strategy in simplistic manufacturing environments. In fact, using a time-advantaged strategy probably fully negates the need for JIT.

All manufacturing plants must deal with two key issues: mix and volume. S&OP is the management process addressing both these issues. The manufacturing approach then implements the volume and mix decisions made in S&OP. So JIT is one of the three major manufacturing practices or systems that can be employed; it is not a comprehensive supply chain strategy. The three manufacturing practices are compared in Figure 2-6.

Time advantage is a strategy because it provides a competitive advantage highly effective for the customer, in the right application and very difficult for competitors to mimic. The strategy requires a specific set of three major characteristics: a market segment requiring and respecting time; collaboratively developed, rapid-fire demand signals; and the value-chain capability to allow manufacturing to deliver as needed without excessive inventory at either the manufacturer or the customer. Most often, a rate-based manufacturing system is employed, sometimes in conjunction with a delayed configuration component to the overall supply system. MRP is never used; it is much too inflexible.

The first characteristic is having the appropriate market segment

Management Factors	Time-Phased Planning (MRP)	Just-in-Time (JIT)	Rate-Based Planning (RBP)
Type of manufacturing where best applied	Job shops only per original design	Simplistic operations	Complex operations
Cost management	Cost drives decisions	Moot due to simplicity	Balanced to asset utilization factors
Inventory management	Big safety stocks	Minimizing drives all decisions	Optimized in all decisions
Throughput management	Not a decision-making factor	Improved using lean techniques	Throughput maximized
Capacity management	Ignored	Highly excessive capacity required	Optimized along with inventory

FIGURE 2-6. THE THREE MOST COMMON MANUFACTURING PRACTICES.
MRP is the most common and most inflexible; RBP is highly recommended for more complex manufacturing.

for time-advantaged competition—one both requiring and respecting time. Many segments are appropriate, including those in which:

♦ Seasonality is significant.

♦ Promotional activity accounts for most of the demand.

♦ Frequent product design updates impact most of the demand (fashion products, for example).

♦ There is a highly complex product mix.

In value segments having these characteristics, the competitive element, which is a strategic fundamental, is recognized. Time advantage is of great importance to the customers in the segment for two reasons. One, they cannot accurately forecast mix very far in advance of the season, promotion, or design change cycle. And two, they cannot afford any inventory overhang at the end of those cycles.

To illustrate, consider a packaged food product sold to retailers, food service customers, and mass merchants. Although the product is identical in each segment, time-advantaged competition may apply only to the food service customer segment due to high product complexity. In the food service segment, many different varieties of the product are required to satisfy the unique needs of a wide range of restaurants and institutional food preparers. The orders in food service are often orders with hundreds of lines, but requiring delivery in several weeks, not in hours. The time advantage is being able to manufacture the full mix inside the order lead times. Seasonality is normally not a big issue for food service customers; for instance, Mexican restaurants typically have the same menu year-round. In the retail segment, a far less complex product line normally exists.

However, if the product is highly promotional at retail, time advantage may apply in this segment, but for a different reason. Order lead times in the retail segment normally are extremely short at the beginning of the promotion, as compared with the food service segment. And demand signals for promotional products are not orders. They are probably statistics from leading indicator stores or very current (a few days or a week old) test-market data. The time advantage is being able to adjust production and ship the necessary volume and mix in days or even hours. In the mass-merchant segment of our food product manufacturer, the time advantage may be of zero value because of low complexity and ready inventory blowout capability. A different competitive strategy is required—probably the other new one, customer connectivity.

The second characteristic of the strategy—the rapid-fire demand signal—is critical. The demand signal is rapid-fire because the time required for acting on the signal is extremely short; thus, one reason for the need to be time advantaged. In many cases, only a day or less is available. The S&OP process must be designed to actually manage to the demand signals, often with weekly or daily meetings during the times when the signals are active. One exception would be in the previous food service example, where the orders are the signals. In this case, the need for a weekly or more frequent *tilt meeting* is desirable in the S&OP design. The tilt meeting is called when the rate of orders is different from the S&OP planned rate.

Demand signals are best developed in collaboration with the customer, who can determine what the leading indicators are and what is happening inside its business to trigger a change in demand. If you try to use point-of-sale (POS) data, several problems arise. The sheer volume of data becomes overwhelming, unless the customer can point out the places where the data are relevant and where they are not. The idea is not to have data but to receive information. I find the executive group tends to be unconvinced at this point, since they do not believe a good demand signal can be developed for the strategy to actually work. Some examples would be helpful to prove the concept.

Cumulative Charts for Seasonal/Promotional Businesses. In seasonal and promotional businesses, the demand signal could be test stores or, in many cases, leading indicator customers. I have managed a business in which we had the sales force present the seasonal product line to leading indicator customers early in the seasonal sales cycle so we could gauge our competitive strength and the appetite of the customers for our products at our expected volumes. The information gained is of enormous importance if placed into the perspective of historical rates. We built a cumulative order chart to understand the data received early in the sales cycle, as shown in Figure 2-7.

In Figure 2-7, Control Point #1 is at a position early in the season when we normally would have received about 27 percent of the orders for product and committed about 60 percent of production. Control Point #2 is a little later, with about 58 percent of orders normally in hand, but still about 25 percent of production uncommitted. When Control Point #1 is reached, the S&OP team adds up the orders—say, 150,000 units—and divides by the historical rate, or 27 percent, to determine what the annual quantity is going to be, or 556,000. If your forecast is greater than 556,000, the team should consider a revision downward or initiate a plan to close the gap between actual and plan.

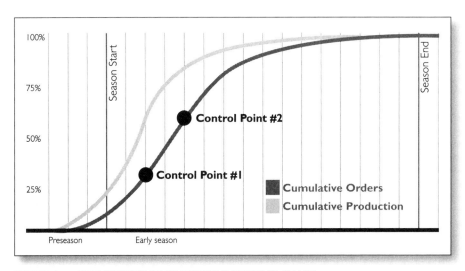

FIGURE 2-7. SEASONALITY OR PROMOTION CONTROL CHART.
The chart shows cumulative data as actually experienced historically.

Contingency plans to reduce production should also be taken. In the reverse case, with the calculated number of 556,000 being greater than plan, production increases should be planned immediately.

At Control Point #2, the same calculation is made. If we now have 340,000 units booked in orders, the calculated annual amount will be 586,000 units. This is a 6 percent increase from Control Point #1, a typical range of results. If a far greater variance is experienced, then you must consider improving the source of the data and pick more representative sources or a larger sample size.

Using this tool, the S&OP team can have a realistic debate about trends and make practical decisions about future production, in time to continue to meet overall demand. I know some skeptics might point to an example of a product that must be totally produced before the season even begins, such as Christmas tree lights. In such a case, a different demand signaling technique must be used. However, in many seasonal/promotional businesses, the situation is exactly as described. One critical thing to remember is this analytical method is done at the market-segment level. When the segments are not defined properly and are way too broad or too small, the problem is lack of homogeneity in the customer grouping, not the analysis.

Leading Indicators for High-Complexity and Fashion-Like Businesses. In businesses characterized by frequently updated design or fashion as well as in businesses with high complexity, leading indicators are the rapid-fire demand signals. Leading indicators may be assessed using POS data, but POS must be turned into information for decision making with well-defined leading indicators. Collaboration with customers to pick the leading indicators is of paramount importance. You want to know which ones they use to make their decisions.

Leading indicators may be demand trends compared to like products or demand trends within a savvy group of customers or in leading indicator outlets. In some cases, the timing of a fashion or design change can be determined by looking at the demand drop-off rates from date of introduction.

The competitive advantage is making decisions in time to avoid unwanted consequences, such as inventory overhang at the end of a season or as the design has changed. Perhaps more important than excess inventory is not having enough inventory to maximize sell-through. In many businesses, such as consumer electronics, new designs or new product introductions can be stopped dead by excess inventory of the old products in the value chain. Choosing the correct demand signals and being able to respond to them is critical to the time-advantaged strategy.

Value-Chain Capability in Time Advantage. The third component of the time-advantaged strategy is having a value-chain production capability that makes the necessary changes to demand signals in time to satisfy the customer without inventory, or at least a very minimum amount, and certainly no safety stocks or inventory buffers. Inventory is the anathema of the time-advantaged strategy. Having inventory means we made something using precious capacity that did not sell through to a customer almost immediately. The time-advantaged strategy incorporates a rate-based planning (RBP) process, which is discussed in Chapter 6.

However, there is more to this strategy than just RBP. The manufacturing process must be totally time-efficient. Every aspect of the value chain must be studied for reduction in time. Forming strategic partnerships with suppliers to have production close, within feet of final production if at all possible, is an essential element. Dedicating production equipment is probably required. Having an organization in the value chain devoted to the strategy and focused solely on the time-advantaged implementation is a major aspect. Products must be made to demand and ideally shipped in hours.

One key to understanding how the value-chain production can be rearranged to become time advantaged is to understand manufacturing aggregates. I mention this now to encourage you to explore this strategic option with confidence. The naysayers try to shoot the strategy down before it has a chance.

The key to implementation is to develop manufacturing aggregates, inside of which are products with common value-chain characteristics. We use the *rule of the 3Ms* to aggregate products: commonality of manufacturing, market, and materials. Heavy use of the tried-and-true 80-20 rule is of great benefit here. Inside a market segment, there are very likely only one or two aggregations of products accounting for the majority of revenue now or planned for in the future. Each of these aggregates can be cycled through manufacturing such that each aggregate is made several times per week. The actual combination of which members of the aggregate are made in one daily cycle is derived totally from demand rates. In practice, items inside the aggregate can be manufactured individually as customer demand requires. Manufacturing would be set up such that each aggregate is made on a separate production line, or a group of a few aggregates have a common line with very little time lost to change from one to another. Obviously, some aggregates do not have enough volume to justify dedicated production equipment. Those may be candidates for being dropped or tackled with a different segment strategy.

In the time-advantaged operation, the production schedule is committed only two or three days forward. In many cases, the schedule is confirmed only hours forward. In the time-advantaged facility, inventory is managed by a different method than is normally used. 'A' items are not just those with the highest volume; they are the items with the most consistent demand pattern. When total demand is less than the aggregate demand rate, the items with the best likelihood of selling inside the next cycle are added to inventory. There are no safety stocks. The discussion in Chapter 6 will further clarify these characteristics.

Customer Connectivity

Customer connectivity removes demand variability by reducing the room for error—error in records accuracy, error owing to delayed knowledge of customers' decisions to change, or error in forecasts engendered by working many steps removed from the market. Customer connectivity is the ultimate in eliminating the bullwhip effect so often discussed but rarely resolved. The benefits to the customer are reduced working capital, lower operating costs, and higher service to their customers. All these benefits come from eliminating variability caused by errors and increasing accuracy. In businesses for which a customer-connectivity strategy applies, managing the basic operating functions with excellence is very important to success. Figure 2-8 lists the five levels of customer connectivity.

At the initial stages, the customer relationship likely starts with accuracy of information. Promise dates, bills of lading, inventory data, pricing information, and all other information exchanged between you and the customer must be right for the customer to begin to have trust. The benefits to your customer are real and should be measured and broadcast widely. For example, most customers know inventory records accuracy is essential for peak performance, yet little work is done to improve the source of what we often find: 50 percent accuracy in inventory records, bills of lading, and receiving-dock documents.

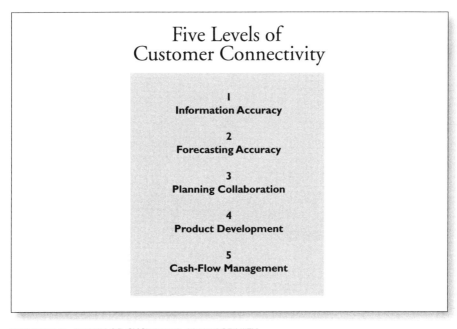

FIGURE 2-8. DEPTH OF CUSTOMER CONNECTIVITY.
The customer-connectivity strategy develops an increasing depth of trust between you and your customer at all levels of management.

Moving forward, the most important and impactful work of the strategy can begin. Forecasting sell-through, or demand from the customer to its customers, is the next level. The idea is to become so good at forecasting your customer's demand that the customer starts to depend upon you for developing business plans. Forecasting sell-through accurately goes a long way to improving cash flow at both your company and the customer's company.

Next comes jointly developing new products or defining how product lines should be structured for everyone's advantage. The ultimate is working together to plan cash flow with the objective of increasing free cash flow in the value chain as a whole. As the trust relationship builds, more senior levels of management naturally become involved. This leads to strategic planning collaboration, joint development of longer range plans for improving the overall business.

The three elements of the customer-connectivity strategy are (1) a proper segment, (2) significant values dear to the customer, and (3) a cross-functional team building trust at the senior management level and below.

The customer-connectivity strategy is best used when the business is more mature and has not created competitive advantage by being the innovation leader or cost leader. The strategy may be used to further enhance a time-advantage strategy, but the original strategy should not be subordinated or it will be lost. The typical segment for this strategy is the one conventional wisdom calls a commodity business, as if to say, "We cannot develop a strategic advantage here." The strength of the customer-connectivity strategy in this type of mature, highly competitive business is that competitors are not often seeking to find competitive advantage, so you can dominate.

The key to success is to find customer-defined values that you can impact with aggressive collaboration. Early success will build the opportunity to find more ways to improve. Often, the process takes several years to blossom. Realize that trust is not readily given to suppliers; you must earn your way. I talk with big brand-name companies that throw up their hands and say there is no way to develop competitive advantage because their customers will not talk to them. I ask, "What questions do you ask, if any?" The answer I receive is, "The sales reps ask, so I don't really know, but probably 'How much are you going to buy and what price is required?'" These are the wrong questions; the sales reps are, in effect, telling and not asking. The key is to ask what you can do to make the customer more successful: "How are you measured? What really counts to senior management beyond price and service?" Those are a given, or should be.

The only way to execute this strategy is by using cross-functional teams working with the sales staff to hold such needed discussions about values. This is frightening to the sales staff, but it is essential to success. The solutions you eventually come up with are ones that the sales function is ill-equipped to discuss, let alone design. The cross-functional team needs to be well trained in effective selling techniques and customer interview methods. You probably cannot just grab the nearest supply chain or logistics professionals and plop them down in front of customers. The team should be composed of appropriately trained staff from finance (commercial terms, contracting); R&D (product development); operations (service initiatives); forecasting and demand planning (statistics); supply chain (cash flow and timeliness); and, eventually, senior management (strategic initiatives).

The customer-connectivity strategy can provide remarkable results in segments often found to be throwaway. Using this strategy, a low-profit segment can become your most profitable.

At the end of the day, the segment-level business strategies are a clarifying force inside the organization, and they free employees to become more aggressive in advancing the business. In contrast, strategy definitions for the portfolio or for a group of segments at the brand or channel level can be terribly muddled as a result of the mix of customer values represented inside the aggregation.

Looking Back

♦ The second guiding principle of market-savvy S&OP design is defining a specific competitive advantage and go-to-market strategy for each market segment.

♦ The strategy is developed to generate new demand.

♦ Portfolio analysis has been the dominating voice in business strategy development to the distraction of the segment strategy with existing, ongoing businesses.

♦ The required value-chain market-segment strategy has five basic parts: segment level, market-driven, advantaged, collaborative, and delivers value. Four traditional segment strategies exist to choose from: lowest cost, highest market share, location advantaged, and innovation leadership.

♦ Two new strategies are available as a result of the dynamics of the on-demand economy: time advantage and customer-connectivity advantage.

♦ A company trying to develop and manage its business at some higher-level aggregation of market segments or using demographic definitions of segments will have a muddled strategy and will struggle to generate new demand and high-growth, high-profit enterprises.

Case Study: VTech

Nick Delany, the president of VTech Communications Inc., attended an education session we held with Oracle Corporation's clients in Napa Valley a few years ago. VTech had already achieved Level IV S&OP. Nick asked us to come to Beaverton, Oregon, to teach his employees what business is like without a first-class S&OP process. We learned a good deal from VTech; I am not sure how much the company benefited from our visits.

Situation. VTech makes cordless home telephone systems. The company is the classic low-cost producer with headquarters located in Hong Kong and manufacturing in China. The U.S. market for home phones is cluttered with low-cost producers, so several years ago, VTech in the United States was having difficulty making an excellent return on investment. Nick decided to develop a first-rate S&OP process. The company formed teams around each major market segment. Because the big general merchandise retailers are the outlets for the majority of cordless home phone systems, the S&OP teams became the Wal-Mart team, the Target team, the Best Buy team, and so on. The teams determined to start to build a trust relationship with their respective customers.

Actions. Cross-functional teams started meeting internally to manage demand, service, and the overall business within each segment. They studied the customers from outside and eventually began to meet with customers to gain an inside-the-customer view of the business.

The teams learned how to improve forecasting for the customer. Today, VTech does not even perform a forecast at the shipment, warehouse, or VMI level. The company forecasts what the retail customer is going to sell through. By doing so, VTech completely eliminates the errors that trigger high levels of demand variation.

As the company became very good at forecasting consumer takeaway, trust with customers increased to the point of full collaborative consideration of product mix, product feature design, merchandising, pricing, and other strategic issues.

The company found many grand ways of increasing the profitability of the customer, while nearly eliminating excess inventory inside VTech.

Results. VTech enjoys a dominant position in share of market at each of the major retailers of cordless home phone systems. The business generates strong cash flow to allow VTech to sustain its product innovations and invest in new businesses, such as expanding to the underserved cordless phones area for small to medium-size business segments.

PART II

Changing Behavior

WE NOW MOVE to Part II of our three-part process to achieve the cultural change required to implement market-savvy S&OP: changing behavior. You will likely find it is fairly easy to have a cross-functional team work together to create a vision, but it may be much more difficult to have the team work on behavioral change and process development. This is, first of all, because it's fun to work on strategy; second, because it's not your normal day-to-day activity; and, third, because it seems more like a project.

Market-savvy S&OP is not a project. It is an ongoing monthly process with high intensity. For a cross-functional team to actually come together, work effectively, and interface boldly with senior management, a nontraditional organizational culture must be realized, and the benefits are astounding. Teams have a great deal of wisdom when working collegially. To create such a team and gain its wisdom in market-savvy S&OP, you need to set a standard for behavior that strongly encourages the team, and this requires a change in traditional functional silo behavior.

Managing by analytics and adopting a customer-centric culture are the two new behaviors that create a strong market-savvy S&OP cross-functional team. In Chapter 3, we introduce our requirements for a team structure and define the set of charts, analyses, metrics, and dashboards required to help the market-savvy S&OP teams operate effectively with all organizational functions working together and complementing each other. In Chapter 4, we explore the benefits of focusing on customer values to accomplish a collegial and collaborative culture inside the market-savvy S&OP team.

Managing by Analytics

NUMBERS ARE FRIGHTENING. Working outside the comfort of your functional organization is frightening. So asking individuals to come together, use numbers to communicate, and achieve complete alignment of their plans with all other departments is very frightening.

Analytics resolve differences of opinion but are often seen as dispassionate. A behavior change is required to make analytics less frightening and even sought after. I have found that people will change their behavior if a consistent and well-reasoned approach is designed. One essential element in the process of accomplishing the behavioral change is to make the analytics standard and familiar month to month. Albert Einstein once said, "It is easy to make things complex; complex to make things simple." Simplicity is the key to familiarity and understanding.

In a collegial team, the numbers are discussed, rather than personalities or opinions. Everyone's opinion is sought initially, but opinions must be supported by the numbers in the end. To have a collegial team, some basic team protocol is required. We define the elements of this protocol as we discuss the arduous monthly planning process design.

The major topics in this chapter include the definition of what constitutes a good analytical tool and a description of the basic analytical tools required for market-savvy S&OP.

In addition, the third guiding principle for market-savvy S&OP design is introduced: managing by analytics. Many companies have what they think are good analytics, but in reality they do not. When we talk about managing by analytics, we mean using analyses that speak cross-functionally and aim to improve alignment, not point fingers. The majority of analytics—those coming from expensive ERP systems—are merely data that detail one functional area's activity. The prevailing culture seems to be very negative about preparing data relating to and aligning what other functions are doing.

Managing by analytics is a major behavioral change for all the companies I have worked with or learned about while in the consulting business. Most often at the beginning of an engagement, management says, "We already use a planning process," and in part it may be right. Once we have gained trust, management is open to having us point out the analytical deficiencies in its current approach.

Greg Hackett, a good friend of mine, is the founder of The Hackett Group, the most successful benchmarking company in history. Greg's approach was based upon providing comparative data against which companies measured their performance. The overwhelming success of this analytical approach proves the need for analytics. Greg has more recently completed research on the underlying reasons for organizational failure, and he has determined that the two major reasons are not using market facts to make decisions and losing touch with customers (the subject of Chapter 4).

The 7 Characteristics of Strong Teams

Great productivity and effective innovation emanate from teams if they are structured according to some disciplined rules. There are seven characteristics of a strong team for use in the month-to-month processes of market-savvy S&OP. A strong team is:

1. Well founded in analytics
2. Broadly cross-functional
3. Capable at problem solving
4. Composed of role players
5. Specifically tasked
6. Jointly accountable
7. Disciplined in approach

Well Founded in Analytics

Teams work best when analytics rule the discussion. In keeping with our management by analytics principle, teams are a natural part of the market-savvy S&OP design. So often we find S&OP run by one department or dominated by sales lore or historical conventions that go unchallenged but drive decision making almost unwittingly. As an example, at almost all the medical technology companies I have worked with, the sales representatives insist that for every one set of devices delivered to an operating room, you actually need two sets just in case a nurse drops something. This doubles the inventory, of course, and causes all sorts of profit and cash-flow problems throughout the supply chain, but the notion goes unchallenged for the most part. If a cross-functional team studies the issue by asking the customer if two sets of everything are needed, the team is surprised to find the answer is almost always no.

When a meeting relies on subjectivity and the opinions of the most articulate, when the less-demonstrative participants are not encouraged to have a voice, when bias and prejudices dominate, it is not a team meeting. The meeting is a power struggle, and the power of the team is lost. A strong team culture calls out these issues and insists on analytics. A meeting that relies on facts presented in a way that encourages understanding and participation becomes a team meeting. In market-savvy S&OP, the team should have a standard set of analytics designed for communication and alignment, as detailed later in this chapter. S&OP is, at its core, all about alignment of each functional area's work to accomplish the strategy. The analytics must focus on alignment. For instance, a basic dashboard showing historical and future sales, production, and inventory is a display of whether or not the work of many functions is in alignment. If sales are going up and production is not following, plans are not aligned.

Given a standard set of analytics used each month, the team becomes comfortable with the information flow and gains an in-depth understanding of the information and its impact on accomplishing the team's purpose. Without a standard set of analytics, the individual members would normally present different numbers from a different set of starting points and assumptions each month, thus greatly reducing the communicative values. The analytics must be generated from a known base of data so everyone is comfortable with the accuracy. The team can then bypass the time-consuming and counterproductive discussions about whether the data are of value to instead focus on meaning and trends in the information.

Broadly Cross-Functional

The market-savvy S&OP team needs to have as senior a representation as possible from each functional area, including legal, finance, operations, logistics, marketing, sales, R&D, and planning. The cross-functional team, over time, becomes capable of looking at problem solving in a way that has strong potential for success because everyone's requirements are being addressed. Of importance is the fact no one is left out, so finger-pointing is minimized. The primary goal of market-savvy S&OP is alignment of each functional area to the customer's planning and operations. No one can be left out of the alignment process if a complete strategic implementation is to be achieved.

Capable at Problem Solving

The team will not be successful if it is always looking outside itself for creative ideas. Many companies find they need to change personnel to satisfy this requirement. In almost all of our engagements, this has been the case. The employees who have become dependent upon their own functional area exclusively for promotion prospects, increased status, comfort, and camaraderie are not good team players. Employees who are basically good businesspersons work well in teams because they seek perspective and insight. Problem solving requires looking for solutions that may be contrary to the accepted methods and policies. Problem-solving skills can be taught; the best approach is the long-proven scientific method. We use this rather than the techniques taught in Lean or Six Sigma (such as the cause-and-effect fishbone charting) because the issues in market-savvy S&OP are normally more complex than the ones for which these techniques are best suited.

We apply the standard method of problem solving using a simple progression DHSSD, which stands for Discover, Hypothesize, Simulate, Select, and Deploy. Simply stated, the *Discover* step is the current state definition. *Hypothesize* is the examination of solution alternatives through a highly participative cross-functional set of discussions. *Simulate* is where each alternative is reduced to numbers, and *Select* is the step in which risk of implementation is balanced with benefit potential. Finally, *Deploy* is when a final decision is made and action is taken. DHSSD is a technique that is attractive to senior managers because it requires financial analysis as well as creative thinking.

Composed of Role Players

A team must have at least one person capable of filling each of the following four roles: a decisive person, a salesperson, a quality control person, and a loyal worker person. These roles are commonly found in a group of people but may not be found in a smaller unit of assigned team members. We actually use personality testing to determine who on the team fits each of the required roles. We then teach how each role works for the betterment of the team as a whole.

Team members must respect the need for each role and actively work to encourage one another in their natural roles. How should you deal with each of these people? To start, recognize that a team will not have its ideas and recommendations heard and approved without the salesperson, but the salesperson may not be the quality control person. The quality control person may be somewhat irritating, always pushing for details and refinements, but he or she ensures that the team is not brushing past important aspects of a problem. The team would work hard but never produce a report without a decision maker who keeps an eye on the bottom line, even though the decision maker may be misunderstood as insensitive. In addition, the team needs at least one, but probably many, loyal workers. These are the people who do the analyses, are always in the meetings and on time, and keep the lid on disagreements. They may also stay in analysis forever unless drawn to a conclusive point by the decision makers and salespeople. Don't ask a loyal worker person to give a presentation; he or she would rather just leave the team. Always recognize the salesperson, and let the quality control person show the numbers. The decision maker may be impatient with the team, so keep on point.

Specifically Tasked

A team needs a very clear charter or purpose. The purpose statement should be a formal one with a good deal of joint thought going into its development at the very early stages of the team's life, such as days one and two. In market-savvy S&OP, each team has sole responsibility for one market segment. The purpose is defined by looking to the go-to-market strategy and the specific benefits defined in the strategy. Each team member should have one page that has the purpose statement written at the top, followed by the quantified goals/benefits, the names of the team members, the team's sponsor or responsible executive, the basic approach to be taken to do the business of the team, and a timeline to establish the monthly processes and to accomplish near-term and longer-term goals.

Jointly Accountable

The team should be seen as a cohesive unit with each member accountable in tangible ways. In many cases, compensation systems need to be changed to fully realize this aspect of the team. Certainly, the team makes joint presentations to senior management and jointly defends recommendations. Team members cannot sit back and say, "Well, I don't agree, but you guys go ahead anyway." There also needs to be accountability between team members. Each person must be willing to submit to the authority of the team and become a team member in good standing.

Disciplined in Approach

Discipline is composed of time commitment, meeting protocol, structure, and an ordered approach.

♦ First, a time commitment is required. The process design must define how much time will normally be required each month from team members, and then the team members must arrange their schedules to meet those commitments. The strongest S&OP teams have essentially 100 percent attendance at meetings by senior members and the profit-center executive. The monthly cycle of multistep S&OP processes must be clearly stated and religiously followed. Market-savvy S&OP has a palpable rhythm and cadence that actually frees up more time than it consumes.

♦ Second, a meeting protocol is essential. Cell phones, e-mail, etc., must be completely banned at team meetings. Having executives pull out for an important conference call or another meeting must be rare occurrences. This is a matter of respect for colleagues and the team priorities. People must come on time and prepared. Reports should be distributed or available on the team's shared website well ahead of the meeting in time for a proper review.

♦ Third, a meeting structure is needed. The meetings should be scheduled months in advance, have specific agendas published at least a week in advance of the actual meeting dates, and have a stated time limit and a formal note-taking and follow-up process. A detailed written record of the proceedings is a requirement. The output of the market-savvy S&OP process each month is very likely to require the electronic equivalent of a full four-inch three-ring binder.

♦ Finally, an ordered approach to the team's work is necessary. If the team is charged with developing a new path for one of the processes involved in S&OP, the ordered approach to the team's work is more of a project nature. If the team is a group meeting monthly on an ongoing basis to lead a process such as S&OP monthly planning (discussed in Chapter 5), the ordered approach is to follow the process design and to continually work on improving the process (discussed in Chapter 7).

The first condition, time commitment, requires a generic structure. I have worked with the High Performance Management System (HPMS) developed by Richard C. Palermo, Sr., in the 1970s and 1980s while he led Xerox Corporation to success in earning the Malcolm Baldrige National Quality Award. I have experienced Palermo's system used very effectively in several major companies, with spectacular results. (You can pick up a book about HPMS for a thorough reading and understanding. I recommend *Leadership . . . A Return to Common Sense* by Richard C. Palermo, Sr., published by Strategic Triangle Inc.) In essence, the practice starts with setting a vision in a fashion similar to our Chapter 2 approach, selecting a destination for the overall business, then selecting high-impact, revolutionizing things to implement. You can look at these revolutionizing things as the "vital few." Palermo points out that for a business to be successful, it must have excellence in three areas, as follows:

**A Successful Business = Satisfied Customers +
Motivated Employees + Satisfied Shareholders**

One right thing or revolutionary idea needs to be defined for each of the three areas of a successful business as stated in the equation above. A *job ticket* is then written for each of those ideas. The job ticket has eight major steps, always the same steps for each thing you choose to be one of the vital few things you do. The eight steps are as follows:

1. Write a purpose statement for the project with a quantified goal, if possible.

2. Define the major work steps, using the generic group at a minimum.

3. Select a team leader with passion about the project, a sponsor from senior management, and team members.

4. Document the current state, including doing benchmarking internally and externally.

5. Define the future state.

6. Develop a transition plan and gain approval from senior management to implement it.

7. Implement with high quality.

8. Monitor results.

These eight steps are always in the plan of work; some specific substeps will likely be needed as well. The first six steps should be completed in about six weeks, or at most nine weeks. Team members should be asked to devote a minimum of 25 percent of their time to the project during steps one through six, and very likely 50 percent or more.

The team approach is always founded on analytics. In HPMS, full participation by team members is required, and analytics are the rule. Teams, whether they are ongoing S&OP teams or project teams, work best when they have a foundation in facts rather than opinions.

The effective team has an abundance of proper analytics upon which to draw conclusions and make decisions.

The 7 Characteristics of a Proper Analytic

Many analyses are simply a total waste of time in preparation and presentation because they do not tell a relevant story. Unfortunately, we see poor analytics done routinely out of some sort of tradition. ERP systems are notorious for generating massive data reports that no one understands or uses. Data overload is a major problem in organizations today precisely because computers can generate data at very high speeds, and do. We must move from big data to the big picture.

There are seven characteristics of a proper analytic:

1. Cross-functional
2. Big picture
3. Relevant
4. Understandable
5. Provides perspective
6. Passes the "so what" test
7. Validated

The market-savvy S&OP team must ensure that the standard reports and analyses presented in team meetings have these characteristics.

In general, a good analytical presentation tells a story that is useful to align the work of the team. The standard analytical presentations used in market-savvy S&OP will be used every month and can be put to the test against these seven characteristics.

Cross-Functional

The first test is cross-functionality. This is particularly difficult, but very important. The analytic must show cause and effect, not simply statistics.

Forecasting is a common function. Companies spend millions of dollars and countless hours on statistical forecasting packages like Demantra to generate detailed forecasts down to the individual SKU level for 18 months or more into the future. (Please note: We mean SKU, or stock-keeping unit, which is an item at a location—for example, a Rawlings RBG 36 model baseball glove at the warehouse in Ava, Missouri. The sum of all SKU forecasts is an item forecast, but it is often called an SKU forecast in error.) When the cross-functionality test is applied, we quickly realize the SKU level forecast is not required. In fact, an aggregation of SKUs to the family level is what is being committed in manufacturing. The 18-month horizon is rarely required, even at the family level for most of the team's work.

What is needed is a forecast for the number of weeks forward required to actually commit to buy materials. Often, the real need is a forecast that projects month two forward or forecasts March in January. Once the team focuses on how and when the forecast data are used, a cross-functional process can be designed. Sales bookings reports, shipment reports, service-level reports, and production reports are some examples of places where cross-functionality is required and significantly enhance the value of the analytics. Nothing is more irritating to the team than to have the sales department report bookings and claim bonuses when the bookings have due dates in far less lead time than is necessary. It is less than helpful to report a successful sales promotion after rush orders were already processed and manufacturing worked the weekend to service them. The practice is a common self-serving approach on the part of the sales force, but it is counterproductive for the team.

Big Picture

The big picture test is closely linked to cross-functionality. As previously mentioned, the analysis must tell a story. Analysis must also rise up from the depths of detail to become important information. Liberal application of the 80-20 rule is essential to help the analyst and recipient gain an understanding of the appropriate time investment. Big picture means having analytics that can be used in short periods of analytical time. If the team must plow through large databases, the analysis simply stops discussion. A food manufacturer we work with has more than 1,000 customers and thousands of ship-to points. However, it has only two or three key customers in each of the five market segments it serves. Every discussion of customer requirements, reactions, or values must start with the top three customers and then all of the others. In too many analyses, the focus falls to the smallest and most unrepresentative by treating each element of the analysis with equal importance. The average of the total is rarely of practical use; the average of the largest 20 percent, which represents 80 percent of the activity, *is* very helpful.

In inventory analysis, all opportunity for telling a story is lost by the sheer volume of numbers. The big picture is seen in those items that represent 80 percent of purchases. We have a billion-dollar manufacturing client that has more than 3,000 raw-material items. The company has avoided making any assertions about how much raw material it needs by simply saying the lead times vary from days to six months and demand variability is very high. In fact, we found that 85 parts account for almost 80 percent of the total purchases. The low number is validated when one takes out all the obsolete parts in the 3,000 item numbers and eliminates the nuts, bolts, and screws that should be expensed because they are very common and easily obtained from multiple local sources. Some 99 percent of the purchases were in fewer than 500 active parts, and 85 of those were the ones that needed to be managed. The others were too small to have financial impact, special orders with no financial impact, or stocked in bulk. The 85 parts were a small enough number to be easily assessed individually during the S&OP meeting. The team members could readily scan the list to see if any individual item was in short supply or excess, and they could segregate the parts into product mix groupings so they could assess the impact of potential mix changes included in the forecast of risks and opportunities. The big picture is being able to use an analysis in an assessment of inventory requirements to support decision making in opportunity management and completion of the analysis in the team meeting in less than five minutes.

Relevant

Analytics must be relevant. Lots of different analytical data can be presented, but we are looking for the vital few analyses that speak directly to the team's work. In market-savvy S&OP, the team is tasked to accomplish a few important goals: generating free cash flow, growing market share, and satisfying the customer's value needs. Only those analyses that speak directly to these few goals should be presented. Supply chain professionals are prone to present service metrics that prove they are doing a great job, such as on-time shipments, perfect orders, and many other internal measures. These are unlikely to be relevant to the team's work.

We need metrics that measure service in terms of the customer's needs. Goodyear measures service in the consumer products business by what percent of customer requests for a replacement tire are filled each day. The metric is calculated by major customers, not by internal processes. The metric does not measure on-time shipment, which could be shipment of lots of things customers did not want. What good does it do to ship stuff that is not selling? The answer is none!

Understandable

A most difficult requirement is that the analysis must be understandable to all members of the team and senior executives. A team cannot use information to improve performance without full understanding. The paramount characteristics here are to round numbers off and to use only significant digits. If accounting reports inventory as $15,746,827.33, the team should report inventory as $15.7 million. All the additional digits and decimal places are totally insignificant and counterproductive to gaining understanding. The team can understand and remember, say, that inventory was supposed to be $15 million, or about 5 percent less than the reported total this month. But team members will gloss over and fail to comprehend that

$15,746,827.33 is more than the goal of $15,098, 652.33. Round and truncate with abandon.

Understanding also comes from making complex issues simple. This requires some work. Again, we can use inventory as a prime example of abuse in this area. I have found CEOs, sales executives, senior financial executives, marketers, and many others who have no understanding of inventory accounting in general. *Absorption* is such a non-normal term that it just confuses executives who are probably embarrassed to ask what it is. So if absorption is low because of low capacity utilization, and the cost of goods sold is adversely affected, the impact on inventory and profit will likely not be fully understood. But it must be.

In some companies, moving away from a standard cost system to an activity-based accounting system may make sense. I have seen financial staff present complex factors as good guys and bad guys to allow nonfinancial executives a level of understanding. For example, it was painful to watch the evening news in the early 1980s during the second oil crisis, when reporters pummeled oil company executives night after night about record profits in a time of severe oil supply shortages. The CEO of Amoco Corporation, one of the largest oil companies, was harassed incessantly by the local news teams in Chicago. Charges of fraud, price gouging, and conspiracies of all sorts were leveled. The underlying issue was that Amoco like all the oil companies used a LIFO, or last in, first out accounting of oil inventory. Under the perfectly legal LIFO method, the barrels of oil most recently arriving at U.S. refineries were considered to be the ones sold. In part because of the world oil shortage, the most recently received barrels were much more expensive than the barrels of oil received in previous periods. As the oil crisis continued, oil reserves were reduced severely, and on paper the expensive oil was gone. On paper only, cheap oil remained. In fact, the LIFO calculations showed that only oil from the turn of the century was still in reserve. As this old oil was sold, the cost was stated in past dollars, which were a fraction of current oil costs. So, cost of goods sold being low, profits were high. Try to explain this accounting on the evening news in 20-second sound bites, when even the CEO had no practical understanding of the accounting.

The CEO of Amoco Corporation stopped trying to explain what was happening and attempted to explain to the press that the profits were made overseas. The problem was that this was not true. As a result, credibility was totally lost. The CEO needed to simply say that cash flow was the measure of his company's business activity in this time of shortage. Everyone knows that it is how much cash you have to spend that is of paramount importance. Then, he could have said that his company's actual hard cash was running negative. The company was actually borrowing to stay in business even though the P&L (profit and loss statement) looked good. This was verifiable at the banks and in the financial reporting. If Amoco had had a market-savvy S&OP process, the CEO would have had full understanding of this critical issue.

Inventory issues have tripped up CEOs often, and seriously. I cannot even count the number of times a year-end audit of inventory found a major inventory shrink that significantly cut profits, and the CEO was clueless on the analyst calls. I bet there are many executives who will read this statement and say, "He's nuts; inventory is on the balance sheet and has nothing to do with the P&L statement." Wrong.

Provides Perspective

A good analysis must provide perspective. The most common analyses merely show a point in time, such as the past month. P&L data is for a period of time. A very useful P&L analysis is a comparison to previous periods, or better yet, to periods of time with the same market characteristics, such as in-season months (for seasonal products) compared to in-season months in previous years. Trends are a good way of providing perspective. Trends look at a statistic over several years or at least many months.

Perspective can be provided by looking at statistics of performance before and after an improvement project was installed, with sufficient time elapsing in the post-improvement analysis to ensure that improvements continue. It can also be provided by comparing an old method to a new one or by benchmarking.

In market-savvy S&OP, I like to see the basic dashboard information presented to show year-to-date this year versus last year, and total year this year versus last year. A good way to make sure an analysis is in proper perspective is to use the 80-20 rule: Look at the top 20 percent of any population, and the 20 percent will represent 80 percent of the total. Some examples: 20 percent of customers do 80 percent of the sales, and 20 percent of the inventory items account for 80 percent of the throughput. If you put the 20 percent into perspective and do not become entangled with the details, you have a good chance of gaining insights.

Passes the "So What" Test

Analytics must pass the "so what" test. If after viewing the analysis, the listeners are asking "so what," then the analysis is probably of little use. The basic issue is: Does the analysis lead to action or a relevant conclusion? So many analyses are dead ends; the team spends time looking at a set of data and charts only to discover they lead nowhere. A good example is the extensive data on customer service normally presented in operational S&OP meetings—data such as on-time shipment percentages and perfect order percentages. The problem is that the data are internally generated and most likely do not show how you performed against customer requirements. In many cases, if you had a high percent of perfect orders, does the customer care? Your policies and lead times may force the customer to place orders with you well in advance of when the customer actually knows its detailed needs. So you ship what the customer may not need, but the orders are on time and complete. If service is measured by the customer, in terms that the customer defines, the service metrics have a good chance of passing the "so what" test.

We had a client that shipped to the major grocery chains. The client had statistics that showed excellent perfect-order performance.

However, the client's customers actually wanted a mix of product on each pallet, rather than full pallets of one item. The client's policies prevented the practice of mixed pallets, so the customers had to take full pallets into their distribution and pick and ship mixed pallets to their stores themselves. In the customers' view, the perfect order percent could have been 100 percent and still been subject to the response, "So what, that supplier does not help us." When we developed a market-in approach inside the client, the company redefined service and began shipping mixed product pallets, cross-docked to the individual stores, on time. The customers rewarded our client with increased business because it was now helping them achieve its strategic goal of hyper-local merchandising.

Validated

Analytics must be validated to be proper. Validated means the conclusions must be cross-checked and proven to be true from independent sources. Averages are big problems, because many people think "average" means acceptable. Average may not tell us anything. For instance, the person who has one foot in boiling water and one foot in ice water is in serious peril, when on average he or she is at just the right temperature. Strategists who do not have market savvy are often guilty of making outrageous assumptions about markets without validating those assumptions.

We had a client that set up a large team to strategically reduce complexity in the product line, working on the assumption that customers simply did not need the complexity. The team members had several examples of individual customers to prove the assumption. Unfortunately, they did not research what customers really defined as unnecessary complexity. They reduced 30 percent of the items in the product line and promptly lost market share. The problem was in understanding what the market was defining as complexity. The market was saying costs were too high and the item offering much too extensive. When the team linked cost to the complexity definition, the rationalization process changed the focus from what the market was saying. The team needed to eliminate whole families of items that were manufactured on high-cost production lines and find lower-cost solutions. Costs could have been reduced by eliminating an entire high-cost production process, such as one that was underutilized, and finding other ways to provide the products required. In the client's approach to item reduction, all production capabilities were maintained, but they became less effectively utilized as market share declined. By reducing families of items, major cost reductions would have been achieved, and overall market share could have been maintained at better profit.

The validated principle applies to competitive assessment also. If you keep losing share to a competitor, you must determine why and not just ignore the trend. Auto companies and airlines have blissfully ignored competitor gains of market share for decades. Most American airlines still do not understand the strategy of Southwest Airlines, even though they have been defeated by the strategy for more than 30 years. Southwest reduces cost by having a higher utilization of equipment, people, airport space, and all other fixed costs. Just walk into an airport at midday. Southwest has flights leaving, while the major brand names (such as American, U.S. Airways, and United) do not. The major brands think passengers want convenient schedules over lower cost and demand planes be scheduled to leave between 7 AM and 9 AM, and then from 5 PM to 7 PM. As a result of this driving belief, their airline gates, personnel, airplanes, and all other fixed costs are underutilized. Their gates are vacant of passengers but stuffed full with ground workers, red coats (supervisors), and airplanes. Southwest proved low cost is more important than schedule for even business travelers. If the major brands had done solid passenger surveys, they would have found the key to passenger thinking. The surveys they did were highly impersonal, or no surveys were done at all. What passengers ever asked the airline to force them to listen to the chairman and CEO give an advertisement early in the morning, as Continental and now United insist upon doing? None! How does charging for the extra checked bag reduce airline costs? It does not, and it probably reduces profit as well, as travelers have dramatically more carry-on baggage, which actually costs more to handle through the manual process rather than the automated processes. The point is to be sensitive to your customers, not enamored with yourself. Validate when the customer tells you they don't like what you are doing and move to a competitor. Southwest is full. Continental and United struggle to fill the seats.

It is difficult to validate analyses, but essential, or the analysis—or at least the conclusions drawn—is simply assumption, not fact.

Market-Savvy S&OP, 70 Percent Analytics

In market-savvy S&OP, the process is a ratio of 70 percent analytics to 30 percent action plans. The analytics required are in three groups:

1. Analytics describing objectives
2. Analytics for planning
3. Analytics to measure performance

Analytics Describing Objectives

The objectives for each market segment must be spelled out in quantitative terms within the market-savvy S&OP process. The team can start with a statement of the vision in more general form, such as "The _____ business will be number one in customer satisfaction" or ". . . the clearly advantaged leader in customer connectivity." These statements of destination for the team's work can be quantified or at least measured over time. Customer surveys are a good way to quantify concepts like connectivity or satisfaction in your performance. The team would build on the values defined in the strategy steps discussed in Chapter 1 and the monthly or quarterly meetings with customers. Questions relating to key aspects of the customer's definition of performance would be graded by the customer or key customers within a customer group. Over time, a trend would develop. The continuous improvement of the overall rating is the quantified trend you would review.

The analytics of objectives also include measures of free cash flow and market share. The free cash-flow metric should be developed for each S&OP team. The finance department will probably tell you it cannot split up balance sheet items by market. But in the end, the finance personnel actually can. You don't necessarily need the accountants to change their formal reporting practices and policies with a more complex chart of accounts. The normal month-end reports of the five elements of free cash flow—margins, accounts payable, accounts receivable, inventory, and capital equipment utilization—suffice. The cash-flow model you desire is a defined set of item numbers, customers, or suppliers making up each segment. This model can be used with reasonable accuracy to split the total balance sheet into pieces using a sampling technique.

Let's look at accounts payable. Each market segment has products that are primary in the segment. These products may be present in other segments to a degree Pareto analysis will identify which segments claim which products. The products have key purchased components or, at the minimum, the percent of each key component assigned to a segment can be determined. Of course, the less you rely on allocation, the better, but in many cases, you can develop a model of purchased items over which the segment S&OP team has primary influence. The best way to make the measure consistent over time is to have a well-documented model or sampling approach and to measure the trends each month.

In accounts receivable, you should break out key customers by segment, which should be very easy if the segment definitions are developed in the way we described in Chapter 1. The key customers should be specifically called out in the dashboard of the segment team's S&OP meeting. Meanwhile, inventory is split by segment in the same way as purchases. Capacity utilization can be determined by assigning major production resources by market segment. I have seen this successfully done in even complex operations. The analysis does not need to be perfectly exact. For example, if a specific process is used 80 percent of the time by segment A, and then some percentage by segment B and segment C, then allocate the capacity utilization variances to segment A. A more complex allocation only reduces understanding and clarity.

Market-share metrics provide a big picture view of the work of the S&OP team. Market share is a good measure because it usually can be verified independently from internal estimates and is relevant to the strategic attainment goals of the team.

Market-share information should come from industry data developed by a third-party industry group or a service company like the Nielsen Company or the SymphonyIRI Group. Many industries have a normal source for this information. The governments in the United States, Europe, Japan, and China have extensive data that can be used to estimate share. Market share should be determined using long-term trend graphs. You are looking for relative changes in market share, not precise numbers. The idea is to identify cause-and-effect relationships.

A few businesses may not have access to real third-party data. They may want to rely upon surveys of customers and to use relative increases from a base market share estimate viewed in perspective of the competitive environment. However, market-share data are normally readily available for those who go to find them.

For example, while at Booz & Co., I served on the Chrysler Corp. team from 1980 through 1981, hired by the board of directors to review the plan of the chairman, Lee Iacocca, as it was being presented to the U.S. Senate in an effort to obtain federal government loans needed for survival. This plan called for a large increase in annual production levels over several years, attributed to the introduction of new car lines. The plan did not include market-share data from third-party sources. The volumes were determined from internally developed market analysis, so the volume increases were presented piecemeal. For example, the plan said the midsize car market is normally three million cars per year (no trend or overall verification to industry totals), and Chrysler's new car would dominate at 300,000 cars sold per year (justified by stating the factory would produce 75 cars per hour, every hour, 16 hours per day, 50 weeks per year). Remember the K-car? (This was a line of fuel-efficient cars that Chrysler launched in 1982.) The K-car was presented in the near-term plan as a new product. When the piecemeal estimates were added together, a phenomenal increase in forecasted volume resulted. Since the auto business is primarily a fixed-cost business, the increased volume corrected all the sins of the past, and a wonderfully profitable company was presented in the business plan. Naturally, we tested the volume assumption with simple third-party market share analysis.

The auto industry has very good overall sales reporting for the industry in total. At the time, the domestic car industry had annual sales of between 9 million and 11 million units over the preceding 50 years. We knew our client's numbers, so we estimated Chrysler between 8 and 9 percent market share over the past 20 years was easy. Thus, the optimistic estimate of annual volume would be reasonable at 9 percent of the peak year, if one expected an overall market increase. At least, this would be a good upper limit for forecasting Chrysler's volume. Nine percent of 11 million is about 1 million vehicles per year. Iacocca's plan forecast 1.5 million units in what was expected to be an average year. Increasing market share by 50 percent had never been achieved by anyone in the auto industry. Fighting for one or two share points was more the case. To increase share by 50 percent, or five share points, would have required a massive increase in dealerships. This was not part of the plan; in fact, Chrysler was losing dealerships. We reduced the estimate and calculated the amount of money Chrysler would then need from Uncle Sam to be more than $5 billion—not the $750 million Iacocca had estimated. We were not very popular at Chrysler for several weeks after our estimate was released to Iacocca's office.

The reader should note the bailouts done by the Obama administration were inevitable given the total lack of market-savvy on the part of auto industry management. Ford is surviving only because they hired an industry outsider as CEO.

These three analytics, strategy or vision statement, cash flow, and market share, describing the objectives of the segment for the S&OP team, in strategic terms, should be sufficient as the analytics for defining objectives. Adding one more is not recommended, nor is subtracting one.

Analytics for Planning

In planning, you are primarily dealing with what-if analysis of the future. Good processes have multiple what-ifs for each planning cycle: a consensus plan, a high sales plan, and a low bookings contingency analysis. The nature of the planning process itself brings certain analytical challenges.

A planning database should be developed. The fundamental processes in planning benefit greatly by having a stand-alone planning database, designed to show all the what-ifs and to capture the historical basis for analytical conclusions in each planning period, made available for further assessment as actual results are recorded. The objective is to have the S&OP meeting focus on the analysis rather than arguments about the data. Major clients of ours have such a database and benefit greatly in terms of planning robustness, continuous improvement work, and reduction in overall planning time. However, most companies—including several major companies, such as top-performing P&G—still use spreadsheets. The major reason is the system of record. ERP systems are transaction-based and designed to efficiently process a high volume of low-value individual data sets. These systems are simply not set up to handle high-level what-if planning functions at various levels of data aggregation.

By planning database, I do not mean a data warehouse or a data extract process, but a separate planning database used specifically by the S&OP team. The database should be capable of handling multiple planning hierarchies, not simply the pyramid hierarchies common in forecasting with preset rules for grouping. The database allows the analyst to drill down along various paths, depending on the issue being researched. The data comes from the formal ERP system, the forecasting system, the point-of-sale software, the operations software, and/or any number of systems of record, including customer systems. The information stored is the detailed data used to sum up to management the reports and analysis used in planning. The information reported each month for all past months should be captured so that comparisons and trends are done using consistent and known data. Extracting data from the big system of record is risky, since in the day-to-day normal flow of data entry, all sorts of adjustments are made or errors introduced to the systems used by hundreds of people. In the planning database, you can establish filters to correct the majority of inconsistent data found in the general systems. Filters for new customers would be added to allow planners to assign a new customer to a segment. Filters for new SKUs or unassigned products or lines would also be used to identify data problems.

In addition, the relationship between the data and the way S&OP planners want to sort by segment can be managed in the planning database, but only with extreme difficulty in the formal database. For example, in the planning database, each product is assigned to a family within a segment. In the general database, you find multiple definitions of family; these numerous definitions can be very confusing and often are used for very narrow purposes. Further, the various what-if plans common in planning can be captured in the planning database with the source or underlying data attached. ERP systems do not have what-if information, only actual facts or the plan.

The planning dashboard is the major planning analysis used in market-savvy S&OP. The typical dashboard is shown in Figure 3-1. The dashboard displays the historical interaction and future projected interaction between sales (shipments, revenue) and production, inventory, service, and margins. The checks and balances features of this dashboard are essential elements of planning analytics.

The dashboard may be an appendix piece with key trends or issues highlighted in an executive summary section of the S&OP information deck. The wisdom of this dashboard is that it compares the basic planning interrelationships between all functions, and it does it in per-

S&OP Dashboard		Segment A								Strategic Vision, Key Customers						
Sales	Last Year	Months								YTD Last Year	YTD This Year					This Year
		1	2	3	4	5	6	7	8			9	10	11	12	
Sales Annual Plan Last Update Current Update																
Production Annual Plan Last Update Current Update																
Inventory Annual Plan Last Update Current Update																
Service Annual Plan Last Update Current Update																
Margins Annual Plan Last Update Current Update																

FIGURE 3-1. THE PRIMARY PLANNING ANALYTIC.
The planning dashboard shows history, the future, and relationships between different dynamics, such as changes in sales forecast and production performance. It also has essential cross-functional metrics.

spective. Look at the criteria for a proper analytic and test this against its requirements.

An executive summary may look like the more detailed dashboard shown in Figure 3-2.

This summary has three major parts corresponding to the three areas of emphasis in S&OP: cash, collaboration, and customer. In the example shown in Figure 3-2, the the symbols of arrows and stop sign highlight issues of good and bad performance, with the up arrows (normally shown in green when using color in slides indicating the good performance and the stop sign pointing out poor results (normally the

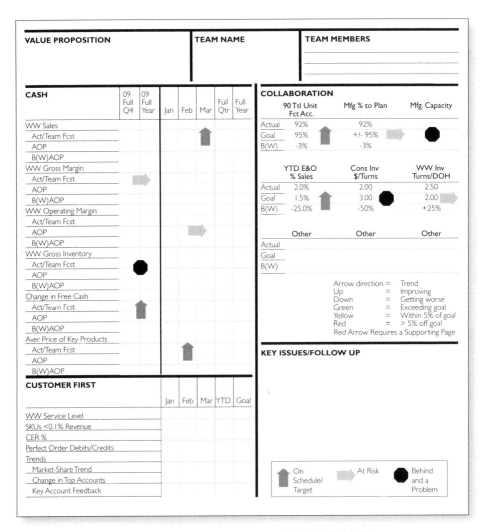

FIGURE 3-2. EXECUTIVE SUMMARY OF THE MORE DETAILED DASHBOARD.
The dashboard shown has a section for cash, collaboration, and customer, which are the three most important focus areas of S&OP.

stop sign is shown in red on a slide in color). This summary would be shown each month and distributed in advance of the executive review to help participants be prepared for the meeting. As noted in the header, a subordinate analysis (a supporting page) is required for each stop sign in the current month. The horizontal arrow indicates a "watch list" or caution situation (normally the horizontal arrow is shown in yellow on a slide in color).

Forecast accuracy and bias must be measured, because the forecast is a key input to planning. The S&OP team is jointly responsible for contributing to forecast accuracy. The team members select the one set of forecast data they will jointly use in individual functional plans and agree to be aligned to this one set of forecast numbers. If the forecast information is presented in a form similar to the one shown in Figure 3-3, the team can readily monitor its performance in improving accuracy and reducing bias. We have always found that a team using this simple type of display does, in fact, improve accuracy.

In Figure 3-3, the analysis of forecast accuracy and bias is shown, with the heavy black line being the actual, the lighter dotted line is Annual Operating Plan (AOP), and the shaded area, or gray shadow, the standard error of the forecast. The goal is to have the actual trend line running within the standard error range or the shaded area. The

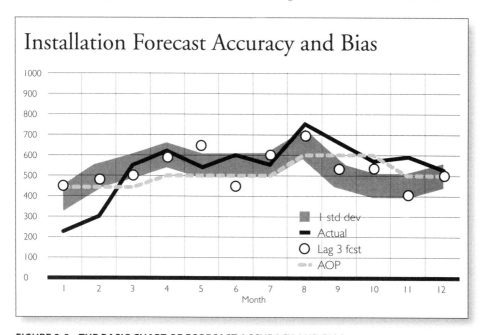

FIGURE 3-3. THE BASIC CHART OF FORECAST ACCURACY AND BIAS.
The chart shows a trend and an easily understandable analysis of joint forecasting performance.

bias is depicted by displaying the actual forecast relative to the forecast trend line. If the forecast dots are always below the trend in actual revenue, an under-forecast or "sandbagging" problem is displayed. The goal is to have as many forecasts as possible above and below the actual trend line. The team needs to select what product grouping or family of products is shown in the forecasting accuracy and bias chart. At a very high level of aggregation, forecast accuracy is more easily achieved, but it may not represent the level at which the forecast impacts planning activities. The major planning families within a market segment may be two to five, but realistically not more. Planning families are covered more extensively in Chapter 5. In brief, a planning family contains products that have a common set of market, materials, and manufacturing characteristics. The major planning work of committing materials for purchase and aligning capacity with revenue is done at the family level. Normally, planning is done for two or three months ahead of the current month, so the forecast chart is a "lag 2" or "lag 3," respectively; that is, you measure the actual revenue against the forecast made two months back in a "lag 2."

The "Eight Reasons for Inventory" analysis, shown in Figure 3-4, can be of enormous value to the team. This analysis indicates the reasons for inventory expressed in inventory days of supply (DOS) requirements. Inventory is perhaps the most misunderstood concept on the planet, certainly in S&OP. Senior management just gets angry about it, while S&OP team members get massive headaches when the supply chain people start dumping massive statistical analysis on them.

On the other hand, inventory analysis can reveal all the sins of a manufacturing company. Excess and obsolete inventory, out-of-stock inventory, overstock inventory, and gluts of inventory are all cross-functional measures of a planning *misalignment* problem, which is precisely the type of problem the S&OP team is supposed to solve. All the second-guessing and arbitrary decision making eventually show up in inventory. For this reason, a simple way of measuring inventory is absolutely required.

Eight Reasons for Inventory

Supply Network Factors	Days of Supply (DOS) Required
1. Information Cycle	Days from replenishment signal to scheduling action
2. Supply Frequency	Days between receipts
3. Manufacturing Lot Size	Smallest lot quantify/daily rates
4. Distribution Network	Days in-transit (only owned in transit)
Variability Factors	
5. Supply Variation	Quantity short/daily rate plus days late
6. Demand Variation	Standard deviation of demand over lead **time/daily** rate
Operations Factors	
7. Quality	$s of **obsolescence/daily** rate in $s
8. Capacity	Peak quantity in excess of **capacity/daily** rate

FIGURE 3-4. INVENTORY REQUIREMENTS ANALYSIS MADE SIMPLE.
This analysis presents a definition of what constitutes inventory that all can understand.

S&OP team members are not going to be inventory experts. The team needs a simple way to determine how much inventory is required and the relative size of the major components. One effective way to calculate and display the inventory requirement is to use the analysis outlined in Figure 3-4.

The actual inventory shown in DOS is a fact typically provided in standard financial reporting. The problem is that actual does not pass the "so what" test. If a standard for inventory is shown alongside the actual, the team has a ready gauge of whether inventory is too high or too low. These two factors, actual and standard DOS, can be plotted and trended over time for even more usefulness. And better yet, the eight factors can be looked at, one relative to another, to assess the root cause of inventory growth and size. The analysis of the individual eight factors provides a guide for team members to start to identify where inventory can be reduced without hurting service.

Using the eight reasons for inventory analysis demystifies inventory and, in my experience, allows even sales reps to begin to see how less inventory means better service. When inventory is expressed in terms of DOS, employees begin to be able to weigh the days against reasonable customer expectations. For example, if finished goods inventory covers four months of daily usage and the variation in demand factor is only eight days, sales will agree you should find ways to reduce the inventory. Of course, additional drill-down analysis is required to identify what items in which locations are the individual contributors to poor inventory performance. But the analysis allows the team to discuss inventory issues, identify where to begin, and monitor progress without getting a splitting headache.

Analytics to Measure Performance

Performance metrics focus on what we are accomplishing for the customer, as opposed to how we are measuring ourselves against our strategy. The actual analytics to be used by the team should be determined by your customers in discussions with the customers or representatives of customer groups.

The list of possible analytics is limitless, so I will suggest only a few that illustrate what is intended.

♦   A medical device manufacturer asked key hospitals to track the percentage of actual procedures consignment inventory serviced off the shelf in the appropriate size. The goal was availability of 90 percent or more, which was found to be difficult to achieve.

♦   A hardlines company received data from Wal-Mart about retail sales missed during remerchandising of individual stores. The customer disappointment index goal was zero, which was achieved in year two.

♦   A grocery manufacturer worked with the top ten grocery chains to measure service levels among suppliers against factors the grocers had defined. The goal was to be number one in customer satisfaction.

♦ A cookie manufacturer was doing store-to-door delivery (SDD) for discount retailers and took responsibility for inventory accuracy. The retailers fed the manufacturer an analysis of errors in receiving documents and inventory shrink analysis. The goal was 100 percent accuracy with zero shrink.

These examples illustrate the principles of customer-defined, customer-measured, agreed goals for performance. The customer centricity discussion in Chapter 4 identifies how these metrics come about.

Looking Back

♦ Management by analytics, the third guiding principle of market-savvy S&OP design, is a behavior change necessary for the S&OP team to function collegially and effectively.

♦ Teams move forward on facts, not opinions and old logic. Analytics are the foundation of an effective team because they eliminate bias, prejudices, and ignorance.

♦ There are many books written about teams. Use the information about teams presented here as a guide. The team may want to print out the list of seven characteristics of strong teams and display it in team meetings. When a team applies these seven characteristics, wisdom flows.

♦ The team should use the seven characteristics of a proper analytic to qualify new analytics and to improve the analytical process.

♦ A small group of standard and repeated analytics, such as the three types suggested (analytics describing objectives, analytics for planning, and analytics to measure performance), allows S&OP meetings to get down to the business of improving performance and to reduce the time spent arguing about whether the facts shown are actually facts.

Case Study: Frozen Food Producer

The frozen food producer in this example brought the jalapeño popper into the limelight in the food service industry. The company had been a small, local fish processor located in the upper central United States. It was a family-owned business run by brothers until it was sold to large single-product food processor after our work there was completed in 2001. In the early 1990s, the family decided to move out of fish and into the growth business of frozen appetizers. The company decided upon onion rings and poppers made by stuffing jalapeño peppers with different types of cheese, with cheese sticks and various other minor product lines to round out the overall offering. The company grew at a double-digit annual percentage rate. Production expanded to nine lines in the main plant, with the onion rings staying in a specialty plant in the southwestern United States. The sales department was the go-go driver of the company. Product complexity expanded to more than 2,000 items.

An outside professional was hired in the late 1990s to be the president and chief operating executive. The brothers remained very active in the day-to-day operation of the business holding executive positions, one as vice president of sales.

Situation. Ten years into the growth plan, cash was in short supply at the company. Wal-Mart, which was a major customer for the appetizers, had placed significant demands on the company for inventory. Food service companies, including Sysco and Arby's, were major customers; they brought with them the demand for a greatly expanded set of product options, as was necessary in the complex food service business. The company had expanded by hundreds of different products with different coatings, using different types of cheese, in a variety of pack sizes, in precooked frozen form for retailers and fresh frozen for food service. The added products increased SKU complexity by nearly double to the 2,000 SKU's and to a nearly unmanageable point.

Operations ran to a detailed forecast generated by a large statistical forecasting software program. Every one of the 2,000 SKUs had a forecast that was updated frequently. Every SKU had a safety stock, meticulously calculated in the ERP system.

Finished goods inventory had grown to more than 60 days of supply, six turns. (For those who are not well founded in supply chain terminology, days of supply is translated into turns by dividing days of supply, 60 in this example, into 360, or the number of days in a year. In this example 360 divided by 60 is 6.) The supply network included a pick and pack warehouse that shipped to several regional distribution centers and some direct customers. Ship from "stock on demand today" was the mantra, the strategy. This strategy was applied to all customers without distinction.

Practical lead times in production were actually very short; however, capacity constraints forced longer lead times from time to time. Any one product could be made in hours, but product complexity and a high requirement for maintaining safety stocks at all the distribution centers meant the time between production batches for any one product could be up to weeks, even though emergency batches were thrown into the schedule daily. The main plant operated at least two shifts and, in several areas, three shifts. Peak production during major customer promotional periods required 24/7 operation.

Costs were out of control, profits were very low, and inventory was very high. Customer service was not as expected. Wal-Mart demanded more inventory to improve availability. Food service customers complained about stockouts of odd items required for key customers—the items that made restaurants unique and, therefore, were of high importance. Product rationalization was tried and failed to produce meaningful results.

Finally, availability of funds from the banks started to evaporate. Improved cash flow was imperative.

Actions. The supply chain team along with some people from marketing began to look for ways to reduce inventory and improve service using advice from my firm.

What were termed 'A' items were attacked first to give fast relief in the cash crisis. We did a Pareto analysis to identify the 'A' items (this was nothing fancy). A big slug of inventory was taken out by heavy management attention, including more frequent production, lower safety stocks, and rebalancing between distribution centers.

The major action was to develop analytics regarding customers, customer definitions of service, and inventory management policies in general. The analytics found that food service was the biggest market served and that the food service distributors were the dominant players in that market for the company. The distributors included Sysco and U.S. Foods, among others.

We then went to the major customers and asked how they operated and how they measured service. To everyone's surprise, we found the food service companies placed orders several weeks in advance of their actual need or selling date to the various restaurant delivery routes. So shipping these customers from stock today not only was not required but was a problem for the customers because they then needed to keep higher-than-necessary inventory of our product.

The team then looked at production and production response times. Since we knew lead times were actually short, how could we manage overall capacity to change the food service portion of the business to make to order from make to stock?

♦ Product families were defined with all items of common major ingredients for food service, those made on the fresh frozen production lines, placed in a separate set of families from those items produced for retail and processed on the cooked or fry and frozen production lines

♦ Only three families of products were found to be required on the two major food service production lines (formerly identified as line numbers and not described by the market served). The "food service" lines designation gave the line workers a way to identify with customers.

♦ Capacity utilization was calculated using various scenarios of major and minor setup and changeover patterns. The sanitation schedule required by the U.S. Food and Drug Administration became an opportunity. Since the FDA required the production line be completely shut down and cleaned with strong disinfectants from scaffolding at the ceiling (even above the ceiling if the ceiling tiles could be removed and down the walls to the floor with everything in between being washed with disinfectant, the line could be restarted with any product family. The production sequence found to be best was one that ran a product family up to sanitation required by the FDA and then used the required FDA sanitation to change to a different product family. Thus, every family was made at least weekly with maximum capacity utilization and the minimum number of extra line changes beyond those done inside the required FDA sanitation time.

♦ A family cycle planning system and philosophy was designed, programmed, and implemented to replace the former master scheduling technique (a spreadsheet process, done manually with little help from the formal and expensive ERP system).

♦ The inventory management policy was changed to make to order.

Business Results Achieved. The management by analytics approach generated very significant results. Inventory turns went up to over 12 or under 30 days of supply from over 60 days of supply, and inventory kept falling. Service as measured by the customer was great. The company received Sysco's number one national supplier award for several years following implementation. In addition, profits were up as a result of production utilization improvements and lower waste, achieved by making fewer unplanned changeovers using the approach of planning by family of product.

Establishing a Customer-Centric Culture

THE SECOND BEHAVIORAL CHANGE required to implement market-savvy S&OP is the development of a customer-centric culture inside the organization. The customer-centric culture brings the market inside the organization itself by defining excellence in behavior toward the customer and the metrics of performance as measured by the customer. For example, at ev3 Inc., a medical device manufacturer that implemented a market-savvy S&OP process in 2009 and 2010, the strategy was to have a customer-centric organization with the "quality of services the customers can feel."

Establishing a customer-centric culture can bring tangible benefits to your organization. The most recognizable will be engagement of nearly all your people in the quest for market advantage and high free cash flow. In most organizations, employees are not top-of-the-mind aware of the impact they are having on the market and the business strategy. Some studies by change management consultants, including Rick Maurer, have found that in a typical organization, eight out of ten management staff members are disengaged from the customer. In a customer-centric organization, we have found that eight out of ten are fully engaged in achieving customer goals with excellence. New clients often ask me, "Who will be asked to participate in the market-savvy S&OP education and process design?" I tell them to be prepared to have all parts of the organization involved, including the fork-truck drivers. Why fork-truck drivers? They are normally the last people who touch the customer by providing accurate (or inaccurate) shipping documents, which either give you a good mark on inventory shrink prevention or a black mark. Actually, we have found that fork-truck drivers normally have more impact on the customer than the CEO in an inwardly focused, traditional culture.

This chapter defines the fourth guiding principle of market-savvy S&OP design: *Organize around customers*, not functions. Just like Chapter 3, on managing by analytics, this chapter is all about actions:

1. Developing a customer-facing organization
2. Establishing collaboration
3. Driving collegiality
4. Designing horizontal management processes
5. Appointing leaders with passion

Developing a Customer-Facing Organization

In the vision portion of the change process, you established a transformational strategy designed to gain competitive advantage. In the customer-facing organization—one that focuses on the customer—you are looking for a structure that supports the transformation. This is a radical change from the internally focused functional organizations that dominate today's corporations. (See Figure 4-1.)

You are looking for a significantly different set of characteristics in the customer-facing organization and a transition to full organizational engagement with the customer. The benefits can and should be measured in periodic analysis, which should be discussed in the monthly market-savvy S&OP meetings.

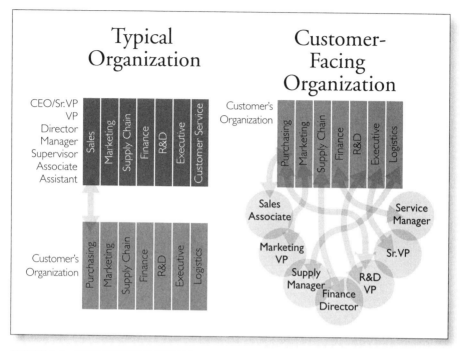

FIGURE 4-1. ORGANIZATION STRUCTURE FOR BEHAVIORAL CHANGE.
The new structure cuts across formal functional organizational silos to achieve broad interaction with the customer's organization.

Attain Balanced Organizational Collaboration

The objective of the new structure is to achieve a balanced organizational collaboration with the customer. The formal organization chart will probably show functional lines of responsibility for some time until the mechanics of the new organization structure can be determined. In the short term, the essence of the organizational requirement will be achieved without the distraction of inventing new human resources policies. The point is to have a strong customer-facing organization cutting across the formal organization lines. One day, management may even replace the functional organization and actually organize fully around the customer.

The benefit of this broad customer-interacting organization is a very significant increase in engaged management that will find as yet unknown ways to benefit both the customer's business and your business with increased services and improved management processes.

This is not just the voice of the customer, or VOC, as is taught in total quality management (TQM) and other productivity improvement programs such as Lean Six Sigma. You are looking for engagement, not just data. The problem with the traditional structure is shown at the left in Figure 4-1. The traditional structure has a very limited number of sales representatives and sales management interacting with the customer, with perhaps a marketing staff member from time to time. The interaction, by virtue of the skill set involved in the meetings, is limited to pricing discussions, volume discussions, and perhaps some talk about service performance. In market-savvy SO&P, in contrast, you are looking for a much more robust interaction across a very broad set of business topics—a discovery discussion in which the customer tells you all. In companies achieving this level of engagement, the very strategic plans of each organization are fully disclosed. What's more, they are messaged to improve both your plans and performance, as well as the customer's.

Balanced organizational collaboration with the customer dispels the myths about what is important to the customer and defines a more well-rounded set of customer requirements with an enhanced understanding. One example of how the customer requirements myth actually harms a business is currently found in the medical device industry. Medical devices are the instruments and implants used in various kinds of surgery. For decades, the medical device manufacturers have had only the sales force giving them insights into what products had to be offered. The sales representatives work directly with physicians. And physicians, many of whom view themselves as godlike, say they want in the operating room (OR) every possible size and configuration of whatever medical device category the sales rep is offering. As a result, the medical device manufacturers have flooded the ORs with inventory. A quick look at a balance sheet for a medical device manufacturer will find inventory DOS eight to ten times higher than in almost any other industry. In fact, the inventory is placed on consignment at hospitals so it remains the financial responsibility of the manufacturer until it is used or, more likely, goes out of date code and is returned for scrap or rework. In our work with several medical device manufacturers, we have found that significantly less inventory is actually required—in every case, at least half the historical amounts. In one instance, senior management of a device manufacturer was called to a meeting of hospital administrators and told it needed to immediately start work on drastically reducing item complexity and overall inventory on location. The hospital administrators knew the cost of the complexity was being passed on, and they wanted it reduced.

Create Cascading Customer Goals

The customer-facing organizational structure will find a rich set of customer-defined goals being communicated from the customer. The individual inside each function represented in the structure is naturally better able to communicate the customer's goals to the others in the functional organization work group. The very communication of these goals, in terms used inside the company, will begin to change behavior. The customer goals can now cascade down to all levels within the formal organization. The customer-facing staff changes the discussion inside the company from an internally defined set of metrics to an externally defined set.

A fully engaged customer-facing organization is also a great deal of fun. Engaged people develop enthusiasm. Look at Zappos.com and Southwest Airlines. These two companies are highly profitable and became so by transforming what were formerly very sleepy and stagnant industry models into organizations that were engaged with their customers. What is amazing to me is that their competitors still do not understand what these companies are doing even after years of watching them gain market share and a competitive advantage. They see Zappos.com as basically a mail-order house using e-mail rather than the U.S. Postal Service and Southwest as just one new airline among many, missing the strengths found in these companies' total customer commitment.

Achieve Transparency

In the customer-facing organization structure, the attitude of the customer toward you is transparent to a wide variety of staff. The reality of your impact on the customer can be understood. You can measure performance inside the company and feel very good about your progress. But often the customer neither cares about what you are measuring nor has knowledge of your performance. A major domestic paint manufacturer measured on-time shipment and complete orders as the primary service metric. The manufacturer was moving up toward 85 percent perfect orders from 65 percent, which was indeed a major improvement. Then one day, the company was shocked when one of its main customers, a major retailer that accounted for more than 20 percent of total business, sent a cancellation notice. The customer was moving its business to a small competitor. The customer measured availability on its shelves and wanted 99 percent in-stock performance. The shipment metric used by the paint manufacturer had no relevance to the customer's availability metric.

The manufacturing and logistics functions made strident efforts to deny the existence of a problem and to claim the customer was wrong, but the reality of the situation hit and the manufacturer was forced to lay off some workers. The functional management had never talked to the customer and was clueless to explain the situation to the laid-off employees. To obtain understanding and regain lost market share, senior management acquired the small competitor to whom the retailer had moved its business. Management kept the acquisition autonomous long enough to find out what that company was doing differently. The key differences were that the small competitor had strong engagement with the customer; recognized the availability metric; and, most important, understood how to make sure the performance goal was both achieved and appreciated by the customer via transparency.

Transform Risks into Opportunities

Often, customer-facing organizations can become risk takers purely by understanding the customer's goals and internal workings. In the customer-facing organization, risks involved with customer changes in product strategies often can be mitigated by having lead time to make a proper response.

A chemical manufacturer began working with the Ph.D.s in its customers' research and development organizations and with the marketing and executive staff to determine how to better align with future plans. Normally, the manufacturer would strongly resist upgrades in technology because of fears of obsolescence and of loss of capacity utilization in existing products and manufacturing capability. By working in a fully engaged structure, the manufacturer gained understanding of the need for the technology upgrades and what changes would be required. The manufacturer had time to bleed down existing inventory to reduce obsolescence and time to convert capacity to the new technology. Internal forecasts of demand using historical data were pointing to the need to keep on pushing the existing product through production. Internally, the risk of change was seen as excessive. By focusing on the customer, executive management was kept fully informed, and an orderly transition was authorized and executed. How often we see companies surprised by the advent of new technology provided by a smaller, more nimble competitor "plugged in" at the customer.

Establishing Collaboration

Simply having a horizontal organizational structure facing the customer does not bring cross-functional collaboration. Collaboration happens when a balance is achieved between functional goals and the overall goals of the customer and the provider.

The balance can be found only inside a specific value-chain definition. We defined value chains in Chapter 2 and will build on that definition here. The important aspect of value-chain definitions, as far as behavior is concerned, is the realization that it takes a full team to accomplish the complex goals of value delivery. Everyone knows it is easy to optimize a particular function's goals and to suboptimize the total.

So how do you establish collaboration? There are three major requirements. You must (1) overcome the fear of change, (2) create common goals, and (3) brand the team.

Overcome the Fear of Change

People have a natural fear of change and a desire to stay inside their safe zone, their own functional organizations. The challenge is to overcome the fear of collaboration. Almost always, fear comes from a lack of understanding, not a basic personality flaw. You can improve understanding with analytics, as illustrated in Chapter 3. In addition, you can show how the individual functional goals are actually in conflict with one another and may well be in conflict with the customer's goals. Everyone should readily agree upon the primary importance of the health of the whole. If not, then everyone should agree that the customer's goals are more important than internal goals, particularly when the customer's goals are objectively defined using a customer-facing organization structure and not filtered through a single point of customer contact.

The first step is to help staff understand the natural tendencies of the functional organizational structure and the conflicting goals inside the structure. Figure 4-2 displays the problem of goal alignment in a functional, silo organization.

Sales organizations normally strive for very high service, as Figure 4-2 indicates, and advocate high inventory and a disregard for cost containment. Finance, on the other hand, pushes hard for lower inventory at the expense of both cost and service. Manufacturing is measured on cost and will increase inventory to gain large lot sizes while hurting service. Each functional area has a different optimum goal, and each area's optimal goal is reversed in the other two func-

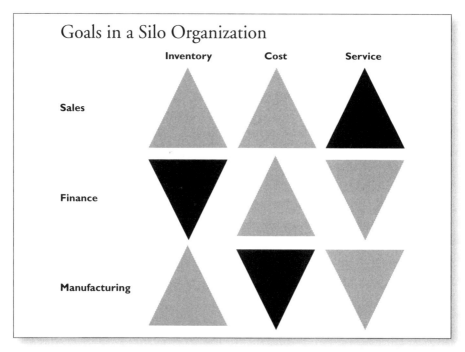

FIGURE 4-2. CONFLICTING GOALS IN A SILO ORGANIZATION.
Each function shown has only one arrow showing alignment with the overall or highlighted goals.

tional areas. When polled, the majority of managers have no idea their functional goal could be in conflict with that of other functions.

The people in each functional area were given performance metrics or indoctrinated with functional performance metrics from the time they started their careers. Internal goals and metrics are safe. Everyone agrees to them, and the way they are measured has been handed down from the managers who perform appraisals and determine raises, promotions, and retention. Thus, going outside the established performance guides and questioning them is cause for great fear. People simply don't do it or appear to be agreeing, while having no intention of actually changing behavior.

Overcoming the fear of change requires two fundamentals: education and customer focus.

I believe education can go a long way toward reducing fear. Using the simple construct shown in Figure 4-2 is a great educational device. Most people have no appreciation for how the overall goals of an organization are achieved or might be in conflict. Educating staff on the way service, inventory, and cost work together does require some formal classroom time, but it is well worth it. For example, I often teach a class on inventory and balance sheet performance in the course of my client work. The lessons are that inventory is an asset only in financial terms. Inventory actually takes money away from purposes of great importance to the health of an enterprise, such as research and development, business growth, acquisitions, and new business start-up, to name just a few. In this age of tight credit and high investor expectations, inventory is a luxury very few companies can afford. In addition, inventory carrying costs are very high.

Having people work together to resolve internal goals is a good way to build confidence. A group of executives should be able to discuss the trade-offs between inventory, service, and cost, discussing where a push for lower costs actually hurts the overall performance of the company.

I worked with a steel manufacturer that had a goal to improve the overall quality of its steel. The CEO had a manufacturing engineering group work on quality improvement, which is an important aspect of customer service. Sales had defined what it thought was important as a quality measure. Engineering came up with new process technology ideas and proposed improvements designed by an outside company. Finance looked at the proposals and held up approval of the improvement programs because of a concern about capital availability. Manufacturing management decided the improvements would require lost manufacturing time with equipment changeover, so manufacturing termed the new projects "counterproductive." Nothing was moving. The CEO asked for help, and we came in.

We first studied the issue from an industry viewpoint to gain some perspective through analytics. The industry was spending up to 8 percent of revenues on process improvement. Our client, however, was spending only 2 percent and falling behind, according to the sales management team. We formed a cross-functional team to study the issues. Everyone had a say and realized they had argued themselves into doing nothing while trying to protect their individual goals. In the end, we did bring some understanding by simply testing the limits of each functional area's argument. Manufacturing began to ask when a project would be financially justified for them. Finance asked the CEO about capital availability and defined a range. Sales became more discerning about quality demands. Eventually, the team defined ways to increase capital projects to the industry norm of 8 percent of revenue. One senior manufacturing executive just could not bring himself to agree; he was transferred to South America. The team defined projects, but it found it now had too many. The team needed to choose between a set of very good projects with acceptable returns on capital.

The company then sent the team out to customers to determine a more specific set of quality definitions. The team members found several large customers, including two of the major auto manufacturers and an appliance manufacturer, which were overjoyed at the prospect of working jointly on steel quality. Confidentiality agreements were set in place, and the discussions started. In the end, our client became the highest-quality provider of specific steel products and ran profitably for a decade. Unfortunately, the legacy costs of the heavy union contracts signed in the 1970s eventually took their toll on capital; the company went into Chapter 11 and eventually into Chapter 7. The failure was due to the lack of cross-functional understanding and collaboration. The union and management could not reach agreement. I cannot say which side was more at fault. The failure was a lack of collaboration on everyone's part.

Create Common Goals

Common goals establish a foundation for collaboration. In our above example from steel manufacturing, we found an industry goal to use as a guideline. Benchmarking is a very good way of setting goals. The principle is to have a goal that transcends the functional areas.

Common goals can be established for the customer-facing organization with responsibility for specific market segments. Senior management then needs to set up a system of reward and recognition around a goal, or a set of a few goals, for the whole team. In fact, we have found all these elements to be important: common recognition and reward practices, a customer-facing organization, one market segment, and common goals. Collaboration is then well founded and can be expected.

The goals should be a combination of internal goals and external or customer goals. Internal collaborative goals are discussed in Chapter 5. They include free cash flow and market-share capture. Achieving these goals requires cross-functional collaboration. External goals for service, quality, and many other areas are equally important, but they must be stated in a balanced, cross-functional level of detail to be effective.

Brand the Team

In all cases of success with collaboration, an enthusiasm for the collaborative process develops throughout the customer-facing organization. An excellent way to generate enthusiasm is to give the customer-facing group a brand identity. The brand should be a simple phrase clearly identifying the goal of the team and the customer focus. Our steel manufacturer client discussed previously developed the "A-1 quality team," which stood for auto industry leadership in flat-rolled steel. An externally measurable set of goals were defined.

Market-savvy S&OP teams should be branded. The brand can identify the new market-savvy S&OP process in terms of the goals and collaboration the team intends to achieve. This is what a hardlines manufacturer did to brand its team:

♦   The manufacturer named its brand "I-4," standing for fourfold improvement in innovation within its market segment. The company wanted leadership in industry patents, but it needed to manage four other areas: cash generation to fund the innovation projects, time-to-market reduction, management of obsolescence, and customer recognition as the innovative leader.

♦ The team members had to be able to explain the brand to those not on the team. They used a suspense strategy to communicate the brand, announcing the team brand, putting up posters around the office, and sending out launch notices prior to revealing what the brand actually meant.

Driving Collegiality

Collegiality is the attitude of members of a customer-facing organization in their approach to one another. Collegial is how we act; collaboration is what we do. Collegiality is the commitment to achieving a common set of goals, possibly at the expense of optimizing individual or functional goals. In the customer-centric culture, the successful segment teams have a high degree of collegiality.

The collaborative process will, in fact, be cut short and stopped if the individuals do not develop a collegial attitude. Members of a customer-facing organization cannot actually visit a customer if a collegial atmosphere is not present. The worst thing that can befall a new collaborative process is to have team members bickering and disagreeing in front of the customer or acting in a haughty or arrogant manner. Employees who are not collegial in their attitude toward others undermine morale, stop very important discussions, thwart teamwork, and shirk responsibility to complete the group work on time.

The customer-centric culture is a consultative culture, not an autocratic or submissive one. The customer-centric culture is rare in business, while the autocratic and submissive cultures are everywhere. The best example of the desired culture in business is a professional management consulting organization where collegiality is essential, both while people are working with other members of the firm and certainly while they are working with client teams. The advantage consulting firms bring to business is the ability to generate fresh insights and to develop transformational plans for improvement. These are exactly the results you are seeking in the customer-centric culture.

Respect Contributions

Respecting one another's contribution and potential to help achieve goals is critical. In a professional consulting organization, unlike the typical functional organization in industry, individuals must bring their talents and expertise together to achieve a high-level result for a paying client. Integrity and ethical standards are of paramount importance, of course, but more crucial to the success of the work effort is gaining the multiplicative effect that is obtained only through a collegial working relationship. I am not talking about having drinks together or socializing; that is not even a factor. I am concerned only with being responsible for thoughtful contributions in team meetings, having an excellent work output, and supporting achievement of client-defined requirements.

Build Trust

Employees will make contributions and will be responsible if they trust their work will be appreciated, not ignored or worse yet ridiculed. Trust is built from the very first meeting of the S&OP design team and in every meeting that then flows forward. Trust can be built through brainstorming exercises. Everyone is encouraged to participate, and everyone has a vote on the final outcome. I have seen collegiality and trust begin and flourish by having the management team develop a set of shared values in an initial meeting brainstorming session. Shared values are, in fact, the components of a collegial relationship. The CEO can go a long way toward making a successful change to a customer-centric culture by leading the brainstorming exercise at the first meeting of the market-savvy S&OP design team. If the CEO is not fully committed and willing, the team facilitator or leader can start. The way this works is for the leader to define collegiality as the expected behavior toward customers, partners, suppliers, stockholders, fellow employees, and the public. The leader can share an example, which should be a positive one.

I have worked on boards of trustees where little is done as well as on one or two boards where a great deal is accomplished. The productive boards have people who share a common set of values related to the work of the organization. The values are stated and well accepted. One nonprofit educational institution on whose board I served grew to be the largest and highest-quality institution in its field. We spent the first several hours of each board meeting sharing personal accomplishments, personal troubles, and/or disappointments. Each person was seen as an individual of value. President Theodore Roosevelt was reported to have started major cabinet meetings by asking participants to walk outside and gaze at the stars together, counting and observing the complexity of creation. He then asked, "Are we now humble enough to work together to solve the nation's problems?"

The management team could start the initial meeting by asking each person to call out ideas of what values represent collegial behavior. You must be sure to seek confirmation from the group as each value is suggested, to make sure you are talking about collegial behavior, meaning working together to achieve goals, and not just socializing behavior. Each person should be strongly encouraged to participate. In some cases, I have seen the leader stop the exercise to talk about energy levels and the need to increase energy in the exercise. Once a good list is written on a flip chart for all to see, the selection process begins. Duplicates are eliminated, like items combined, and a ranking of very important or less important completed. Once the list is down to, say, 15 to 20 items, the voting begins, with everyone having perhaps three votes. A final list of no more than five key values should be the result.

Design a Measurement Process

Just having a list of values does not necessarily develop collegiality. You need to put serious structure to the values. The group should

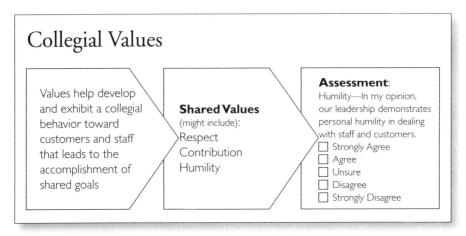

FIGURE 4-3. TAKING A VALUES ASSESSMENT.
The commitment to the collegial values should be measured periodically with a survey.

design a periodic measurement process in which each individual is asked to assess the collective performance to achieve the values. A survey should be designed and taken within the first few weeks of the initial meeting. The survey may include sections like the one presented in Figure 4-3.

You want results indicating "Strongly Agree" or "Agree" at 90 percent or better. The measurement results can be shared without finding specific fault with a group or an individual. The employees participating should discuss the results and talk about ways to improve. This should not turn into a finger-pointing exercise or an intervention. The measurement and discussion itself is an exercise in collegiality. The group can discuss how to collectively handle the assessment discussion as a way to identify improvement actions.

Include Collegiality in Performance Reviews

Individual performance in adopting the collegial behavior values should be part of the annual performance review. Performance reviews in general should be a professional development tool. I have experienced good and very bad performance review practices. In the consulting business, a major emphasis of the performance review and assessment is adherence to collegial values . For a time, Booz & Co. did a great job of preparing performance reviews using a peer assessment methodology, along with client interviews. The process worked well, as long as the assessments were positive and aimed at building rather than tearing down.

In my business, we use an educational tool to help define a healthy way of handling collegiality building and assessment. The system, called "Sharpening Your People Skills," was developed by a friend of mine, Bruce Cook, the past president of Leadership Dynamics International. Bruce is a Harvard Business School graduate who became fascinated with leadership development. I served on the board of Leadership Dynamics and saw firsthand how powerful the system is in developing collegiality. The "science" behind the system is in the recognition of four basic personality types in humans, termed D-I-S-C. The recognition that the four types exist is ages old, having been originally described and used by the ancient Greeks. Bruce's system has a strong emphasis on understanding how your behavior impacts others. Each person takes a personality evaluation test and determines his or her major strength in a group of four standard types. *High D* personalities are decisive, *High I* personalities are imaginative, *High S* personalities are submissive, and *High C* personalities are correct. A summary description of the four personality types is shown in Figure 4-4.

The participants learn that a good leadership team needs all four types. *D*s make decisions, *I*s sell ideas outside the team, *S*s hold the team together in times of stress, and *C*s make sure the work is of the highest quality. Certainly, individuals can irritate others if their personality traits become obsessive. *D*s can cut people short in the quest for a bottom-line answer without all the frills, while *I*s can be distracting with their constant need for recognition. The point is to educate everyone in how they interact. Each person has strengths and perhaps faults. The education helps form a language useful in correcting team members gently when their collegial values tend to slide down. For example, you might say to a *High S*, "Your submissiveness has shut you down, and we need you to tell us your ideas," or to a *High*

	D	**I**	**S**	**C**
Value to the Team	Takes initiative	Salesperson	Builds relationships	Focuses on detail
Major Strength	Purpose-driven	Enthusiasm	People skills	Thoroughness
Time Perspective	Now, to the point	Future, rushes ahead	Present, interacts well	Past, works slowly
Major Weakness	Impatient	Impulsive, no focus	Harmony before results	Overly cautious
Motivated by	Results	Recognition	Relationships	Being right
Decision Making	Jumps to goal	Intuitive	Relational	Reluctant
When Challenged	Autocratic	Attacks	Acquiesces	Avoids
Effectiveness Improved by	Listening	Pausing	Initiating	Declaring

FIGURE 4-4. UNIVERSAL PERSONALITY TYPES IN TEAMS.
The objective in using the system is to build acceptance and respect.

D, "Your *D* is over the top. Let's discuss the issue in more depth, so back off."

The education system is also used to make performance reviews positive. Periodic refresher courses may help to remind everyone that each individual has intrinsic value. If you find a person who chooses to take the whole collegiality value idea lightly or chooses to ignore it altogether, you should probably encourage that person to find another place to apply his or her talents. I am aware that some very talented people are not willing to be collegial. If your number one sales representative is one of those, you may have a dilemma in the short term. Over the longer term, the drive to collegiality should win, or you risk losing the momentum. I have worked with clients who have an anti-collegial culture. I can say with great confidence that such a culture does not produce strong business performance results.

Collegiality is essential to developing revolutionary ideas and implementing the next part of the customer-centric culture, which is horizontal management processes.

Designing Horizontal Management Processes

Most management processes are vertical. They are built around the linear information systems model, which passes data up and down, within, and between functions. Information technology (IT) is the new name for what was formerly known as data processing. The process has not changed, and the activity is still data processing. Processing optimizes functions but suboptimizes the whole organization. Horizontal processes are the antithesis; they convert data into information, which is then integrated across the organization. Horizontal processes are a requirement in the customer-centric culture.

Make Processes Executable

In the typical management process, massive amounts of data are gathered from transaction processing systems such as ERP or customer relationship management, then summarized and sent upward to the top of the organization inside a function. These systems are good for efficiently gathering data and mechanically passing it up. They are very linear and bland, lacking depth and color. Process analysis experts can use a simple SIPOC (source, input, process, output, and customer) technique for describing a transactional process. SIPOC analysis, from the Lean Six Sigma field, is very useful in analyzing vertical processes with single-point data processing because the process is very linear and moves vertically. Inputs are mechanically gathered, used, and passed on. SIPOC analysis is not possible in highly interactive processes because of the many feedback loops and also because of the changes that inputs go through as the process moves. While I have a great deal of respect for Lean Six Sigma professionals, they always have difficulty using their linear process analysis techniques to describe horizontal processes.

You need processes that are executable and support decision making. Decision making is about assessment, judgment, trade-offs, optimizing the whole, and—for sure—action. Processes are neither linear nor vertical; they involve creativity built on analytics and information, not merely data. The management processes you need are horizontal ones that allow a free and open consideration of ideas. The flaw in the vertical process is the absence of what-if thinking, consideration of alternatives, openness to opposing interpretations of the data, and interactive assessment.

I have often heard senior managers say things such as, "Don't second-guess my forecast," or "I passed you the decision, just follow it." These are autocratic remarks made to force conformance to vertical processes; they thwart constructive assessment and lead to limited planning effectiveness, as found in the predictive and presumptive planning models described in Chapter 1. Predetermined planning, the desired model, is a discovery process that requires exploration of multiple inputs from a diverse set of sources.

Horizontal processes, when combined with the customer-facing organization, support the customer-centric culture.

Create a Common Language

Horizontal processes require a new language for cross-functional communication. The language is the recasting of data into a form that multiple functions can understand and make into executable plans. We have emphasized the need to have the entire operation working in market-segment teams. So, the language you need is one limited to the complexity of the market segment; therefore, it is not very difficult to design.

The language should be formed around the rule of the 3Ms: market, manufacturing, and materials. When you have families of products that have commonality across all three factors, you have a basis for a productive discussion or a language you can all speak. The opposite is when sales speaks in terms of sales regions, which are foreign to manufacturing's production lines and do not relate to procurement's supplier types. A common language of 3M families allows everyone to understand the families' impact on the work.

An easy example is in food manufacturing. Food service customers are found in all sales regions. They buy most of their needs in the form of bulk packages, such as gallons rather than 12-ounce cans, and the products they buy are produced on segregated production lines due to package size. So, we now have common market, one M and common manufacturing, a second M. The third M is the raw materials. For food service, the ingredients are normally commonly used in the production facility, only needed in higher volumes. In addition, many specialized items are required to provide the high complexity of products normally required by these food service customers. So, separating the food service market from other markets is helpful when the family also includes items made on the bulk lines as well as the special purchase items. We have a set of 3M families. In frozen food, the food service items are often not fully cooked, as the retail items are, prior to freezing. Vegetables for food service often are grown to have thicker skins, which helps them survive the warming tables in restaurants without becoming mush. Investigation of the market characteristics, manufacturing alignment, and materials almost always yields discovery of a set of planning families with a common language.

When working with a paint manufacturer, we found that the 139,000 different items it made could be organized into 39 major 3M families making up more than 80 percent of production. All the different brands were ignored, since labeling was done with indifference to brand changes. The big discount retailers purchased only base paint, which was then colored in-store. The specialty retail chains purchased pre-colored paint and specialty bases with higher-quality ingredients. Thus, the pattern of production-line segregation emerged from the 3M analysis. Procurement of the bulk of the standard ingredients was strongly aligned with the discount retail family.

Procurement of specialty items was the exclusive territory of the specialty retailer family.

This language makes it very easy to understand cross-functionally and makes integrated planning actually possible. A team of time-challenged executives can discuss a small group of 3M families very quickly and effectively.

Insist on Bold Interactivity

Horizontal processes use the language of the 3Ms to become interactive, greatly expanding the depth of understanding across the organization and leading to consensus and decisiveness. The horizontal process results in a multiplicative effect in decision making, which is impossible in a linear process.

The general model for the horizontal process replaces the IT model. In fact, the data transfer processes are best stopped altogether.

The horizontal process model is distinctly different. The model has a rhythm rather than a beginning and an end. The model as shown in Figure 4-5 moves information and decisions across and inside the collaborative organization.

The four design elements shown in Figure 4-5—communication, collaboration, execution, and follow-through—are unique to a decision-making process. Communication is achieved using the language of the 3M families, with ranges instead of single-point data and insights recorded as the information is passed. Asking a sales rep to send up a three-month forward forecast for the quantity to be sold each month is simply naive. The sales rep will provide the numbers when asked, but he or she will quietly laugh at the request because it is far too simplistic. A better way is to ask for the range or 80-percent-confident interval. Also, ask for what is going to drive the high forecast and the low forecast. When the forecasts from many sales reps in the same market segment are combined, the management group has the beginning of a risks and opportunities analysis, as well as the midpoint and range of the forecast.

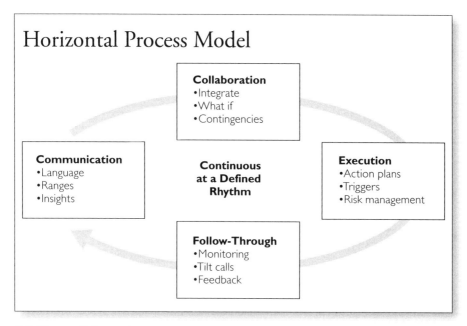

FIGURE 4-5. GENERAL PROCESS DESIGN ELEMENTS OF THE HORIZONTAL MODEL.
The design includes four sequential phases with rhythm and cadence

Collaboration is achieved when the information from several sources is integrated to form a larger story. What-if scenarios can be formed from the insights provided in the communication phase and the contingency plans that have been formed. Let's continue with the forecasting example we started when we were talking about the communication phase. Forecasts from field sales would be considered along with forecasts of industry trends and market share from marketing; forecasts based on historical analysis in a statistical forecasting process from demand management; forecasts developed from competitor analysis; forecasts from past calendar periods; forecasts from strategic planning or IBP (integrated business planning) processes; and other forecasts. In many cases, you want to see 10 to 20 different forecasts being communicated in the collaboration phase. The participants would then integrate the forecasts, defining the patterns with some very rich color, making judgments about confidence, and eventually coming to consensus. The consensus is reached in part by considering capacity constraints. You certainly want to know the unconstrained forecast, but you must have contingency plans made when capacity constraints force a lowering of the consensus forecast. You don't want manufacturing and procurement, or for that matter sales, going off independently and deciding how to respond to capacity constraints. Sales might start placing phantom orders to reserve scare capacity for customers, or purchasing might decide to order a different mix of materials than manufacturing may plan to use. So contingency plans are required, and then a specific consensus forecast is completed. Once subsequent processes are completed, the consensus forecast may change, as rough-cut constraints are removed in more detailed planning.

Execution is achieved when action plans are formed. The action plans normally have trigger points identified for each contingency plan option. Again, building on the forecasting example, as the actual orders begin to come in against the rates defined in the collaboration phase, a trigger to move production higher or lower would be defined to occur at some future date based upon new experience weighed against the consensus plan. Risks and of course opportunities are managed by knowing when the specific drivers identified in the communication phase are realized. The management team is forewarned to be on the lookout for risks materializing because of the richness and color of the communication from many sources.

The follow-through phase is critical to the success of the horizontal process. Decisions about specific actions are not just allowed to continue without the monitoring of updated experience over short intervals. Some horizontal processes are monitored daily and some weekly, but they are all monitored. As actual orders come in, the trends are measured against the plans, and if the trends are particularly adverse to expectations, a tilt meeting is called. Tilt meetings are breaks in the rhythm of the process caused by outside-in recognition. Tilt meetings are a major replan inside the process, a new collaboration phase. Feedback is sent for higher-level executive review once the tilt meeting comes to a new consensus. While tilt meetings are not expected to happen very often, they avoid having major surprises in the normal rhythm of the market-savvy S&OP monthly process.

Test for Broad Inclusiveness

The process is inclusive of all functions in the customer-facing organization. Each function takes away different information to use in other horizontal processes. The insights gained in each communication phase have impact in myriad ways. This is where the multiplicative effect takes place.

The participants in the horizontal process should be at a decision-making level. They are not the most senior people in each function, but they are able to commit to following through inside their own functions. The processes cannot be complete if everyone moves forward without commitment and allows second-guessing. Once the consensus is reached, the action plan is the responsibility of the participants, and all are held accountable for the decisions as a combined team.

Fully Document

The horizontal process needs to be documented in a simple form. We like one-page, single-sided, normal-letter-size documents. In the document, name the participants, define the objective, identify the timing or rhythm elements, and include a brief description of the contents of the process.

Complex documentation is not effective. Since horizontal processes are fluid, decision-making processes, a step-by-step exact definition of the work is not possible. You want the documentation to be used and to be an active guide. If the documentation is very specific and lengthy, then people simply ignore it.

I was once sent to Woodward, Oklahoma, to develop a process for natural gas pipeline safety. The assignment seemed strange at first. Why would a company hire Booz & Co. at very high billing rates to write safety processes? When I arrived in Woodward, I found large books of written safety procedures inside locked filing cabinets with red tape outlining the doors to signal the importance of the contents. I asked to read the books. People spent several days looking for the file cabinet keys, and finally a locksmith was called to pull the lock. The books were covered with dust (not uncommon in far western Oklahoma), and cobwebs showed they had not been taken out of the cabinets for a long time, if ever. When I began to read, I learned that five men had died in a tragic breach of safety when a crew fired up a welding torch in a containment pit under an active gas-holding tank. It seems they had a new piece of pipe and valve to install. Gas from the tank had been flowing into the holding pit unnoticed by the crew, since they were close to the well heads and the smelling agent is not put into the gas until it is moved much farther up the pipeline. The explosion left the concrete pit liner completely eradicated, the tank nowhere to be found, and five families left fatherless. The line management crew had not padlocked the valves shut, and the welders were macho men who were not afraid of gas explosions, so they ignored all safety procedures. Management had no way to supervise because of the distances between sites, and no one had read the safety procedures. This goes to show that documentation by itself was not effective. What is needed is a horizontal process and lots of senior management support.

I have also worked in the construction of fire protection systems in complex structures such as high-rise buildings and nuclear power plants. For a long time, bad accidents and even deaths were accepted as part of the cost of doing business in these areas. Then the Japanese automobile companies came to the United States to build major assembly plants. They had very strong horizontal processes for safety implementation. They demanded effective communication, collaborative planning, action plans, and feedback loops. Safety was discussed and demonstrated in daily meetings, at which attendance was required. A culture of friendly reminders between fellow employees replaced the macho-man arrogance found in most construction crews. All employees were active participants in designing safety procedures, and simple written documentation was the norm. I experienced a totally accident-free major construction program. I was told by some longtimers that this was a first in the country for all of them. I might also point out that my firm had a very profitable experience as well.

Measure Meeting Time Saved

Horizontal processes produce tangible benefits. Time spent in seemingly endless meetings is the bane of major companies. Significant competitive sluggishness is the result. Tangible reductions in profit attainment and cash-flow generation are experienced to the frustration of senior management.

Horizontal processes with the four unique design elements in place, though, eliminate hundreds of meetings each month in companies having predominately vertical processes. Clients implementing market-savvy S&OP report that an enormous amount of time becomes free as the pronounced rhythm and cadence of the horizontal processes organize everyone. Employees report finding hours per day of open time for needed research, essential analysis, and expanded thinking.

Employees experience a significantly enriched job experience as they move from being attendees at boring meetings to interactive thinkers. At a consumer products company, Fred, the manufacturing master scheduler, was found to be severely time-stressed. He carried two cell phones, had a business line next to his bed at home, played his beloved golf only every other weekend (and then only one round), and was harassed all day long by multiple change requests for the master production schedule. Fred was near a mental breakdown. Daily expediting sessions held at lunchtime—a formerly open time set aside by some for eating—were the norm and grew to meetings of more than 30 people. Fred's time was taken up with change meetings, and the company's profits were taken away by constant schedule changes and the material waste that resulted. Once we put in the horizontal processes of market-savvy S&OP, Fred had most afternoons free. His golf handicap went down steadily to his college career level of two. In addition, the company's profit improved very substantially, and the business was soon sold, at a very handsome profit to the shareholders.

Appointing Leaders with Passion

The customer-centric culture is implemented by people with a passion for continuous improvement in value delivery. A true leader is a person who works through others to accomplish a purpose. A passionate leader accomplishes transformational change and finds ways to communicate a purpose and to contribute with a sense of urgency.

In the seemingly endless candidate debates that precede U.S. presidential elections, the most stirring moments are the ones when a candidate expresses thoughts with passion. The winners of a debate are those who make an impact and are remembered for remarks delivered with enthusiasm and knowledge of purpose.

Identify a Leader with Passion

We often use examples from the orchestral world to illustrate points for managers outside the United States, where baseball and U.S. football are not well understood. The Cleveland Orchestra is considered by experts to be one of the top two or three orchestras in the United States. It has benefited from leaders with a passion for excellence, from George Szell, its music director for 24 years, to Christoph von Dohnanyi, who held the baton for 18 years. I attended a Cleveland Orchestra concert where the principal music was a piece very often played by the Boston Pops, another highly regarded orchestra. The person giving the lecture about the concert prior to the performance was a development professional who had been with the Boston Pops for more than a decade and had recently moved to the Cleveland organization. He said, "I have heard the score being played tonight many times in Boston. In fact, it is a signature piece for the Boston Pops. However," he continued, when he had heard the Cleveland Orchestra perform the piece the night before, it was "the first time I have ever heard it performed with excellence. The attention to the excellence of tone, accent, entrances, endings, dynamics, and pitch accuracy in the presentation by the Cleveland Orchestra is astounding, truly a transformational experience." After hearing the orchestra that night, I fully agreed. We were blessed with an outstanding and competitively advantaged company in the form of a classical music performance organization. Both Szell and Dohnanyi had special talents and highly developed skills, but their main quality as leaders was a passion for continuous improvement.

Excellence in this case is defined by the customer. Leaders with passion help change the organization to the customer-centered culture by making the case for achieving the customer's goals. There will be a great deal of inertia inside a company to stay the existing course, even if the existing course is leading to ruin.

Many change management experts describe the "burning platform" effect as being the driver of change, as if all the employees must immediately see the flames to be motivated. Some say the employees will not truly get on board with change until the actual heat of the flames is so intense that the skin on their feet starts to blister. The employees may see burning platforms and feel the heat, but unless a manager with passion leads them in how to change, the employees will just keep doing the same old thing. Look at all the staffs who work in large organizations that have failed. They doggedly stayed the course to eventual ruin, even while seeing some flames and certainly feeling some heat, as droves of fellow workers lost their jobs. General Motors lost half its market share to the Japanese and European car makers over 20 years, yet its employees stayed the course of high union benefits, even higher management compensation, not one innovation of consequence developed for the customer, and near-zero attention to quality as defined by the customer. Eastman Kodak, once very proud and highly successful, failed to make the digital transition. The company did not move from film to digital storage disks in the 1980s, when it had plenty of time and could have been first. Instead, Kodak employees lost sight of the customer and watched complacently while more than 50,000 fellow workers lost their jobs in Rochester, New York, alone. Don't tell me no one noticed.

Strong examples of leaders with passion are hard to find, but there are some. Robert J. Palmisano, CEO of Wright Medical, of ev3 Inc., and several other major companies, is a great example. I have had the privilege of working as an S&OP process consultant for him for more than twenty years. His passion for excellence in delivering customer value has resulted in major financial turnarounds at four companies, primarily in medical technology. His work saw stock prices of these companies move up in several years to three to nine times the price from when he started. Bob has the passion and the emotional sensitivity of a great leader. He uses the HPMS (High Performance Management System) pioneered by Richard C. Palermo, Sr., of Xerox Corporation in the 1970s and 1980s. Like Palermo, his contemporary, Bob started his management career in Rochester. One of the main principles of HPMS that Bob applied in the companies he turned around was to find people with a passion for change to be leaders of the process improvement programs implemented under the system.

Apple Inc.'s cofounder is a more famous example of a passionate leader. Steven P. Jobs had a passion for innovation at the crossroads of technology and humanity. He brought valuable innovation from many places, some developed at Apple and some stolen, into reality in a way customers perceived as valuable. At one point in the 1980s, Jobs was forced out of Apple by a professional manager. Jobs went on to apply his passion at Pixar Animation Studios with remarkable success. Meanwhile, Apple shrank to near oblivion before Jobs came back in the 1990s and fired up the troops with his passion for the customer. Certainly, Apple's innovations were great, but supply chain execution was the key to success. Many very good ideas die of poor supply chain execution. For example, Xerox innovations were applied with great success to the Macintosh computer, but they were also applied to a Xerox offering that sold only 30,000 units. Innovation is only part of the equation. Bringing innovation into use requires someone with both genius and a passion for the customer. For a number of years, Apple has won top spots in the Gartner Supply Chain Top 25 for best-in-class performance in supply chain, with supply chain correctly defined as the broad coalition of functions from technical, commercial, and operational disciplines.

Starbucks Corporation was successful despite many very smart financial people turning down its leader, Howard Schultz, saying $4 cups of coffee would never sell. The experts were wrong, because Schultz had a passion for customers and created a customer-centric culture in every store. The price of the coffee was secondary. Starbucks lost the passion when Schultz went into retirement. He had to return to rescue the company from sure ruin—and he did.

In highly successful companies, the passionate leader is focused on value delivery. However, there is a caution: People with passion that is focused somewhere else can lead a company to ruin. Lee Iacocca was a person with a passion for his own ego. I met him several times. He seemed to be a difficult person and a very poor leader in every regard, except giving a public impression of positive action. He always took personal credit for everything positive, even the K-car and the mini-van, which were the passions of another Chrysler executive, Harold K. "Hal" Sperlich, a truly inspiring individual.

Reward Passion

We mentioned earlier that annual personnel reviews should include measuring and encouraging collegiality. Another major element of the review should be passion. People with passion for excellence in value delivery to customers will be the agents of change. People with passion have rewarding careers.

The ultimate in employee empowerment is having employees motivated by a leader to act with passion to implement the strategy. Empowerment is not passed out. It is inspired.

Looking Back

♦ The third guiding principle of market-savvy S&OP design is to organize around *customers*, not *functions*.

♦ The customer-centric culture broadens effective management engagement in strategic attainment from two in ten to eight in ten.

♦ A customer-facing organization replaces the formal functional organization in practice.

♦ A basis for collaboration needs to be established with common goals and common accountability.

♦ Collaboration is how the work is accomplished; collegiality is the attitude of people toward one another in the new culture.

♦ Horizontal management processes are essential to achieving the value delivery sought in the customer-centric culture.

♦ Horizontal processes save a significant amount of time by eliminating hundreds of redundant meetings.

♦ Passion for excellence in delivering customer values should be strongly encouraged in the new organization. Leaders must communicate passion at a personal level to overcome the myopic malaise that plagues most companies.

Case Study: Goodyear North American Tire (NAT) Consumer

I began working with Goodyear North American Tire (NAT) Consumer when the company started to think about transitioning to a higher level S&OP in 2008. I now do the S&OP performance audits for the profit centers globally. The audits allow me to see firsthand the progress made in S&OP implementation and the results achieved. While many of the profit centers have achieved world-class performance, NAT Consumer is the strongest.

Situation. Since its founding in 1898, Goodyear has had a long tradition as the leading tire manufacturer, especially in the United States. But when Michelin entered the U.S. market in the 1970s, it started to change the order of competition. Goodyear has always been an innovator, leading the American conversion to radial tires and introducing such products as the first all-season passenger tire.

Even so, Goodyear felt the impact of a foreign brand that produced high-quality premium products to challenge the company's domestic dominance. Years later, Goodyear also was forced to fend off a credible takeover threat that increased its debt and hindered its ability to invest in the business. At the same time, manufacturing costs rose and fixed costs were not fully absorbed at lower throughput rates.

Several very talented senior executives from outside the tire industry were hired by the board of directors to try to find solutions. Stanley C. Gault was one of the executives hired by Goodyear, after he had a very good career at Rubbermaid Inc. and GE. The new Goodyear executives made many changes and improvements. However, the basic competitive disadvantages were not solved, and a major cash shortage started to emerge. The cash shortage was due to very high legacy costs associated with past contracts between Goodyear and the United Rubber Workers of America.

Goodyear had a basic level I S&OP. The company used forecasts to plan the ticket given to manufacturing. The focus of the whole organization was on manufacturing costs to the exclusion of almost everything else, including outside influences such as real consumer demand. In fact, the company was so inwardly focused that the executives in manufacturing would call marketing after an S&OP meeting to ask, "Why are you not selling what we are making?"

In 2003, Robert J. Keegan was named Goodyear's CEO and faced many immediate and major challenges. Among them were rationalizing the overall portfolio of businesses, returning the emphasis to the company's core tire businesses, and leading a turnaround that included moving from a manufacturing-driven culture (selling what they made) to a market-driven culture (making what they sold).

Actions. The management team created the many horizontal processes required in S&OP, developed a strong collaborative planning approach, and implemented analytical practices. The team had to put aside IT systems work until the horizontal management processes were fully developed. Eventually, parts of the SAP system installed at Goodyear were adapted for use in S&OP.

One of the most significant challenges was to develop a way for sales and marketing to talk with manufacturing in meaningful ways. The manufacturing process for tires is extremely complex, so finding commonality in what I have described as 3M families was a major task. Concurrent with the economic downturn in the early 2000s, Goodyear felt a sense of urgency, particularly in its North American Tire business. The company had not introduced a new, successful replacement consumer tire since the early 1990s; relationships with dealers were contentious; and competition was getting even more intense. Clearly, the traditional manufacturing-driven model was not the answer. Goodyear had to bring the customer (retailers who sell Goodyear tires) and the consumer (drivers who bought tires) into focus throughout the organization. P&G's CEO, A. G. Lafley, defined his company's cultural driver as "the customer is boss."

Goodyear took that sentiment to heart, establishing a customer marketing department in North America, defining "high-value-added" product segments, identifying desirable channels and product categories, and beginning the process of instilling a new language for cross-functional communication. Goodyear changed its strategy and began functioning more like a consumer-products company than a traditional auto supplier. Using product, customer and, process groupings, Goodyear began to manufacture, market, and sell tires that responded to the needs and demands of the market. In early 2004, the company introduced the first of a series—a series that continues today—of innovative, "market-back" Goodyear brand tires, reclaiming its position as the industry's innovation leader.

The NAT consumer business became a customer-facing organization and operated market-back from forecasting and manufacturing to sales and marketing. The installation of and commitment to S&OP

fostered a new process culture. Where manufacturing, supply chain, finance, and sales once produced their own differing forecast numbers, they now all operate with one set of common, shared data. In 2012, Goodyear's North American consumer business became the company's first product business unit to earn three straight Class A S&OP ratings.

Business Results Achieved. Thanks largely to the success in its consumer business, North American Tire was profitable in 2010, reversing a trend that was exacerbated by the global economic downturn in the prior two years. It followed with $276 million of earnings in 2011, the region's most successful year since 2000. In addition, 2011 marked the eighth time in the previous nine years that NAT saw a share increase in consumer tires in the Goodyear brand.

Cash flow improvement has been remarkable, despite the fact that the legacy costs continue. Inventory was reduced to several months from many quarters of inventory. The company executives believed if the inventory ever got down to 60 days, they would be out of business; now they are striving for less than 60 days as a way of achieving even better customer service.

PART III

Designing
New Processes

THE THIRD AND FINAL PART of change management is design and implementation of new processes. In Chapters 5 through 7, which form Part III of this book, I describe how this is accomplished.

As you read in earlier chapters, there are three processes composing market-savvy S&OP: integrated business planning (IBP), the monthly collaboration process, and rate-based planning (RBP). Chapter 5 covers the monthly collaboration process, which is founded in the vision from IBP and extended to the value chain through RBP. RBP itself is described in Chapter 6. The three market-savvy processes are sustained through the work of consolidation and transitioning to the new culture, which is discussed in Chapter 7.

Often, companies fail because they are people-heavy and process-light, meaning lots of people spend all day running from meeting to meeting, rather than using a management process to achieve results. For example, prior to its failure, International Harvester had 22 layers of management in corporate planning, but no process to organize activity into productive planning. The company merely collected, summarized, and passed data, in myriad different forms, up and across the organization. The Booz & Co. team I was part of tried to implement S&OP at International Harvester, but we ran out of time. Divestiture was forced, as the economy deteriorated and the normal cyclical upturn in the farming sector was skipped in the mid-1980s for the first time since 1900. As Stephen R. Covey observed in his book *The 7 Habits of Highly Effective People®*, "It is not the problems we have that stop us, it is the process used to solve them."

The analytics of Chapter 3 and the customer centricity of Chapter 4 are key building blocks to the three overarching market-savvy S&OP processes. Analytics and customer centricity keep the team focused on facts rather than on conventional wisdom, which is most often wrong. In addition, the customer focus helps the team produce a result that is commercially viable. History proves that 50 percent of innovation is the invention itself, and 50 percent is bringing it to market. The S&OP process focuses on the second half of the innovation story.

As you begin process improvement programs in S&OP, your emphasis at the beginning should be to work on the behavior changes required first. Since most companies have some form of S&OP, starting with creating vision and changing behavior is best.

CHAPTER 5

Designing and Implementing Collaborative Planning (Segment-Level S&OP)

WE NOW TURN TO MONTHLY COLLABORATION, the intermediate of the three major processes in market-savvy S&OP, as shown in Figure PI-1. This chapter describes how monthly collaboration aligns the essential horizontal processes of the customer-centric organization. We make clear that the segment-level S&OP process moves the business strategy from the executive suite through the entire organization and down to the shop floor, as well as out to the customers.

The guiding principle of design described in this chapter is *Process Heavy, People Light*, the most important aspect of the principle being *collaboration*. Only a truly collaborative process can bring management together in such a profound way to achieve the most profound results for shareholders, employees, and customers. The teams we described in Chapter 3 are put into effect to design and implement segment-level S&OP. All the team characteristics discussed in Chapter 3 are required. A leader with a passion for excellence in delivering value to the customer is put in place. Now the team accomplishes the process design in detail. It is useful to show this in management summary form as a high-level process map, as shown in Figure 5-1.

People participate in the design process in earnest if they see a big picture win. The process design overview can be developed in concept at the very beginning of the design process to help the team see where it is going. The integration of functional planning has an important overarching goal of developing wins for all three of the key constituents of a corporation: employees, customers, and shareholders.

Employees win by being empowered to participate with management to deliver customer value. Winning employees become passionate leaders and perpetuate the processes. Shareholders win when key financial metrics are achieved and the corporation has cash to invest

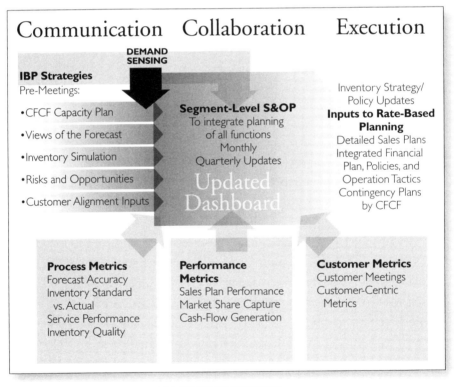

FIGURE 5-1. COLLABORATIVE PROCESSES IN OVERVIEW.
This chart can be used as a one-page handout to show monthly collaboration in segment-level S&OP, aligning all functional organization planning.

in new products and market share growth. Shareholders win financially with positive stock-price growth as calculated and powered through the generation of free cash flow. The cash in your collaborative model is used to keep the company healthy.

I do not intend to mean you should run the corporation only for the benefit of the employees or to give cash to the investors to extract. Those two practices can very quickly drive you to destruction. The whole leveraged buyout practice of so-called investment bankers, as forced on many companies in the past 20 years, has failed in large part to produce healthy companies. These investors were not intending to build an enterprise to produce value; they were interested only in wantonly removing cash to gain excessive returns on their meager investments. Running companies for the employees is just as shortsighted. Just look at the disaster of the major U.S. airlines, such as American, Delta, United, and U.S. Airways. They now are totally ignoring customer values and instead promoting only employee satisfaction. I travel more than most airline employees, have traveled by air for more than 40 years, and have witnessed the switch from a business model focused on customer satisfaction to a new model that eliminates the customer from the equation and operates the company for the privileged employees. In the end, the employees are actually losers, because they will lose their jobs as general aviation and regional new-breed carriers such as Southwest Airlines take more and more market share.

On the contrary to trying to benefit only employees and shareholders, collaboration is aligning the major constituent values to produce a positive win for all, including customers. In Chapter 4, we described how to set the foundation for collaboration in customer centricity. In Chapter 5, we describe how collaboration is achieved.

Design Starts with Education

Almost all S&OP implementation efforts initiated by the best-known S&OP consultants fail. Almost all S&OP process improvement efforts started internally by a company go nowhere. I am defining *failure* and *nowhere* as producing few significant benefits, as well as lacking in sustainability, scalability, and reproducibility. These unsuccessful implementations follow a well-traveled "path forward." In these unsuccessful efforts, an outside organization or one functional department runs the pilot, writes a design document, and then drops responsibility on employees who have little to no actual training. Sadly, implementation stops after great expenditures of money and time. The majority of all S&OP processes installed in major corporations never progress beyond the basics of scheduling and determining some estimate of future volume and mix. Basic S&OP resides in one function, with poor engagement by all the other functions, and senior management is not involved.

A much better design and implementation approach must be used if you wish to be successful and make your company a financially viable and high-growth enterprise.

You must work through people—not just with them. Successful implementation requires ownership of the process by many different functional organizations. Ownership is gained by working through the various functional organizations, rather than having one function as the lead and asking for representatives to work withit. When you work through each functional area, the functions are treated with respect and are trusted to design a process that works for them; thus, they will have ownership. If you have the behavior changes in place from Chapters 3 and 4, the process design developed by the combined group of process owners will work for the whole.

Guided Participatory Education Approach

Working through people starts with participative education. Education allows some people from all functions to actually participate in the S&OP design process, rather than just being handed a process in prepackaged form. The guided participative approach uses business simulation games, case studies, and directed discussion to increase knowledge. The opposite approach is the one we often find throughout the higher education system, with the exception of the few places that use the case study approach, such as Harvard Business School. The approach seen in many other institutions, where professors "hand down" their wisdom, often fails to engage the imagination of the students, because it treats them as know-nothing beginners. However, students in college are for the most part not know-nothing beginners. And, for sure, executives in major global corporations or small domestic corporations are not know-nothing knuckleheads, which is why the guided participative approach works.

In guided participation, the initial emphasis is to train trainers. The new trainers then in turn train other members of the organization into people who are engaged in a customer-facing organization of S&OP; and they do so as no other approach possibly can. Most likely, leaders will develop who are outside the supply chain function. Through this educational approach, leaders with a passion for the principles of market-savvy S&OP will surface, and they should be appointed to trainer status. In one of our client companies, the initial group of 15 people in participative education went on to facilitate participative learning with 150 new people, who then went on to facilitate sessions with 1,450 people. Eventually, more than 3,000 senior and middle managers were personally and respectfully brought into the inside of the S&OP design process. Talk about sustainability, scalability, and replication, with 3,000 well-educated and motivated people on the design team.

Guided Participatory Process Appraisal Approach

Education leads to a guided design process to encourage cross-functional participation, rather than a dictated process design. The education should focus on the principles of S&OP that can or even should be adapted to your company's unique requirements; education should not hand down a set of completed design documents. Benchmarking and having examples of best-in-class processes are good ways to spur thinking and to avoid groupthink, which usually results in the design of only a slightly different version of the current process.

The various horizontal processes in S&OP are outlined in the education to facilitate the participative appraisal of current processes in the company. Many of the necessary processes will not even be found in the current state. You will find that some are done poorly, while you may find a few that are done well. (The horizontal processes that could be included in your S&OP are covered later in this chapter.) Further work in defining what needs to be done may include visiting companies with very strong S&OP processes and/or having experts such as myself come to address your group.

The guided education principle was described by Paulo Freire in his book *Pedagogy of the Oppressed,* published in 1968. Freire calls traditional pedagogy the "banking model" because it treats the student as an empty vessel to be filled with knowledge, like a piggy bank. However, Freire argues for treating the learner as a *co-creator of knowledge*. The dialogue among a group of cross-functional leaders is more important than having the exact curricula or benchmark designs.

A good friend of mine who is a cultural change expert applies the principles of guided design to his work with East African communities fighting to overcome the scourge of HIV/AIDS. Dr. Gil Odendaal is a pastor with Saddleback Church in Orange County, California. He is responsible for the implementation of the global PEACE Plan (see www.thepeaceplan.com), with a special focus on East Africa. Saddleback Church was founded by Rick Warren, the author of the best-selling book *The Purpose Driven Life*. Saddleback itself is a good study in successful cultural change. Warren held the first church service there in 1980 with 205 people. At the 25th anniversary, 50,000 current and former members attended a service held in a professional sports stadium.

Odendaal has been working in Rwanda to develop civil societies (code words for "church") to prevent the spread of HIV/AIDS and to care for those living with the virus. He has taken Warren's PEACE Plan (plant churches that promote reconciliation; equip servant leaders; assist the poor; care for the sick; and educate the next generation) to the people of Rwanda. Odendaal started in Bwishyura, a sector in western Rwanda with a population of 30,000. Using guided education principles, he first held seminars for 124 church leaders and trained trainers inside the civil societies. Thirteen churches signed up for the train-the-trainer program. Through the use of participatory learning activities and participatory rural appraisal techniques, they developed home-health plans and community support programs working through local civil societies. The leaders, all Rwandese, trained trainers, also all Rwandese; thus, 225 trainers were developed. Each trainer then went into seven homes. The community was profoundly changed, and the program has been very successful. The government even asked to have its community workers included in the training programs. The program has moved on to five other sectors of Rwanda and now has 2,400 trainers trained and implementing home-health programs.

Odendaal describes the guided participation process as midwifery rather than fathering. The midwife is there, helping many mothers (think *teams*), and ownership of the product almost always results. Fathering with many mothers is bastardization, and the product is most often abandoned.

Design to Implement Strategy

The segment-level S&OP process is the most important tactical planning process inside any business. The purpose is to implement the business strategy in each market segment. The go-to-market strategy comes to real life inside the S&OP process. Each functional area has a specific role and is engaged in the overview of the whole business.

Design S&OP to Run the Business

S&OP is the way you run your business. Like no other process, S&OP can bring the functions together. It is not one of many management activities or regular meetings the CEO uses to manage. One of my clients, Thomas C. McDermott, is the former CEO of Goulds Pumps Inc., a global commercial and industrial products company. He summed up the first market-savvy S&OP meeting he ever attended by announc-ing to his staff, "This was the most productive meeting I have ever attended in 40 years of management. Attendance at this monthly meeting is now mandatory."

Through the S&OP meetings, pre-meetings, and horizontal processes, the work of each function is fully vetted, with decisions made and accountability shared. The team determines how to inter-pret forecast inputs, and the team determines the consensus action plan. Thus, the team takes responsibility for the results of the decision-making process.

Design to Enable Customer Centricity

Market-savvy S&OP is centered on the customer through the go-to-market strategy. We discussed the go-to-market strategy form and con-tent in Chapter 1. Now you must put it to work. The first process design required in S&OP is communication of and feedback on the go-to-market strategy. The process should have a one-page statement of the strategy using all the content shown in Chapter 1. Each func-tional area's responsibility and approach should be briefly described. In the S&OP meeting, the strategy itself will be discussed, as will the progress in implementing it. You need to have specific metrics describ-ing strategic implementation.

Regardless of which strategy you choose, the general customer metrics should be measured and reviewed in a strategic implementa-tion process in each S&OP meeting.

The metrics or strategic goals will be very different than in tra-ditional S&OP, which is centered on internal operations. Market-savvy S&OP considers enabling concepts, which may be anathema to internal goals. The customers want many results from your work that, on the surface, may increase cost, complicate service perform-ance, and increase inventory. The customer in concept wants the results shown in Figure 5-2. Let's look at each of these goals.

The S&OP process should enable *complexity*, as defined inside a market segment. How often have you heard manufacturing executives

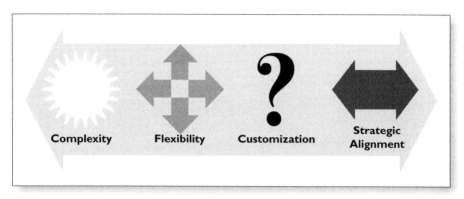

FIGURE 5-2. CONCEPTUAL GOALS OF THE CUSTOMER.
Customer groups think differently than internal managers about goals.

say they need to rationalize (reduce the complexity) of the product line? The goal of S&OP is to find the correct complexity for the market and align your product complexity rationalization to the collaborative standards developed with customers.

The S&OP process should provide maximum *flexibility* to meet the variability in the customer's actual demand profiles. Note: Building massive inventory does not substitute for flexibility. The goal needs to be to meet customer demand variability without inventory at either your locations or the customer's locations.

Customization is almost never allowed in make-to-stock manufacturing companies. What if you collaborate in the design of products so that what the customer sees as customized is actually an alignment of your product design with customer design criteria in the standard product?

Strategic alignment should be accomplished through market-savvy S&OP. Each of the options in the strategy discussion of Chapter 2 will be implemented well when your strategy is aligned with the customer's strategy. Most often, senior executives develop strategy and tell the world what it is. But in market-savvy S&OP, you want to change the telling into asking and adjust your go-to-market strategy definition at the segment level to accommodate the customer's strategy. The S&OP

process for all strategies picked in Chapter 2 must include a strong horizontal process to achieve strategic alignment with customers. If the strategies cannot be aligned, you should go back to Chapter 2 and rethink your segment strategy.

Each of the customer-desired goals outlined in Figure 5-2 should have a metric within the context of the value proposition and go-to-market strategy. As an example, working inside the 3M families we discussed in Chapter 4, a complexity goal may be achieved by offering new products and rationalizing products to provide a product complexity mix defined by the customer without increasing the number of 3M families, thus not increasing overall cost of production.

The strategic implementation process should have a dashboard matrix that shows the overall segment strategy and then the metrics for each relevant customer value, perhaps by family, as shown in Figure 5-3.

Market Feedback

Segments	High Touch	On-Demand	Mass Market	Premium Gold
Segment Strategy				
Key Customers	**Your goals and action plan**			
CUSTOMER GOALS	**for each segment;** **Quantitative and**			
Complexity	**Qualitative Goals should be**			
Flexibility	**in each box**			
Customization				
Strategic Alignment				

FIGURE 5-3. DISPLAY OF MONTHLY REVIEW OF STRATEGIC INITIATIVES.
Monthly updates would feature feedback from customer interviews or metrics.

The goal is to show planning alignment to the strategic plan and to the customer's goals. The description of the customer group should describe how they interact with their customers or how they are grouped by market characteristic; high-touch providers have great interaction with their customers to achieve a pleasing shopping experience, on-demand providers need significant technical support and special services with short notice, mass-merchants are just that, and premium gold may be those providers who only offer our premium products and are our best customers. The process includes gathering feedback from the customer on a regular basis. As we have discussed in previous chapters, the feedback should be gathered by having customer-facing teams meet regularly with key customers in each segment. Each functional area should be ready and able to discuss its practices to achieve the business strategy for the segment and to present metrics related to customer goals. Not every functional area will have input in every box shown in Figure 5-3. The discussion should center on the functional areas having primary responsibility for each strategic initiative.

Design to Align All Planning Processes

Segment-level S&OP is a comprehensive planning process. The plans of all functions are fully aligned in the market-savvy S&OP process. Planning alignment is unique to segment-level S&OP in the following ways:

♦ The alignment itself is uniquely different with market-savvy S&OP, since all other forms of S&OP do not even consider full alignment across all functions.

♦ Alignment at a segment level is specific and uniquely different from segment to segment.

♦ The alignment being tied to the customer's goals and strategies is unique to market-savvy S&OP. Voice-of-the-customer (VOC) processes are just surveys sent out with an expectation of a 20 percent or so return; these may be useful, but they do not constitute alignment.

♦ Alignment being done at the market-segment level is unique to this form of S&OP.

Align Up to 26 Horizontal Planning Processes

All the planning is done in the segment-level S&OP process, which is made up of 26 horizontal processes. Some of our clients find they have some of the 26 different horizontal planning processes already in place, at least in part. The 26 are shown in Figure 5-4; all are pulled together in the segment S&OP meeting.

In Chapter 7, we will discuss the three additional processes required when you expand beyond one segment level market-savvy S&OP to a profit center, or Global S&OP process. The first is executive S&OP, commonly characterized incorrectly as the place where major decisions are made. The executive S&OP in our approach is really an FYI (for your information) session. You use the executive S&OP to keep senior management apprised of your progress, but not to push all decision making to the top. That would be eliminating the employee empowerment you are seeking in the collaborative processes. The other two processes involve import and export families; these processes are required to bring alignment in planning globally. In these two processes, one segment level S&OP team is the provider and another is a receiver of production from capacity owned by the provider. Often, other segments are either suppliers or customers and can be handled without any additional processes. We do single out annual operating planning (AOP), which is process number 14 of the 26. AOP is a separate process even though it is simply an extension of the monthly process, with perhaps some emphasis on a longer time horizon and more formal emphasis on new product planning.

Each process shown in Figure 5-4 is important. Implementation

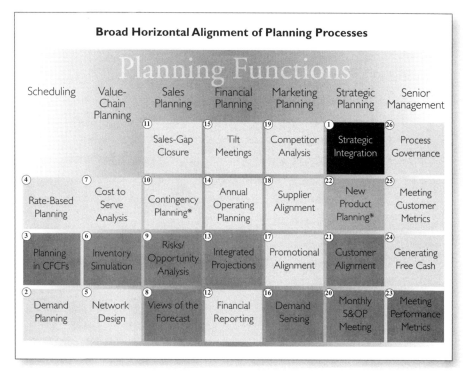

Broad Horizontal Alignment of Planning Processes

FIGURE 5-4. THE 26 HORIZONTAL PLANNING PROCESSES IN SEGMENT-LEVEL S&OP.
The 26 horizontal planning processes are brought into alignment within the monthly
collaboration.

of market-savvy S&OP builds upon certain processes that most
likely are already being performed, but not fully aligned. Network
design, demand planning, and financial reporting are the processes
most companies include in a low-level S&OP process. Moving to
market-savvy S&OP requires adding the sentinel processes of collaboration. The eight sentinel processes, highlighted by the shadow
in Figure 5-4, plus the monthly S&OP (the meeting in which the
eight sentinel processes culminate) will most likely require extensive
process design work. Since this is a book on the change management
process in implementing market-savvy S&OP and not a process
design manual, I will not go into detail here on each of the 26
processes. I will describe the eight sentinel processes to help you to

understand how to accomplish the planning alignment through process design.

Planning in CFCFs

Cross-functional coordinating families (CFCFs) are the families defined using the 3M process described in Chapter 4. These are highly aggregated families of items (SKUs) used to promote communication. This is no more striking than in scheduling. Normally, a company with thousands of SKUs has zero communication between the S and the O in S&OP, because it cannot communicate about thousands of items in a monthly meeting. However, inside a market segment, you can consider the eight to ten CFCFs that will emerge from the 3M analysis covered in Chapter 4.

Scheduling normally starts with a demand plan for every SKU, and MRP takes over to accomplish the planning, the schedules of future production, and purchase orders. Having taken a deep dive down to the item level of detail, no one can comprehend the resulting schedules. All enterprise management systems do this, and they are all flawed. We pointed out the basic flaw earlier in the book: The validity of the demand plan at the SKU level is zero for the vast majority of items. Just run a simple statistical significance test—something that is never done—to prove it. In addition, the SKU forecast is simply not required at the planning stage. Manufacturing does not need detailed forecasts for every SKU to accomplish its scheduling requirements. SKUs are combined into individual items, and then items are combined into individual groups or families. Scheduling using a rate-based planning approach is the subject of Chapter 6. The reason you do not want to schedule by item is that item forecast inaccuracy leads to errors in calculating safety stock. As actual demand comes in different from the forecast—which it must since the forecast is wrong—false triggers for requirements are generated. Since more than 50 percent of all items are 'C' items by definition, and forecast error is most profound in 'C' items, then the scheduling done using the forecasts in SKU detail will have a very large number of erroneous triggers, causing scheduling chaos.

To see a full picture, you should use highly aggregated forecasts, and in fact, multiple views of the aggregated forecast. We will discuss the specifics of multiple views below, but think about industry views, customer views, salesperson views, and others. The forecasts are aggregated at the level of the large CFCF families. With multiple views and this aggregation, you will be able to accomplish several important goals without causing problems in scheduling. This last point—not causing problems in scheduling—will be a point of contention with old-timers in manufacturing who can come up with endless examples of "one time" when not having a detailed item or SKU forecast makes a difference in some small cost factor. Please apply the significance rule to handle these objections. Not all costs are significant. We know from some of the better lean manufacturing work that aggregation into large families is very practical and significantly increases overall utilization, reduces unplanned downtime, and improves overall throughput.

The collaboration goals achieved using CFCFs are significant. They include:

♦ Communication of capacity constraints and opportunities to the team

♦ Understanding of near-term scheduling difficulties or lack of issues

♦ Assessment of contingency plan complexity

We have found that CFCFs can be defined for very complex, job-shop-type manufacturing. Pumps, tires, and cosmetics processing all have thousands of SKUs, hundreds of specialty manufacturing processes, and many process variables. However, in each of these businesses, we have been able to aggregate the items into a handful of CFCFs and accomplished the collaborative goals.

Views of the Forecast

Forecasting should not be limited to just a statistical forecast, as is most often the case. Multiple views should be added to the straight statistical forecast. Perhaps you would even change the name of the statistical forecasting process and call it *multiple view of the forecast*. We have some clients that have up to 12 or 14 different views of the forecast. Let me mention just a sampling: econometric model forecasts, trade association forecasts, salesperson forecasts, sales management forecasts, historical trend forecasts (basic statistical), marketing forecasts of promotions, marketing forecasts of market share/segment sales trends, forecast from AOP, forecasts from key customers, and past period forecasts. All the views of the forecast should be displayed in a comparative chart to foster discussion and lead to a consensus of the forecast to be used in the S&OP meeting, as well as for defining inputs to the risks and opportunities process.

Inventory Simulation

Planning the physical movement part of the value chain is an area of significant collaborative difficulty. The sales side of planning wants every item stocked in many different locations, while the supply chain managers want few stocking locations, and on we go. Often, logistics cost is the driver of the network design decision. In reality, it is inventory, and perhaps more important, the utilization of capacity that should drive the decisions on network designs, along with significant consideration of the business and go-to-market strategies. The problem is that the standard models used for network design are not capable of assessing the capacity utilization impact, nor the full inventory impact, of the network design alternatives. The senior technical person at one of the most popular network design companies, located in Atlanta, told me he assumes away the capacity utilization issue and thinks about variation in demand simplistically. The common models used in network design are LPs, or linear programs. They do simplistic cost trade-offs and ignore capacity and demand variability problems.

Using inventory simulation modeling to determine the number of stocking locations significantly improves the network design. Since inventory simulation can be intimidating in the sheer size of the data requirements, care must be taken to summarize the outputs.

Some of the simulation models we have used have very clear graphical outputs, which display the results of the simulation in a way senior management can absorb and appreciate. We described the eight reasons for inventory approach in the analytics chapter, Chapter 3. This is a simple form of inventory simulation summary output. In fact, several of the eight factors discussed there can be calculated using simple Microsoft Excel methods. (The sixth factor, the impact of demand variation, may require a more sophisticated modeling technique.)

Simulation has major benefits in inventory analysis. Using simulation, you can model the highly variable demand patterns of most products using random distributions and/or other discontinuous distribution patterns. Simulation has been known to business managers for decades. It was used in World War II to solve some of the distribution issues in marshaling war materials. In addition, it was used to determine the mixture of elements in the atomic bombs built and detonated in WW II. The actual mixture problems were very small in mathematical terms. However, the simulation had to be done manually since computers were not available in WW II. It took several months to complete using hundreds of mathematicians. Today, we have solved very complex simulation problems for companies with more than 100,000 items using laptops with large hard drives and fast processors. A very complex simulation model can be solved in a few hours.

Inventory simulation using a simulation modeling technique shows the impact of the full variation in customer demand on the inventory for each scenario of one or more stocking locations and also shows the impact of the demands on manufacturing capacity utilization. Intuitively, manufacturing must see a significantly increased range of daily demand, higher peaks and lower valleys, as the number of stocking locations increases. The effect is ignored if you are using linear models. In contrast, inventory simulation allows you to prove that fewer stocking locations are the most cost-effective when the entire network cost is considered. Using inventory simulation modeling, the resulting networks have performance characteristics in the live case nearly equal to those predicted in network design modeling.

Risks/Opportunity Analysis

In the area of planning sales activity, a demand-planning process is becoming very popular. Demand planning tries to convert the statistical forecast, the field sales inputs, the econometric model data, and other inputs into a plan reflecting the best forecast of actual demand.

Ideally, demand planning is trying to develop demand expectations at the time horizon most critical to manufacturing and suppliers. Often, the focus is on the next few weeks only or a month or so out, which is far too shortsighted to be of use to manufacturing. If we use the rate-based planning techniques that will be described in Chapter 6, this issue becomes moot.

The real breakthrough in demand planning comes when demand projections are augmented with assessments of higher-probability risks and opportunities. The output of demand planning can be one consensus set of future demand predictions. However, it would be the rare case to not have upside potential and downside risks. The demand planners must know about some of them. The sales force and other members of the customer-facing organization must know about additional risks and opportunities. Having a formal process to aggregate the upsides and downsides, apply probabilities, and have a fruitful collaborative discussion about the impact will be of significant importance. This process will then lead to comprehensive contingency planning and sales-gap closure analysis.

The director of supply chain at Goodyear, Ken Fletcher, observes that the risk and opportunity process, coupled with contingency planning, "makes lead time your friend." You plan ahead, rather than let a somewhat predictable event just happen, which would cause you to jump to respond with little lead time. With a proper risks and opportunities analysis process, you identify and act upon opportunities to gain market share.

Integrated Projections

Certainly, financial managers make financial plans; it's in their DNA. The market-savvy S&OP process provides them with all the information they need to make the projections that are a critical part of the financial planning process.

In my experience, companies finding themselves in severe difficulty with their banks are most often guilty of using only historical data to prepare the cash-flow forecast. The process is easy to understand and uses numbers accountants like, historical facts. The process also is not very useful in recognizing a potential cash-flow problem in the future, because all the future variability is assumed away. However, using the S&OP data, you have all the information required to make a cash-flow forecast, including the expectations of actual labor costs, actual purchase commitments, and actual sales mix. The cash flow based on integrating the plans of each function will be of significant value.

Senior managers, like bankers, do not like surprises, but when historical data are used to make the cash projection, surprises are unavoidable. Again, using integrated projections, lead time becomes your friend, as you identify and can adjust plans for future cash-flow issues. All the senior managers and bankers will be very pleased with a "heads-up" on future cash flow.

Projecting ahead using S&OP, particularly if the S&OP has an 18-month time horizon, makes annual operating planning (AOP) a routine extension of the monthly process, rather than a grueling year-end exercise of starting with a blank sheet of paper and developing "new" plans for the coming year. In fact, people who are good at S&OP can develop the AOP in less than a week.

Demand Sensing

We described how the market strategy is developed in Part I of this book. The monthly process involves keeping track of the progress of the strategy. Demand sensing is the starting point of the monthly process.

Actual demand is captured in the demand-sensing process. We call it *sensing* because the process is one of looking for key indicators, not necessarily one of capturing daily every scrap of demand data in databases of terabytes. Some companies do try to capture terabytes of data for consumer products; in the majority of cases, a much-simplified approach is appropriate.

Demand sensing can be done by identifying leading indicator situations and interviewing industry experts. Leading indicators could be key retail sites for several major retailers. We have seen companies take POS data from key Wal-Mart stores as demand-sensing data. Often, consumer packaged goods companies that successfully perform demand sensing are gathering regional data in summary to use as measures of actual demand trends. The regional summary data can be captured in trend-line form and presented in a short, powerful update presentation for the S&OP team to review. It is important to have concise summaries that show significant trends compared to your strategic expectations, rather than detailed store-by-store daily demand data, which even analysts—let alone an S&OP team—will not be able to comprehend. Industrial products companies can use actual demand from key customers to sense demand trends. A factory automation manufacturer can show trends by collecting data from customer groups; for example, it can collect data from early adopters, distributors, sophisticated OEMs, and other groups to sense demand trends for new technology, older technology, and its products versus the competition. Test marketing and sampling of randomly selected selling sites also works.

Industry experts may be senior management of major customers or representatives of customer groups. Having monthly or quarterly meetings with decision makers inside your customer organizations will tell you about their internal plans. Often, future demand is affected more by the customer's decisions to increase or decrease inventory or to run promotions than it is by actual selling trends. We have an industrial products client that has meetings quarterly with two major distributors handling nearly 60 percent of its total business. The client has learned to sense changes in demand by understanding the distributors' cash-flow issues and service interpretations. The distributors are very different. Just looking at orders received at the plant does not provide the necessary insight to near-term and longer-term trends.

Starting with demand sensing will lead to further collaborative planning with promotional planning, alignment to supplier plans, and competitor analysis. As you project demand using demand sensing, you can signal your internal and external partners to improve alignment, and you can sense when you need to look at a competitor more closely.

Customer Alignment

Customer alignment is the beginning of the strategic update processes. On a monthly basis or at least quarterly, the S&OP team should have formal meetings with customers to keep track of changes in their strategic thinking and forward planning. The alignment also includes gathering and interpreting customer-defined performance metrics.

Our "customercentricity" discussion from Chapter 4 covers this alignment subject well. The team needs to have a formal process developed to accomplish the monthly alignment. The process design should include who meets with the customers, how specific customers are selected, what topics should be discussed, how the relationship is maintained, and what senior management involvement should be. The customer-alignment process should lead into the new product planning process, which would be done in collaboration with the customer.

Meeting Performance Metrics

The planning process related to achieving performance results requires methodically measuring and responding to performance indicators. The dashboard that is central to the monthly segment-level S&OP would be maintained in this process. (The dashboard was discussed in Chapter 3.)

The high-level process overview in Figure 5-1 shows three groups of metrics to be included in this process: process metrics, performance metrics, and customer metrics. The team needs to define a specific process for gathering, maintaining, archiving, and managing to the metrics.

The process design should describe each metric to be used and the process for evaluating performance and action planning. For example, when is it necessary to perform a root-cause analysis of a change, either good or bad, in a metric? For the forecast accuracy and bias metric, the process design may call for root-cause analysis when the forecast falls outside the plus-or-minus-one-sigma limit on accuracy for two months in a row. For the sales planning metric, an action to initiate the sales-gap closure process may happen when demand forecasts show a potential to fall more than 3 percent off the AOP.

The archiving portion of the process of meeting performance metrics is an important part of the analytics. A formal history of the metrics and an action plan archival approach is necessary. As you go through the S&OP process and discuss update requirements, action plans, and information, all the information needs to be kept for future reference. The information exchanged during the monthly collaboration processes will be useful for future root-cause analysis, such as "Why did we take that action anyway?"

Action plans should be captured on a single page with a cross-reference header. The action plans could be set up in a database in which people who know how to make queries can find what they want. Better yet, the action plans can be placed into subfolders in a directory for easy access by team members who may not be IT-oriented. In either case, you need multiple archival references, as follows:

A. Archival record storage sorts
    ♦   By category (related to strategic goals or performance metrics)
    ♦   By primary name of action
    ♦   By alternative name (generic naming)
    ♦   By meeting type (S&OP or pre-meeting on forecast, etc.)
    ♦   By date

- ◆ By milestone date/event date for progress or reporting
- ◆ By person assigned

B. Description of action

- ◆ By standard phrase categorizing the background
- ◆ By key metric chart involved
- ◆ By data reference (e.g., April 4 forecast input at Step 2 in S&OP cycle)
- ◆ Description of the action required in a paragraph or two

Process design is a team effort. The On-Point Group offers an S&OP process design workbook that you can purchase and may consider using to help expedite your design process. The seven principles of design, individually described in each chapter of this book, should be a guiding factor. Benchmarking is always a good way to assess your current processes and to define improvements. However, in the end, the team must define processes that work for your business. It is important to start with a well-thought-out process design emphasizing collaboration. You will not be perfect at the beginning, but you will move forward in a matter of weeks, rather than dwell on the design step for many months or more than a year. (Chapter 7 describes process clubs, a continuous improvement approach that may help you in your efforts at process design.)

Design with Interlocking Cycles

Market-savvy S&OP is actually a group of planning cycles for each of the integrated planning activities as depicted in Figure 5-4. Seven planning activities individually plug into the monthly cycle of pre-meetings and the segment-level S&OP meeting itself. These are shown on Figure 5-5; the seven are financial planning, sales planning, schedule planning, market planning, customer integration planning, business results planning, and value-chain planning.

The Main Cycle

The basic S&OP meeting cycle sets the rhythm and cadence of the integration. The rhythm is the assurance that a meeting bringing each planning activity to a conclusion will be held on a certain workday each month. The cadence is the pace of the series of pre-meetings in specific, prenumbered steps that march along on the same successive workdays each month. Figure 5-5 is an example of the monthly cycle.

The cycle chart in Figure 5-5 is one of the three key overview charts describing the monthly collaboration. The other two charts are the high-level process map (Figure 5-1) and the list of horizontal planning processes (Figure 5-4). These three charts should be posted and visible on every analyst's and manager's desk.

The monthly cycle in Figure 5-5 has seven major steps. The first four steps plus Step 7 integrated projections at the end of the previous month are pre-meeting steps—pre-meetings to the segment-level S&OP meeting. Each of the pre-meetings is actually the conclusion of a planning cycle in each of several planning activities.

Step 1: The Month-End Review. The first pre-meeting is the month-end review meeting, which is supported by the financial planning cycle. The financial planning cycle goes along from Step 7, specifically, from the integrated projections shown on workday 10 through the month-end close and publication of numbers for the Step 1 review. In the monthly cycle for finance, many work steps are completed, including financial analysis, closing preparation steps, and other normal financial work steps. The two critical aspects in your monthly collaboration with financial planning are (1) the absolute deadline of workday number 3 for the review of last month's numbers, and (2) work Step 7. The timing is such that Step 7 is done after all the S&OP information is known. The projections going to shareholders and even to Wall Street analysts should come directly from the S&OP. The information that finance needs to make all its financial projections can be taken directly from the S&OP output in a greater

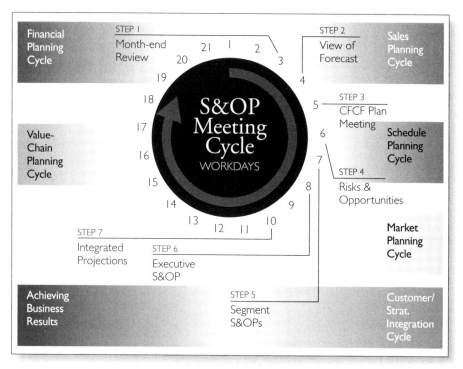

FIGURE 5-5. MONTHLY PLANNING CYCLE AND ALIGNMENT.
The whole organization knows in advance how its planning activity plugs into one integrated set of pre-meetings and the S&OP meeting itself.

level of detail than would normally be used for shareholder projections. The advantage is that both the CEO and CFO will have confidence that the whole organization is working toward achieving the numbers being projected. This, in essence, is the whole basis of the concept of "one set of numbers." S&OP does not have just one set of planning numbers; it has ranges of forecasts and operating numbers. But it also has one consensus plan. The "guidance" given investors in the calls to Wall Street is the consensus plan. It is guidance, not guarantee. The critical aspect is that the guidance is developed from realistic operating plans.

Step 2: Views of the Forecast. This is the end of the sales planning activity. Step 2 starts the CFCF planning, which is supported in part by the old demand plan. The sales planning cycle has many steps that probably start near the end of the previous month, including gathering input from field sales, having coordinating discussions with sales management, reviewing inputs from groups outside the company, and compiling the various views. Prior to the Step 2 meeting, some analysis will be required to explain differences in the forecasted rates of sales from different views. During the Step 2 meeting, the decision is made regarding which forecast you will use as the consensus forecast.

Step 3: The CFCF Planning Meeting. This is where you discuss the impact of the newly configured consensus forecast coming out of Step 2. Normally, Step 3 is the end of a monthly cycle of schedule planning, where capacity updates are considered and assessed, attainment to schedule data is assessed from the Step 1 review, and inventory performance is assessed. During this meeting, a new manufacturing and procurement master plan for several months forward is agreed upon—another consensus plan. The output of Step 3 is the data used in rate-based planning to establish a cycle plan (discussed in Chapter 6).

Step 4: The Risks and Opportunities Analysis Meeting. Here, you compare the consensus plans for sales and manufacturing to the output of the market planning cycle. Demand sensing will have been pulled together over the few weeks prior to the Step 4 meeting and may even be one of the feeds into Step 2. The purpose of Step 4 is to use the updated sales plan, inputs from demand sensing, and the updated manufacturing CFCF plan to identify areas of supply or sales concern. Contingency planning is initiated out of the Step 4 meeting, and sales-gap closure may be started so that it is completed prior to the Step 5 S&OP meeting.

Step 5: The Segment-Level S&OP Meeting. Everything finally comes together here. During the Step 5 meeting, you discuss customer input from customer team meetings held in the previous weeks in the context of the newly updated consensus plans. The metrics of your achievement of business results can also be addressed in the same context. Decisions are made in Step 5 about actions required to mitigate risks or to capitalize on opportunities. Decisions also are made to take corrective action or to start root-cause analysis in the area of a particular metric. A summary of the Step 5 decisions is then prepared as input for the executive S&OP meeting.

Step 6: The Executive S&OP Meeting. Step 6 is a meeting with senior management and a group of representatives from each of the segment S&OP teams. During the Step 6 meeting, actions proposed by individual S&OP teams are discussed. The senior managers normally are merely gaining a comprehensive set of information about the businesses. Some allocation of resource decisions may be necessary during this step if multiple teams are proposing actions different from the AOP. Normally, the Step 6 discussion is just keeping management apprised of developments and avoiding big future surprises. Each segment management team is responsible for gaining the required approvals in appropriate form.

Step 7: Integrated Projections. Step 7 is the end of the financial planning cycle. The data from the previous meetings can now be pulled together into one combined projection to shareholders.

The value-chain planning cycle is shown in Figure 5-5 as not connected to a specific meeting or workday event. The activities of value-chain planning are not done monthly. Normally, they are quarterly or even annual planning processes. The inventory simulation, when performed with formal modeling software, may be done monthly as an input to the process of achieving business results and calculating goals for metrics. In that case, it would feed into Step 5.

Multiple Cycles

The seven categories of planning as shown in Figure 5-5 each has its own planning cycle. A chart similar to Figure 5-5 should be prepared for each one. The individual cycles should be coordinated fully inside the overall segment-level S&OP. The individual planning cycles will house some of the 26 horizontal processes in the segment S&OP group.

The essential part of the individual cycles is that they conform to the basic S&OP cycle as shown in Figure 5-5. You cannot have separate one-off planning being done in any form within the enterprise. The segment S&OP is the only planning function and is run by the only cross-functional team doing planning.

Predictable Rhythm, Fewer Meetings

Earlier in Chapter 5, we discussed the rhythm and cadence that results from planning according to the processes and cycles shown above. The overall picture looks like a good deal of meetings and processes. In fact, your enterprise probably currently has more meetings by a multiple of three to five and even more disjointed processes. In every case where we have installed this S&OP structure, people comment that the number of meetings is vastly reduced.

At one client, the supply chain people went from working six days a week, 12 hours a day, to having many afternoons available for actually performing analysis, rather than attending poorly run meetings. Executives at another client, a global manufacturing company, expounded on the benefits of knowing the rhythm, and thus, being freed from the hassle of having to call meetings.

I will not claim a reduction in planning personnel from implementing the monthly collaboration process and segment-level S&OP. I will claim a 30 to 50 percent reduction in time spent in meetings. We measured the actual productivity improvement for one client and found that we increased the productiveness/engagement of meetings from an average score of 4 to a 6 on a scale of 1 to 10, with 10 being high. When combined with holding 30 percent fewer meetings, the overall productivity gain for all managers was nearly 50 percent.

You will use the time savings to find ways to improve value delivery to the customer and achieve business results.

Mandatory Participation (Encouraged)

Because of the productivity improvement people will experience—and to help achieve improvement in the short term while there are many nonbelievers—you need to make attendance mandatory at the meetings of Steps 1 through 7. As noted earlier in this chapter, the CEO at a pump manufacturer claimed the meetings were the most productive he had ever attended in his more than 40-year career. He had his administrative assistant make sure people were attending the meetings. You could not miss more than one out of five meetings. If you missed more, you would be called in to explain the absences.

I had the privilege of working with Sam Walton when I was president of Rawlings and a supplier to Wal-Mart. He held management meetings every Saturday morning in Bentonville, Arkansas. Every store manager was required to attend all but one per month, and then an assistant had to be in attendance. I can tell you for sure that getting to Bentonville on a Saturday in the 1980s was no easy task, but the meetings were extremely important to Sam (and very much like an S&OP meeting for retail). The mandatory attendance rule worked, and the results are obvious.

Design with Collaborative Goals

Market-savvy S&OP is a very different process from anything an enterprise is doing now in 95 percent of cases. The emphasis is on collaboration embodied in the guiding principle "process heavy, people light." Of course, the other six guiding principles (first discussed in the Introduction, and as part of each chapter's introduction) are also important. Once the design process is started, the high-level process map is conceptualized (Figure 5-1), and you make a good pass at the horizontal process definitions, your team should name the new process. Do not use SIOP (sales, inventory, and operations planning) or S&OP or anything similar to whatever you currently call your planning process. The name needs to be representative of a new and aggressive planning process.

Claim the Goals in the Branding of the Process

The new process being designed should be branded or named. The name should communicate goals, and then those goals should be communicated throughout the company. Future participants will have a common affiliation with the goals.

We will discuss transition planning in Chapter 7, but here is a preview of one concept: communicating the new process and its goals. You can use a 5x5 communication process in which you pick five key messages and spread them in five different communication vehicles. The five messages describe the key elements of the new processes, the expected impact on the organization, the monthly processes, and the impact on customer value delivery.

Be creative with the five messages and the vehicles of communication. Here are some suggested venues to help in your brainstorming. (Note that only five are needed, although more are suggested here.)

♦ A letter from the CEO for each message, probably one and a half pages long and including his or her own examples of effects on cash flow and share gains

♦ An e-mail blast to all employees for each message

♦ A one-page high-gloss sign in every restroom for each message

♦ A colorful posting on the company intranet for each message

♦ A sticky bun meeting (an informal gathering, normally at the beginning of the workday where simple rolls, Danish, or actual sticky buns would be served along with coffee and perhaps juice, tea, and water) for each message

- ⬦ Have a three- to five-question self-test sent out prior to the meeting
- ⬦ Everyone who answers all the questions correctly receives free sticky buns and coffee (the answers are found in the first two or three messages)

- ◆ Town-hall meetings with all employees for each message
  - ⬦ Perhaps a ten-minute presentation by the team with follow-ups
  - ⬦ Be sure to hold the meetings on all shifts
- ◆ Teleconferences or Web meetings for each message
- ◆ Tweets announcing the messages and directing people to where to find them
- ◆ Use of social networking tools to invite people to an informal outing at a bar or restaurant to discuss the messages

Specific Collaborative Goals

Collaboration is cultivated by having goals that cannot be achieved without collaboration. There are three such goals: free cash flow (FCF), market-share growth, and customer-defined goals.

FCF is an excellent collaborative goal. First, the goal must be defined, and by doing so, people learn what FCF actually is and is not. By defining FCF, you automatically engage people in trying to improve it when they could not have done so in the past, simply because they were not accountants and did not understand. I have seen engineers become very excited about FCF when they learn that new-product development projects are funded only through FCF. FCF becomes a job-security factor for them. Even accountants learn the difference between FCF and cash flow as reported in the third basic financial statement (the first two being a balance sheet and a statement of operations performance, or profit and loss statement).

FCF comes from making a permanent, systemic change to the operations that generates cash. Certainly, you will generate cash by reducing inventory by crunching 'A' items down, or by deciding to delay paying vendors until 15 days later, but both of these tactics would not be included in your definition of FCF, because they are most likely not sustainable. Making a new inventory policy as part of the go-to-market strategy will be a contributor to FCF. Working with suppliers to improve collaboration and decrease cost will reduce accounts payable permanently. To make these FCF improvements requires a fully collaborative cross-functional effort. The FCF benefits are real, and the team members working at the problem will find they are empowered to become real business partners.

The second collaborative goal, increasing market share, is an obvious goal. Most people don't even know what their market share is and know even less about how to improve it. By setting market share as a common goal of the segment-level S&OP team, the market-share numbers become understandable and manageable. The team needs to work together to devise provisions that increase share in the go-to-market strategy. The improvements to market share will be measurable at the segment level.

The third collaborative goal, setting customer-defined goals that are practical at segment-level S&OP, can be a strong stimulator of collaboration. People who focus on the outside world will work together with far less friction. The individual silo organization goals become secondary to the customer-defined goals, or at least the silo goals are focused and put into a healthy context, which reduces the friction caused by arbitrary and parochial goals set inside a functional area.

Looking Back

♦ The guiding principle of market-savvy S&OP design discussed here is collaboration.

♦ Monthly collaboration is the middle process group of the three processes in market-savvy S&OP, as defined in the Introduction to this book.

    ◆ A high-level process map can be used effectively to communicate and share the inclusion of all planning processes in this segment-level S&OP design.

    ◆ The design process starts with education, to gain ownership by working through the formal organization.

    ◆ Two basic, important phases of the educational approach are accomplished with a guided and participatory technique:

        ◇ Guided participation education

        ◇ Guided participation appraisal of existing process and future requirements

    ◆ The business strategy defined in Chapters 1 and 2 is the foundation for the monthly collaboration process.

    ◆ Alignment of all planning processes in the enterprise is the goal of segment-level S&OP.

    ◆ There are 26 horizontal planning processes in the overall S&OP plan.

    ◆ There is a specific seven-step cycle of monthly meetings in the overall S&OP plan.

    ◆ At the segment level, you can define clear and understandable goals that encourage collaboration. Any planning level other than the segment level will have highly generalized goals that people can easily avoid.

Case Study: Wright Medical Technology

Wright Medical Technology is the fifth company my good friend Bob Palmisano has managed as CEO. Bob's trademark approach is to implement HPMS (the High Performance Management System), which I touched on in Chapters 3 and 4. In many ways, HPMS is an IBP (integrated business planning) process. At a very early stage in Bob's tenure at Wright Medical Technology, the management team went through an overall strategy definition meeting. The customer was defined, and the overall businesses the company was going to keep were determined. Then, the team defined revolutionary goals for the customer, the shareholder, and the employees. Sound familiar? The overall strategic goal for Wright Medical was "#1 in Customer Satisfaction." The goal is a destination—a BHAG, or big hairy audacious goal. This goal reflected the overall strategy of the growth business for Wright Medical, foot and ankle orthopedics; it was also the customer-connectivity strategy for the segment. The strategy also applied to the low-growth, low-market-share business of hip and knee orthopedics, even though this segment was not being relied upon by Wright Medical for significant revenue improvement.

I worked with Bob and his management team to implement the HPMS goals, including implementing a market-savvy S&OP.

Situation. Communication between operations and commercial functions was nearly nonexistent at Wright Medical. S&OP was done by the supply chain people at a very detailed level, with very little input from the commercial side. Some 150 different product lines or product brands were discussed without regard to strategic impact. In fact, 86 of the product lines were very small; they represented less than 10 percent of the business overall but took up more than 25 percent of the inventory investment dollars.

Revenue was declining, cash flow was negative, and inventory was very high. Overall, the company had nearly two years' supply of inventory. Most of the inventory was located in fixed consignment locations at hospitals or at distributors under the control of salespeople who had no training and no interest in good inventory management. Consignment stocks had items that were never used. In fact, nearly 8 percent of the inventory was in items that had no sales at all. Field locations often had excess quantities of many implants and shortages on other commonly used implants. Popular implants were "hoarded" by salespeople who were motivated only by a desire to increase their own commission checks.

The inventory was not going to work for the company. The cash invested in the inventory was excessive; this was starving new product development programs and stifling any thought of an acquisition program. The inventory was not deployed to enhance sales growth prospects.

The factories were well managed and able to supply replenishment stock overnight in the United States and in two days for Europe and the rest of the world.

Actions. HPMS teams were formed to study the situation. The steps in HPMS are as follows:

1. Write a purpose statement
2. Form a team
3. Adopt a disciplined process of teamwork
4. Document the current state
5. Determine the future state
6. Plan the transition
7. Implement
8. Monitor

A team was formed to generate free cash flow and eventually a new S&OP process with the following purpose statement:

> Develop and gain approval of a plan that, when executed with excellence, will result in a dramatic reduction in inventory/ instruments and product line optimization that results in dramatic sustained improvement in cash flow worldwide while maintaining a high level of customer satisfaction.

The team completed the first six steps in HPMS, with the following actions:

♦ Internal benchmarking was done to identify well-functioning distributorships and sales management practices.

♦ The problems with the current state in ten major processes involved in inventory management and S&OP were identified.

♦ Analytics were completed.

♦ A future state was defined with three major areas of focus:

1. Pro-growth inventory management through a monthly collaborative planning process (market-savvy S&OP)

2. Product life-cycle management

3. Market-driven implant kit configurations

♦ The transition plan included branding the new process to extol the goals of collaboration and generating free cash flow.

♦ The implementation began with a pilot of the market-driven supply chain design in one major market.

Business Results Achieved. The following results came about:

♦ The work is ongoing as this book is being published.

♦ The BHAG in inventory reduction is to initially cut inventory in half, to less than 12 months of supply. The project is proceeding well against plan, the reduction target should be exceeded.

♦ The HPMS team took charge of 14 implementation programs.

♦ The emphasis is currently on education.

♦ Field salespeople were given the facts about the current inventory practices and the "hoarding" going on that restricted sales growth. They went from demanding more inventory to fully supporting the new market-driven culture.

♦ Plans were formed to use the cash expected from the program to achieve market-share leadership in the high-growth foot and ankle market.

♦ Double-digit revenue growth plans were formed and executable because the cash required to support sales growth was being generated internally, not by new equity or debt.

♦ When the program is successful, Wright Medical will be the fifth company Bob Palmisano has managed to triple or more increases in the stock price.

Designing a Rate-Based Planning Process

RATE-BASED PLANNING (RBP) is a significant departure from conventional S&OP and the conventional scheduling practices of MRP (material requirements planning), as imbedded in all ERP (enterprise resource planning) systems. Using RBP can have a transformational impact on your business, increasing cash flow and delighting your customers with excellent service.

MRP, JIT, and the so-called pull systems that ERP has added all start the production process when a new order comes in and trips a replenishment signal, either a safety-stock level or a Kanban trigger. This trigger is not limited to any capacity consideration, nor is it sensitive to order trends; it just starts new production even when the trend would say you have enough already. In RBP, you use expected order rates, as determined in S&OP, to gauge whether a series of orders are as expected. When the rate of incoming orders is higher or lower than expected, you reexamine the situation and determine whether you want to change the master schedule. Most often, you will wait for further information before changing the schedule. This is the principle of "don't make a decision until you have to."

These two guiding principles are the basis of rate-based scheduling:

1. Build to an order rate, not to an order.
2. Don't make a decision until you have to.

Chapter 6 describes the applicability of RBP, the history of scheduling schema, and the process tools and key elements of RBP.

RBP Applicability

RBP can be applied to almost all manufacturing businesses, the true job shop being the most notable exception. However, only a very small portion of manufacturing is truly job shop. MRP, safety stocks, and forecasting still are necessary in scheduling capacity-constrained job-shop operations. However, RBP is the proper scheduling tool for the type of job shop in which extensive use of cellular manufacturing is in place.

RBP schedules production to demand—true demand, not the demand surrogates that come in the form of replenishment orders from upstream stocking locations or from forecasting. Before all the forecasters go crazy, forecasting still is used for longer-range (12 to 18 months or more) capacity planning. RBP plans to the end-user takeaway rate. For manufacturers that sell through distributors, this is not distributor stock replenishment orders; it is the actual purchases of end users such as OEMs (original equipment manufacturers). For those manufacturers that sell to retailers or brokers, it is the rate the retailers sell to consumers, not the rate of replenishment to retailer distribution centers. For medical device manufacturers, demand is the number of devices used in surgical procedures, not the shipments to consignment stock or to distributor safety stocks.

RBP works for both make-to-order (MTO) and make-to-stock (MTS) businesses. The preference would be to convert an MTS business to an MTO one by reducing the master-schedule horizon to a few days and producing very close to the actual consumer take-away rate and mix. In some businesses, particularly consumer products or food manufacturing, MTS is probably required. However, you still replace short-term SKU-level forecasts and safety stocks with family-demand rates and inventory balancing. The objective in both MTO and MTS situations is to eliminate or drastically reduce finished-goods inventory and to use manufacturing flexibility to produce to true demand. Ideally, you eliminate not only your own finished goods inventory but also the inventory in distribution, except for goods in transit or being cross-docked. Certainly, some companies have seasonality-forced capacity shortages. In those cases, RBP would have a prebuild strategy resulting in some finished-goods inventory. In the prebuild strategy, you use a zero-zero inventory strategy, committing only the inventory guaranteed to sell during the season and leaving open the ability to adjust production to actual demand for a substantial part of the season.

In an MTO business, the RBP process manages variability in demand by managing order backlog, rather than inventory safety stock. This is not new to highly engineered MTO businesses. What is new is operating as an MTO business in traditional MTS situations. We have converted food manufacturers to MTO, as well as medical technology businesses, consumer durable businesses, and commercial products companies.

In an MTS business, the RBP process has a totally new inventory replenishment strategy. Rather than produce to replenish stock at a location when the individual-item forecast predicts a safety-stock violation, RBP selects an SKU mix each time a family is to be produced, such that a balanced inventory results. In RBP, you produce the items with the highest probability to sell in the very near term.

RBP Versus Traditional Scheduling Methods

RBP is a pull process. Many managers think they are using a demand-pull process, because demand pulls inventory down. If inventory initially was put in place to a forecast (which is a push concept) and is maintained using safety stocks calculated from a forecast (another push process concept), you do not have a pull process. In RBP, you set the expected rate of capacity usage to a highly accurate aggregate forecast of all members of a 3M family. The rate comes from the monthly collaboration, but you actually make to the mix and volume of true demand. There are no individual SKU forecasts at all—none—and there are no safety stocks. In cases in which manufacturing cannot produce to true demand inside customer lead times, you calculate an inventory standard, which is a range of acceptable inventory but does not work as a safety stock, only as a balancing factor. All items within a family should have the same stocking level in days of supply at the end of a family production run.

RBP Supports the Time-Advantaged Strategy

I introduced RBP in Chapter 2 as the method required to support a time-advantaged strategy; that is still true. However, RBP has a much broader applicability and is far superior to the traditional scheduling methods commonly used and included in supply chain software. Figure 6-1 shows how RBP differs from traditional methods of scheduling at the concept level.

MRP is the Push System Inside ERP

The MRP process was defined in the 1960s, as computers were just starting to be applied to manufacturing. It has stayed in the software designers' application set through many upgrades, but it stays the same. All MRP applications are designed for a true job shop. ERP systems of the 1990s and the MRP II, MRP, and PICS (production and inventory control system) systems of the 1970s and 1980s were written by computer programmers who simply copied the scheduling concepts designed in the 1960s for the job shop. The "modern" ERP is just a copy of what the pioneers at Warner & Swasey Company and The Stanley Works came up with in their job-shop applications. In fact, in the late 1960s, I was a member of the teams designing the systems for

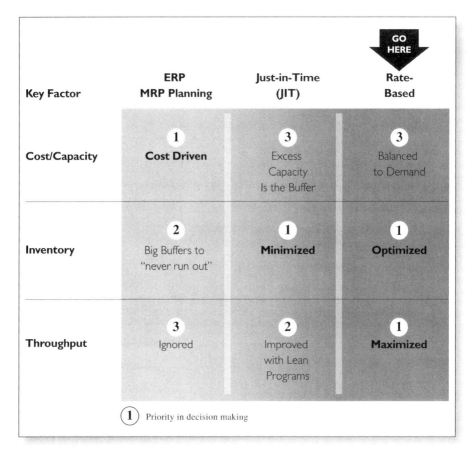

FIGURE 6-1. COMPARISON OF SCHEDULING SCHEMES BY DECISION-MAKING PRIORITY.
RBP optimizes inventory and maximizes throughput; both produce free cash flow.

Warner & Swasey (W&S), which was the ultimate job shop. IBM's
PICS system came directly from the work we did at W&S. Later, the
Arista System was adapted directly from the W&S system. Since the
1960s, the logic for scheduling in MRP has not changed significantly.
MRP is widely accepted as the way to schedule any and all types of factories, even though we knew from the very beginning that it applied
only to job shops. One significant group of manufacturers did not
accept MRP: The leading Japanese manufacturers use a very primitive

form of rate-based processing that employs Kanbans to accomplish the demand-based signaling that MRP is incapable of producing.

MRP was designed to explode the bill of material for an assembled product into individual parts. The parts were then planned over a lead time to be produced in time to be available for the assembly operation. Assembly was planned using an S&OP process in an MTO environment. MRP ignores capacity constraints completely. Supposedly, the assembly master schedule was developed to allow for capacity constraints, but in the job-shop environment, individual parts compete for capacity on feeder production equipment, so it is very difficult to predict capacity usage. Elaborate finite scheduling processes were developed to deal with the problem and were successful to some degree. All is well with this approach.

However, when the so-called independent demand problem was presented to the MRP designers, the scheduling problem became complex. Demand for individual parts came from customers, as well as from the assembly schedule. The MRP designers tried to add independent demand forecasts to the exploded expected requirements from the assembly schedule. In a job shop, lead times for parts are very long. Forecasts over long horizons typically are very inaccurate, so as the actual demand came in and was different from the forecast, major schedule changes happened. The schedule changes continued—and continued to be magnified. This problem was even named back in the 1970s as the "bullwhip effect." The solution was to add large safety stocks and to try to develop the "perfect forecast." The only economic benefit of this historical struggle fell to software manufacturers, which were and are rewarded for providing ever-more-complex and costly MRP software, forecasting software, etc. Manufacturers gained high inventory and high obsolescence. The big failings of MRP are poor cash flow and the inability to plan collaboratively. MRP is driven by the drum of forecast error, not the demand rate of S&OP.

Managers decided to put in pull processes to stop the tyranny of MRP. This was a good idea, but it was poorly implemented. It was interesting to see all the software companies almost instantaneously offer a pull-process application in the 1980s. All they did was dress up MRP.

In time, a pull process called just-it-time (JIT) was developed. The origin of JIT was the popularity in the 1970s of the Toyota Production System (TPS), with its Kanbans and pseudo-pull processes. One large consulting firm purported to know how the TPS worked and could be applied widely. The firm was paid large sums of money, but it rarely had a successful installation. The problem in applying the TPS is that auto manufacturing is very simplistic, while the vast majority of man-ufacturing is much more complex. Toyota makes one product in each plant, a vehicle, with a set manufacturing rate determined in large part by the design of the factory. If the factory is designed for 35 cars per hour, then it produces exactly 35 cars per hour. In Toyota's case, the company offered very few options or only a standard option package, so predicting the demand for parts was much easier. The Kanban sig-naled for replenishment only when small variations in the rate changed the supplier schedules very slightly, so the process worked with low inventory. The problem comes in when a company's manu-facturing does not mirror the Toyota model.

JIT is a Push System Inside a Make-to-Order Manufacturing Design

JIT tries to minimize inventory to the exclusion of all other factors or goals. In practice, JIT does two things, both of which are counter-productive. First, the manufacturers that employ JIT as a scheduling strategy end up with massive amounts of excess capacity. JIT says any-thing, anytime, and any quantity. Only the most simplistic manufac-turing operations could possibly do this. These would include some manual assembly operations, with flexible workforce characteristics and very limited capital equipment requirements. Second, the manu-facturers using JIT for supply force inventory downstream to suppliers. They have the least possible chance of producing to true demand, and thus, end up with massive amounts of inventory, which leads to higher costs, higher prices, and eventually may cause bankruptcy. Sometimes, these supplier-JIT arrangements are called vendor-managed inventory, or VMI. This is interesting phrasing, as the word "vendors" calls to mind people who sell hot dogs on the streets of New York, not critical business partners. Manufacturers that try to work with major retailers through an arms-length VMI process—typically managed by the sales department, where there are no inventory management skills—become frustrated and end up with large inventories, massive manufacturing schedule changes, and very high costs relative to other non-VMI customers. The excuse is "we will make it up in the volume," but of course they cannot.

In the big picture assessment, neither JIT nor MRP are collaborative processes. They do not work within the capacity as defined by S&OP, and they do not signal when planned capacity is being exceeded or is unutilized. Both exaggerate the peaks and valleys of demands on capacity by overreacting to short-term demand variations that should be ignored. They are anathema to an efficient and effective market-driven process. Demand is variable and S&OP, along with RBP, deals with the demand variability effectively. Any scheduling scheme that builds inventory and/or requires excess capacity is not optimal.

The other major problem with MRP and JIT is that they operate at a highly detailed level and way into the future. MRP deals with individual components for every product, all the time, and so does JIT. Consider the problem of 'C' items. (Note that to keep the problem simple, I have only 'A' and 'C' items in my definition of the way the world works. Some people follow a strict Pareto distribution, with its 'A,' 'B,' and 'C' items; I find this much too complex. I even had a client who used 'A,' 'B,' 'C,' 'D,' and 'E' items. Using an 'A' and 'C' item definition is sufficient.)

'C' items are 80 percent of the finished goods items, but only about 20 percent of the total throughput. In MRP and JIT, all items are dealt with as if they were equally important. Since 'C' items have significantly more volatility, they trip a replenishment signal much more often than their 20 percent would indicate. They totally consume your time because the sheer number of them is overwhelming. Literally every day, a mess of 'C' items have orders come in differently than expected, and the MRP or JIT responds by triggering production. In practice, schedules are chaotic. Employees who work down in the plant and deal with MRP every day know exactly of what I speak. Unfortunately, they are shouted down by the IT wizards and senior managers who spent millions of dollars on "the system" and are emotionally wed to it, even if it does not work.

My advice is to throw MRP out, stop thinking about JIT, and install an RBP process without delay.

RBP Scheduling Strategy

The remainder of Chapter 6 is for companies that have significant setup time or line-change time. Even if you are able to become almost MTO using Lean or Six Sigma, and matching the manufacturing lead time to the customer's need, you will need the tools described in the following sections. Some companies can have dedicated production lines and can make whatever is required every day; the beverage manufacturers were like this until they exploded their product offerings tenfold. So, almost all manufacturers that are not true job shops will benefit by using RBP tools.

As I pointed out in the introduction to this chapter, the basic principles are building to rates and not making decisions until you have to. In RBP, super 'A' items or order backlog become the buffers to variation in demand, not safety stock on all items and not safety stock on the super 'A' items.

The strategy for scheduling in RBP is to use capacity to make what will sell in the near term. That is, make those 'A' items that have the least amount of demand variability. This is a new concept for most managers. 'A' items normally are defined by a Pareto ranking of sales revenue or some other volume-related factor. Some managers even use item sales value, i.e., the most expensive items are the 'A's. Both of these methods to define 'A' items are of little use here. The ones you want to commit to stock when you don't have actual demand information are the ones with the lowest variability, the most stable items. The idea is to conserve capacity. If you make high-volatility items, you risk having put up finished goods that will sit in inventory. In that case, you have wasted capacity on something you did not need right away, made it before you had to, and have no scheduling buffer from those items. If you make low-volatility items, you can be assured of having demand tomorrow that can be satisfied from already-produced items, and thus, you have capacity available for the items actually in tomorrow's demand mix.

Let's look at an example:

♦ There are 300 items in the family.

♦ Some 20 items equal 50 percent of total demand and are in the actual demand mix almost every day.

♦ As a group, they account for a minimum of 30 percent and maybe as much as 70 percent of every day's actual demand.

♦ You can then make some of these 20 super 'A' items into finished goods.

♦ You schedule capacity for this family to the aggregate average daily demand. The accuracy of your estimate of average daily demand is high, because it is at a relatively high level of aggregation. However, you can deal with some volatility in the daily family demand, as you will see later in this chapter.

♦ On days when the actual demand is below the aggregate average, you fill up the production to planned capacity with the super 'A' items in the worst stocking position (worst will be defined using *inventory standards*, discussed below).

♦ On days when the actual demand is higher than the aggregate, you make all the non-super 'A' items in the actual demand mix and satisfy the excess demand from the stock of the super 'A' items built previously.

By following this strategy, the peaks and valleys of production are eliminated, and 'C' items are made when they are required, without disturbing the overall production allowance for the family.

'C' Item Strategies

If 'C' items are too much of a problem to handle in daily production within a family, or if they have their own families because of raw material issues (which is often the case), you want to eliminate their impact by simply making a quantity of three to six months' supply early in the overall production cycle (an annual cycle or the seasonal cycle for the product line).

I don't like to make 'C' items in more than about three- or four-month quantities because of the demand variability. Three months may become eight months or a year very easily as a result of the inherent error in future planning.

When significant setup or line-change time is involved, you should try to batch the 'C' items in an off-season period or in the low production months.

Another 'C' item strategy is to reserve capacity for 'C' families in the cycle plan, which we discuss next.

Cycle-Plan Strategy

When setup is significant and many different families are made on the same production line, a cycle plan is used to implement the RBP process. Cycle plans have a horizon of two to three weeks at maximum, and perhaps only two or three days, as is the case in many food-processing businesses. Cycle plans show what family is made during each shift of each day. 'C' families can be grouped together and scheduled for about 20 percent of the normal capacity, or about one out of five days per week. Cycle plans are updated once a week or perhaps more frequently. On the update day, the 'C' families that have the lowest number of months of supply are chosen for production. The total production is whatever 20 percent of the week's capacity is planned to be. Then, if the 'C' families as a group start to trend so that they have more than the planned months of supply, you skip making 'C' families for one week. If the 'C' families start to drop below a few months of supply and threaten stockouts, you may want to add a half-day or so in the next cycle plan.

Some people worry about 'C' items within an 'A' family or 'C' families with very long lead-time components. Normally, these are not a problem. You can either stock the long-lead component if it is not too expensive and has a long shelf life, or more likely, you keep a little more than three months' worth on hand, so when the long-lead item is found to be needing more production, you have time to add it to the cycle plan a few weeks forward, without creating a stockout. If the 'C' item is not really that important overall, consider getting rid of it altogether.

In job shops, cycle planning is used to manage the capacity-limited operations. Take a printed circuit board (PCB) operation, for example. The PCB plants make double-sided boards and multilayered boards. The double-sided and multilayer PCBs use drilling capacity, which is an expensive and capital-intensive part of the operation. Multilayered PCBs use more drilling than double-sided PCBs by a multiple of two to three times. So, the planner must feed new orders from backlog to match the available drilling capacity. The cycle plan comes in when deciding the mix of double-sided and multilayered PCBs each day. The inner layer department (the area of the factory where the multiple layers of circuits inside a multilayered PCB are aligned and assembled) is also expensive due to the need for highly trained staffing. The department may not be staffed every day, so the orders for multilayered PCBs must be released to production inside the restrictions of the cycle plan. If the backlog of multilayered boards builds, more shifts of inner layer department capacity must be added and vice versa.

In food manufacturing, the filling lines run to one cycle plan, and the labeling lines run to a second cycle plan. The inventory available for labeling is not known in detail until the production in filling is completed and the mix of individual items is known to labeling.

Because labeling may take place several days after filling, allowing for incubation time in quality control, the actual demand for each labeled item is determined at the future date, not before. In labeling, you often have not only different brand labels but different packaging configurations, from six packs to cases, and so on.

Zero-Zero Inventory Strategy

The term "zero-zero inventory strategy" comes from a technique I first learned from Harry Figgie, the CEO of the parent company of Rawlings Sporting Goods Company, the first zero refers to rebalancing production to demand early in a season to zero at the end of the season and the second zero refers to doing the rebalancing again later in the season when demand for the total season can be projected more accurately. The idea is to have zero inventory carryover at the end of the season.

Often we find a business has a natural seasonality or promotional activity. Both situations present the opportunity to employ a zero-zero inventory strategy. Some managers do not think about seasonality because they are in a hard-goods business, but many businesses actually have an off-season, and thus, a beginning of a new season. Some businesses have a natural or customary time of the year when product-line changes are introduced, so there is a beginning and an end to the cycle every year. Businesses that have production in, say, China, with very long transit times, may need to be committing production far ahead of actual demand. The zero-zero strategy works exceptionally well in these cases. This strategy can also be applied to new product introductions when the business does not have a customary introduction period and launches new products whenever they are ready.

The situation appropriate to a zero-zero inventory strategy is when there is a beginning and a ramp-up. The shape and size of the ramp-up is always fraught with unknowns. How will competitors respond? Which customers will convert from a competitor's product to ours or participate in the promotion? How will the products sell through to the end user? What is the actual market size and your share of market? And there will be many more unknowns, as yet unknown.

The primary tool of a zero-zero inventory strategy is the demand-sensing and balancing chart, as shown in Figure 6-2. A reference or typical historical pattern is used to predict the cumulative demand curve, as indicated in the chart by the dotted line. Actual demand is then plotted at significant points. Typically, when the season or

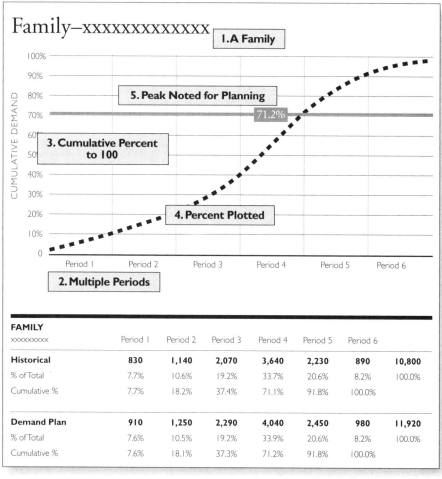

FIGURE 6-2. EXPECTED CUMULATIVE DEMAND PLOTTED OVER THE SEASON.
Actual demand is plotted against the historical expectation or demand plan.

promotion is about 25 percent booked, per the reference pattern, a comparison is made, and the total season or promotion quantity is adjusted.

As an example, in the chart, the 25 percent experience has been about halfway into Period 3. We are anticipating the demand at that time to be 2,980. If we have actual demand of 3,500, we should adjust the total season or total promotion quantity up by 3,500/2,980 = 17.5 percent. The production schedule would be increased by an amount equal to the 17.5 percent increase, such that inventory would be zero at the end of the final period.

The zero-zero strategy gets its name from the common use of this tool. At the 25 percent point, you would plan to have no more than 40 to 50 percent of the total production fully committed. The first zero adjustment in production would be to calculate the production required to zero out the inventory at the end of the last period, using the newly adjusted cumulative demand plan. However, at the 25 percent point, you would authorize to produce up to only 75 to 80 percent of the total. You would leave about 20 percent of production uncommitted until the second zero point, which would be at the last possible time period for making the production commitment without causing excess costs or risking stockouts. If the production department requires one to two periods for normal lead time, the second zero should be done during Period 4 in this example. If the production managers are committing raw material to rates, the rate of production is adjusted, and lead times often are not a factor. The capacity is reserved in a RBP process, and items with long lead times are planned out of the situation.

There are, of course, some products that have such short selling seasons as to make this process unworkable, for example, Christmas tree lights. We recommend that manufacturing lead time be cut drastically with a final assembly postponement strategy or a strategy of making the final production in a somewhat-higher-cost facility with flexible, short lead-time capability. For example, laptop computers assembled in China have six- to eight-week lead times for transit. If the last piece of the production is made in the United States, the lead time for transit and assembly is about three days. In that case, the components could be used to support off-season sales, so the component inventory risk is low. The much bigger factor is the risk of making the wrong configuration of the laptops. Configuring the final 20 percent of production to demand in the United States can reduce inventory risk considerably.

So, you can keep production running smoothly over long periods of time and make schedule adjustments to the rates only twice per season. The mix of items within the family would be adjusted to demand, with a 'C'-item scheduling strategy employed.

I have used this technique with all sorts of consumer products, hardlines products, food production, industrial pumps, and many other industries. It is close to magical. The major benefit is a drastic reduction in expediting, production changes, and excess inventory— all factors that increase free cash flow.

Capacity Definition

In all our scheduling strategies, the one underlying requirement is an agreed capacity or daily rate. The rate you want is the demonstrated rate, not a theoretical rate. A fun exercise for the design team would be to ask four different functional areas what they think capacity is and then do an analysis of actual throughput.

We did this at a food production facility with nice, clean, stainless steel production lines. I asked the master scheduler what he used for a daily rate in his production planning, and I asked him to show me the calculation; he said he used 20,000 pounds per day as the three-shift capacity. I asked the design engineer what the line was capable of producing in practical terms; his answer was 25,000 pounds. I asked the plant manager what he felt the production line team should be held accountable for; his answer was 18,000 pounds per day. I asked the foreman what he thought was a reasonable daily rate; his answer was 15,000 pounds per three-shift day. The actual throughput was 12,000 pounds per normal three-shift day.

We agreed to study why we were losing over half the design capacity. We found we had unplanned downtime of more than 20 percent, rejects for quality of 8 percent, and poor work practices that kept the line below full speed at the beginning and end of each shift and during breaks and lunch periods. The 20 percent unplanned downtime was nearly impossible to measure except in aggregate. The major factors were material jams, missed production steps, and equipment stoppages. To solve the problem, a Lean team was assigned to come up with ways to eliminate the unplanned downtime, and an unplanned downtime metric was added to the daily assessment meeting. The work practices were changed. Tag teams were used to make sure the line kept running at full production. A good deal of resistance was encountered at the beginning. The S&OP design team worked through the resistance by doing some education and by using analytics to help the production staff see and solve the problems.

The tools used in RBP are shown in Figure 6-3. The whole idea is to plan the next level of detail only when you must and not before. There is no need to worry about SKU-level detail in planning until the family is scheduled to run the next day. This is a major time savings when compared to an MRP schema. The reason the planning strategy works is because the members of the 3M family all have commonality of materials or consist of materials that can be planned to the cycle plan within the plan horizon. The differences between members of the family can be handled with minor changes in dies, stocking a few different raw materials, or using different packaging or pack sizing.

Cycle Planning

Cycle planning is an advanced master scheduling or capacity planning tool that has been around for many decades, but it was never built into the ERP systems. We know why. ERP systems were designed for the true job shop.

Cycle planning is the manufacturing manager's friend. With cycle

Rate-Based Planning Tools

Tools	Frequency	Horizon	Level of Detail
S&OP	Monthly	6 to 18 months	By CFCF family
Cycle Plan	Weekly	Few days to two weeks	By shift
Rate-Mix Plan	Daily	Next day	By SKU
Inventory Standards	Twice a year	Season	By SKU

FIGURE 6-3. THE FOUR PRIMARY TOOLS IN RBP.
This is a hierarchical ordering of planning activity.

planning, the decisions in S&OP are directly translated into manufacturing schedules. Cycle plans, unlike any other scheduling techniques, maximize flexibility in production while maintaining manufacturing economics.

In cycle planning, you calculate the maximum number of batches of the 'A' families you can make within the economics of setup time, a non-value-added function in total capacity. You should continue to add setups, making each 'A' family more frequently, until the annual line availability is used. The goal is to make the 'A' families multiple times per week, if possible. You leave 20 percent of the production line availability to the 'C' families.

From S&OP, or AOP to begin the year, the annual production quantities of each family are planned. In cycle planning, you take that information and calculate the number of batches you can make of each family. In fact, you normally set the S&OP output to have a specific number of shifts or batches for each family planned directly from the S&OP dashboard (as shown in Figure 3-1). The number is then held in the cycle-plan tool and reduced as the planner actually includes a family into the cycle plan.

A cycle plan would then look like the diagram in Figure 6-4. I normally like to see the capacity division as shifts per day. It is useful to have the line management for a shift held responsible for producing the planned quantity of each family in an easily accountable form. When responsibility for performance to schedule is limited to one management team and can be measured immediately during and after the shift, clear communication of capacity utilization can be achieved. The cycle planner needs to know if a shortfall or overproduction event has occurred so he or she can adjust the next cycle plan and definition of capacity, if necessary.

The cycle-plan diagram is self-explanatory. Each division of time—normally a shift—is set, and the family number is shown in the slot. The actual planned number of units of the family is also shown. All the planned downtime is shown in the cycle plan, including maintenance

Cycle Plan Concept Diagram

Line 5	Shift	1	2	Day 3	4	5
Families A-001 A-002	1	A001	A003	A001	A002	C???
A-003 C-102	2	A001	A003	A001	Sanitation	C???
C-103 C-104 C-105	3	A002	Sanitation	A002	A003	C??? Preventative Maintenance

FIGURE 6-4. CYCLE PLANS DISPLAY ALL PLANNED LINE ACTIVITY.
The cycle-plan horizon is the minimum time necessary for acquisition of materials not to be taken from raw stocks.

and line changes or sanitations for food production. We suggest doing cycle-plan updates once or twice a week. The plan is a rolling set of days and shifts. So for a plant with a horizon of three days, the planning can be done on Monday for Friday through Tuesday, on Thursday for Wednesday through the following Friday, and so on.

An exception report comes out of cycle planning. The planner is given a list of families that have low or high aggregate inventory.

The basic requirement to make the cycle plan a practical solution is to plan the raw materials in a fully collaborative fashion. The objective is to have all raw materials received on or just before the shift during which they are to be used. That is planned by the supplier directly from your cycle plan.

At Anchor Foods, we had a cheese supplier that produced fresh cheese for jalapeño poppers using about 70 percent of its total capacity. Anchor seemed to always have three or four days of cheese on hand in a refrigerated holding warehouse. The maximum shelf life was right at four days, so the limits were always pushed. Sometimes, a lot went past date code and had to be trashed—an expensive occurrence. The supplier talked about the ability to supply on demand. Basically, it could produce white cheese easily to the demand. The problem was with yellow cheese. When the supplier ran yellow cheese, the equipment had to be cleaned thoroughly before it could start up on white again—a cleanup that used an entire shift, which was very expensive. We collaborated on the cycle plan and were able to schedule the yellow cheese families in such a way as to have them all produced on consecutive shifts and then switch to white. By sharing the cycle plan every few days, the supplier was able to plan to have cheese delivered at the beginning and the middle of each shift, on demand. The inventory went down to less than one shift, and the refrigeration requirements dropped to near zero.

There are four kinds of raw materials to be planned. All except type (4), which is discussed below, can be planned to the cycle plan directly. Briefly, most materials should be ordered to the actual cycle plan date and shift. We call these type (1), which are planned to the rate. Some materials are low enough in cost and space requirements to carry in stock. We call these type (2), stocked materials. Some materials can be manufactured on demand. We call these type (3), to requirements. Packaging suppliers normally are type (3). These suppliers need to plan their own production to your cycle plan and very likely have some inventory. Finally, some suppliers need to be scheduled over a longer lead time than the cycle-plan horizon. We call these type (4), long lead-time items.

Significant work is required to move all items possible to delivery on demand within the cycle plan's planning horizon. Those are the type (1) and (3) items. Basically, you can receive these materials per the cycle plan. The suppliers should have ready access to your cycle plan and should be able to plan their production in close collaboration with your cycle plan. You set up real-time, online applications in SEQUEL software to communicate with the suppliers (but do it manually first to prove the design).

If you find some type (4) items, try hard to eliminate them by moving them to type (1), (2), or (3). If you cannot, consider changing the design or dropping the product. In no case should you have more than 5 percent of the raw materials in any family in a type (4) situation. The 'A' families should have no type (4) items. You simply must find a way to collaborate with the suppliers for the materials going into an 'A' family.

The managers who do RBP well have almost all their suppliers located within walking distance, or at most, within a few hours of the point of use. Procurement needs to be encouraged to complete a full analysis of the cost versus the benefit of having suppliers nearby. In many cases, we have found suppliers' manufacturing processes to be very flexible and/or nearly dedicated. Do not assume the lowest-cost situation is to buy from a foreign supplier. Be sure to count the transportation cost and the inventory holding costs of both finished goods and raw materials in the analysis. Use a 30 percent per year inventory carrying cost. I know accountants want to use the borrowing rate as the cost of capital, and thus, inventory carrying cost, but that is wrong. Go to the Internet and research the studies done by experts such as those at the Ohio State University to learn about inventory carrying costs; 30 percent annually is actually on the low side. Inventory is way more expensive than direct labor. In the actual Toyota Production System, having suppliers near the plant is a requirement. One of the major reasons the Japanese auto manufacturers have dramatically lower costs and inventory than the U.S. manufacturers is precisely because the supply location is very close to the use plant. Ford and General Motors run the socks off the parts before they even come close to being used.

Inventory Standards

When you must use some inventory to maintain high-capacity utilization or to manage shipping lead times to a regional warehouse, the RBP process employs an inventory standard. If you are able to produce to customer requirements within the customer's desired replenishment window, then actual orders should be used instead of the inventory standard.

Inventory standards are calculated best using an inventory simulation model. Simulation develops a reasonably accurate expected demand pattern out into the future using what is called in Operations Research (OR), a Monte Carlo simulation technique. The technique is commonly taught in operations research programs at major universities and in many MBA programs. I learned about simulation as an undergraduate at Iowa State University in the 1960s.

Why Simulation?

Simulation is a "what-if" technique, not a simple linear plot. Demand is nonlinear. In fact, our studies find well over 90 percent of the items in product portfolios have demand patterns that do not follow a normal distribution at all. Many items are random in demand or have a statistical pattern like Poisson, beta, or another of the many different types of distributions describing more randomly distributed demand patterns. Simulation allows you to study the effects of the random demand and not be fooled by the assumption of an average or normal demand pattern.

A senior executive who was a client of mine challenged me to provide an answer to a question that had perplexed him for his entire career (a long career at that). He asked, "Can you tell me why I have a very large inventory and still have stockouts on many items?" The answer I gave was by way of an example. In standard supply chain software—his company was using one of the most popular brands—safety stock is estimated using average demand and the three-sigma limit of the variation in demand. The software did not automatically check to see if the statistical calculation of a three-sigma limit had any relevance or fit inside a reasonable range of err. If the software had done the checks for relevance and calculated the err range, the company would have found the calculation did not provide much protection against a service failure. Consider an item with a demand pattern per week of the following: 3-0-0-0-0-0-5-0-0-0-0-0-0-0-3-0-0-0-5-0-0-0-0-0-0-0-3, etc. The average over the six months shown, 26 weeks, is .73 per week. The three-sigma limit would be 2.5. So the system would carry about three or four in stock. For 21 of the 26 weeks, the safety stock would be considered excess inventory. But for each week in which there is demand of five, the safety stock does not satisfy the demand, and there is a service failure. It could be that one customer has a rule to order in lots of five and another in lots of three. These are not average or normal; they are arbitrary. Thus, you carry excess inventory and still have stockouts. When I finished giving the executive this explanation, he hired us on the spot; he was overjoyed at finally having an answer to his question. Simulation would have suggested a stocking level of five and replenishment to five after each week in which demand was determined. If lead time was longer than a week, I believe the system would most likely have ignored that fact; the users probably don't understand the requirement for safety stock to be variation in demand over lead tine. This is not the users' fault but is a software training deficiency.

Another common technique for calculating what system inventory should be is so-called optimization. The technical term is linear programming (LP). The word *optimization* is used as a marketing term. Who would object to having their inventory optimized? The problem with linear programming, though, is that solving for "optimum" inventory in a random demand world is not linear. Linear programming was used before we had nearly free memory in laptops and massive amounts of computing power. The laptops today are many times more powerful than the computers in computer rooms in the 1970s and the first laptops in the 1980s. Since LPs are simple and reasonably small, the old computers could handle them with ease. The programs provided useful information, given the limits of computing power 30 years ago. A small simulation problem would have overwhelmed the computers of the 1970s and 1980s, when most supply chain software was developed. Today, it is not unusual to have a laptop with sufficient memory and computing power to solve even complex simulation models. We had an automotive client with 180,000 items stocked in more than 30 locations. We ran a simulation model to solve for the inventory requirements in a matter of a few hours. All the "what-if" scenarios were completed in a few days. The emphasis is on analysis, not crunching numbers.

Inventory Standards Replace Safety Stock

Inventory standards represent the inventory level that results from the cycle plan's expected frequency of production versus the Monte Carlo–simulated future demand by SKU. The inventory standard is set based upon the desire to avoid stocking out. If you wish to have no chance of a stockout, set the standard at double the level the simulation calculates as safe. If you want reasonable inventory levels, use the basic inventory level the simulation calculates.

The simulation runs through "what-if" scenarios to calculate the resulting inventory. As production frequency increases or initial inventory is increased, the occurrences of a projected shortage are reduced. The cycle plan restricts the number of batches of a family to be allowed over the planning horizon, say, a season or more than six months. So the inventory level will be increased and then float from a very low level to a higher level. The inventory standard is usually chosen to be such that at 50 percent of the standard, a projected shortage never happens or is so infrequent as to be irrelevant. The inventory standard then sets the mean with 50 percent being the lower control limit and 150 percent being the upper control limit.

Inventory standards function as a barometer of inventory, not as a safety stock. The actual production is to demand when the cycle plan has a family scheduled to be produced. The inventory standard never triggers production by itself. Production is always planned with the cycle planner, and inventory deployed is by SKU through rate mix.

Rate-Mix Planning

Rate-mix planning is done the day before production, per the cycle plan for each family. The planning tool schedules the quantity required by the cycle plan. The individual SKUs, if produced to plan, have the same stocking level as compared to their individual inventory standards. That is, they should have the same exposure to a stockout and the same probability of having the actual demand satisfied with minimal inventory.

The form shown in Figure 6-5 is a snapshot from a rate-mix planner programmed into a homegrown planning system by one of our clients. We developed the logic and detail in Excel first and then let the IT staff go to work once the process was fully vetted.

The figure shows a simple example of a production line that is making four different families of product that day with specific products in each family. In the example, family 211, with product number 983, is scheduled for production. The product is stocked in three different locations, or has three SKUs. The planner determines how much to send to each of the three locations. Note the information displayed:

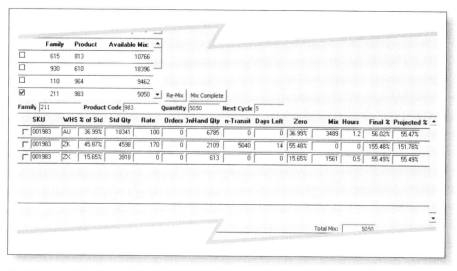

FIGURE 6-5. THE RATE-MIX PLANNING TOOL.
The rate-mix tool balances SKU inventory. It can be set up in a database or in Microsoft® Excel with minimal effort.

♦ The percent of the inventory standard on hand now.

♦ The most recent calculation of daily rate of consumer take-away.

♦ The on-hand quantity.

♦ The in-transit quantity from the last batch of production or another source, such as released from quality hold.

♦ The days remaining on hand or in transit now.

♦ The percent of inventory standard that would be remaining if you produced zero.

♦ The calculated mix the computer is determining: a total of 5,050 units, with 1,561 going to one SKU and the remainder to another. (None is going to the third SKU.)

♦ The two SKUs produced will be balanced at about 55 percent of the standard. The middle SKU will have an excess as a result of the in-transit quantity.

♦ The final percent is the inventory balance after the production day.

♦ The projected percent is the expected inventory level at the next scheduled batch of this family, which is in five days per the header information.

The rate-mix planner runs in minutes and shows the detail for each item being produced tomorrow. Once the planners are comfortable with the process, very little intervention is necessary, and detailed production orders can be written. In most cases, the planning output becomes input to whatever existing transaction software is being used to generate the electronic instructions for the production lines.

You will have an exception report coming out of rate mix, similar to the one from cycle plan. If the percent to standard is below, say, 50 percent, after the production plan is set, the planner is notified to consider moving the family up in the cycle-planning process. If the family's inventory is more than 150 percent of the standard, the next cycle plan may see the family moved out.

Why It Works

Rate-mix planning works because the raw materials are required only when the products into which they go are being manufactured. This is a simple fact, but one that is often overlooked. Most mangers think they need to have a decoupling of the supplier and the manufacturing line. Another term for this decoupling is an inventory. However, if the supplier can operate at the same rate as the manufacturer, only offset by a few hours or a day, then there is no need to decouple and create an inventory. The major raw materials for most products can be arranged to operate at a collaborative rate rather than be built to inventory. This is true even if the lead time between the supplier and the manufacturer is very long—for example, if you are buying a large component from a source in Hungary, which is three weeks away by boat from the assembly plant in the United States. If the assembly plant works to a cycle plan, then the supplier can predict the timing and delivery day required for each component with a high degree of accuracy.

We had a client that made a complex capital equipment item for banks. The company sourced one major component in Eastern Europe and another in China. Lead times were long. The practice was to use MRP and safety stocks, ignoring the idea of using a cycle plan and building to rates. Raw materials inventory was large, because the company calculated safety stock in the standard MRP method of variation in demand over lead time. The company assumed lead time at its worst, 22 weeks, which was the time from the Eastern European supplier's start of procurement of materials to the time of delivery to the U.S. factory. If the client had used the rate-based method and rate-mix planner with a cycle plan, it would have been able to carry only the in-transit inventory that it did not own, or zero inventory on the balance sheet. There is no variation in demand in cases such as this, because the raw material is used only when production is scheduled. The client also carried a great deal of finished goods inventory, so it had truly no need for safety stock in raw material. Thus, a major inventory reduction opportunity was found.

This process is designed to let inventory for items within a family actually float inside a control limit, so the production plan for the next few months is not constantly being disrupted.

The possibilities for extension of the rate-mix process into logistics management are significant. We have used the SKU detail, which is by stocking location, to plan warehouse operations. You can run a planning report from the rate-mix detail that tells you how many truckloads or less-than-truckloads (LTL) of product will be loaded for shipment. The warehouse employees can spot trucks into loading bays and then let them sail when they are full or hold them until the LTL load is finished for the day. Packaging lines managers can be told how many boxes, labels, and the like should be staged ahead of production the next day. Quality control can make its plans for sampling and so on.

Major Benefits

RBP and rate-mix planning specifically can provide a significant reduction in the planners' daily workload. Take, for instance, a company with 1,500 product items stocked in eight warehouses, with both company and customer VMI locations. In an MRP world, the planner deals with the total number of SKUs all the time, or with more than 12,000 SKUs. On any given day, the demand for many of the SKUs is different from the normal distribution assumptions used automatically in the computer software. A planner will be given exception reports with perhaps hundreds or thousands of line items. In practice, the exception reports are ignored because of their sheer volume, and they are just passed on to production, where changes in production schedules are very frequent. In one client of ours with approximately this level of SKUs, the production scheduling staff held meetings with production twice daily to discuss major schedule changes of eight to ten different production orders each time. The client also had high variability in production orders not yet released. The result was much chaos and confusion. In the rate-based world, the planner handles two or three families of items each day and nothing more. The level of schedule changes is almost irrelevant, and the planner can focus on improvements and refinements, rather than the non-value-added functions of expediting and handling objections from foremen and suppliers who are being disturbed with schedule changes.

In the rate-based world, suppliers are truly collaborative partners. The suppliers see a much more stable production requirement than is found in the MRP chaos. Suppliers often discover they can reduce changeover costs, eliminate costly inventory, and find available capacity. They will then be open to reducing prices.

Looking Back

♦ These are the principles of rate-based planning (RBP):

   ◇ Build to an order rate, not to an order.

   ◇ Don't make a decision until you have to.

◆ RBP applies to almost all manufacturing types.

◆ RBP replaces MRP and JIT, which do not respect capacity limitations and work independently of S&OP.

◆ MRP and JIT require excessive capital expenditures and excess inventory investment. Both methods are counterproductive to good business management.

◆ The scheduling strategies in RBP reduce the peaks and valleys of demand variation by using 'A' items or order backlog as buffers.

◆ A zero-zero strategy reduces inventory overhang in seasonal and promotional businesses.

◆ Cycle plans flow directly from S&OP and maximize production flexibility without violation of manufacturing economics.

◆ Inventory standards are a barometer of demand, recognizing changes in demand rates to expectations, while maintaining production line schedule stability.

◆ RBP generates the SKU-level inventory flow by managing to demand—ideally "at market" demand, not some intermediate surrogate.

◆ The benefits of the RBP approach are better utilization (more throughput), less time spent doing non-value-added clerical functions like expediting, and lower raw material costs.

RBP delights customers, provides cash for investment, and enables employee job enrichment—a win-win-win situation.

Case Study: Canned Food Manufacturer

A client of ours in the food manufacturing business has applied RBP to good benefit. The company manufactures canned products in a modern, stainless steel canning facility. The company uses a complex process involving food preparation on three separate sets of equipment, filling on automated conveyor-fed lines, and cooking in large continuous-process cookers, followed by a labeling process with multiple labeling equipment and packaging types. The plant was only a few years old and was already running at capacity, as current output determined.

The owners thought they had paid for a factory with considerably more throughput capacity than was being realized. The owners wished to have throughput increased and factory management had no idea how to comply.

Situation. The company asked several firms, including ours, to prepare a proposal to improve the low throughput situation, as defined by the owners. Each firm did some studies and prepared a formal analysis for presentation to the full management team.

The JIT consultant suggested a strategy of maximum flexibility with little inventory. It advised making anything, anytime, and in any quantity. To accomplish this, the consultant wanted to do a major capital expansion at the facility. While the approach may have improved customer service, the capital cost was totally out of the question for the board of directors, who were not at all convinced the current facility was giving them what they originally paid for.

Our proposal, not surprisingly, was to install an RBP process that would maximize throughput and keep inventory at an acceptable level below the current level, even as the business grew. We proposed an educational program followed by a design and implementation plan. The company accepted our proposal.

The company had a strong brand name with high brand equity among the major grocery chains and with Wal-Mart. The management team was not interested in inventory reduction at all, particularly if reducing inventory could result in lower service levels.

Customer requirements were not well understood. Marketing did work in the field with customers, but rarely knew about customer promotions in advance of receiving significant changes in customer-order patterns. Further, major retailers were asking the company's sales team for support of their new "hyper-local" merchandising strategies. The sales force did not really understand what was required, and the supply chain managers were highly resistant to customizing the supply strategy. The practice had always been to send full pallets of one product per pallet to the grocery chains' main distribution centers.

Customer service was also not well understood. The order-entry staff calculated service statistics, which were excellent. However, order entry also asked customers to change their orders to include items in stock and exclude items currently in short supply, so the real inventory availability and on-time shipment statistics were not known.

The product mix was very large, with more than 1,300 items and five major stocking locations. Customers were prone to pick up loads at whichever warehouse fit their logistics situation on any given day, so demand variability at the warehouses was accentuated and very high.

Manufacturing had to deal with the demand variability resulting from each of these factors. The result was chaos, as the planners tried to use MRP at the SKU level to manage inventory in the individual warehouses.

Did I mention the business was also highly seasonal? In fact, the company had two different product lines, one sold during the summer and one in the winter.

We had to understand these impacts on manufacturing. In the analysis leading up to the design phase, we and the team found many opportunities for improvement that were not obvious to management. The key opportunities were as follows:

♦   Planned downtime for line changes and sanitation were running very high as a percentage of overall time over three shifts in a six-day week.

- Schedule changes were the main factor in excessive planned downtime; changes of five or six times per day were not uncommon.

- Unplanned downtime was also very high, at almost 20 percent of the planned production time.

- Quality and R&D had requirements for specific cook times for each product.

  - Some items needed 72 minutes, some needed 103 minutes, and so on for about 18 different cook-time categories.

  - Changing from one cook time to another required completely unloading the "continuous" cooker and changing temperature, then reloading; the time required was nearly an hour—all non-valued-added time, of course.

Actions. A guided education participation program was completed for hundreds of employees in the office and in the manufacturing plant. The education program included three major courses on market-savvy S&OP topics. The three courses were customized versions of our standard education, which included a business simulation game for S&OP, another business simulation game for cycle planning and rate mix, a set of case studies on manufacturing to demand and scheduling strategies, and case studies on developing a go-to-market strategy. All the educational materials used the client's own products and actual business statistics. Thus, the participants in the education were not required to think about theoretical "widgets."

Following the education, a guided participation assessment of the current processes in manufacturing and supply chain was completed. A future state definition of the processes was completed. The design team came up with a set of scheduling tools, as we had introduced in the education program. Action plans and transition plans were developed. The list of actions was very long, including the following:

♦ Cycle planning for filling and labeling was developed and installed.

♦ Rate-mix planning was employed.

♦ The team worked with R&D to clarify tolerances around the cook times and to try to find ways to consolidate cook times without compromising product quality.

♦ A set of 25 cross-functional coordinating families (CFCFs) was defined to allow good communication between marketing, supply chain, and manufacturing.

♦ A scheme to provide "custom" pallets, which would be cross-docked to the major retailers' stores at full truckload costing, was devised to support the hyper-local merchandising strategy. The collaborative team of manufacturing, marketing, and sales was able to find an economical solution once everyone understood that the alternative was to lose the business.

♦ Inventory standards were calculated using a simulation application developed by the client's IT department, with some help from us.

♦ The scheduling tools were also developed by the client's IT department.

♦ A planning database was developed to pull data from Oracle, PLCs (programmable logic controllers) in manufacturing, and other software used in the company.

Business Results Achieved. The main objective was increased capacity utilization. For the three years following implementation of the new processes, the company experienced double-digit growth and did not build a new factory or do a major capital expansion.

Unplanned downtime was cut in half, as stable production schedules allowed factory management to find and resolve the problems that caused the small disruptions in schedules.

Planned downtime also was cut significantly, due to the cycle-planning scheduling and use of inventory standards. MRP was thrown out.

The company was recognized as a high-service provider by the major retailers. It was able to increase margins, even in a tight economy, because of benefits the customers received via the collaborative planning process.

Transitioning to a New Culture of Market-Driven Supply Chain

CHAPTER 7 TAKES US from setting up the cultural change to the actions of transition in implementation. This chapter also describes the follow-on work required to consolidate the gains, to expand the application globally, to formally update the vision, and to continually improve the processes.

The guiding design principle of Chapter 7 is *change culture*. You need to have a culture of change, and you need to change the culture. You need to start the transition.

The Transition Plan

Transitions to new cultures do not happen by the principle of "if at first you don't succeed, try, try, again." They do not happen if you just start something and believe that you will thus just get better. I have heard this principle espoused by the leading S&OP consulting firms. The approach has been tried over and over and succeeds only a very small percentage of the time. The approach of "let the system do it" also fails. That approach assumes that some software developer knows your business and your people well enough to have come up with the perfect solution to your problems. These two principles have failed repeatedly. This is why some 90 percent of all companies with S&OP do not have the commercial side fully engaged and do not produce significant business results.

The transition to the new market-savvy S&OP culture must be methodically planned using proven culture-change techniques.

Change Agent Model

The approach we espouse is a transition planning technique combining the best-known culture-change approaches and a basic cause-and-effect analysis technique. The change agents in our model are powerful: leadership, strategy, communication, money, metrics, and education. All six of these agents are required. The cause-and-effect relationships are shown using a familiar Ishikawa diagram, used so effectively in Lean Six Sigma and adapted to our purposes. The chart shown in Figure 7-1, and as depicted in the HPMS program described in Chapter 5, has six fixed boxes (three on top and three on the bottom) representing the agents of change or causes in our cultural-change situation.

The figures in this book are all in black-and-white. This chart is normally shown in color. So, I will describe what the colors should be and what they represent. When used in actual practice: The box at the extreme left, the one with the north-south lettering, represents the current state, or the S&OP process you have now. Unless you found your process is working well, the color should be red. If you do not currently have an S&OP process at all, then this is whatever you call your current planning process and you should also color it red. Everyone has a planning process even if it is "seat of the pants." The box on the extreme right, again with north-south lettering, is the future state, or where you have determined to go after completing the design work of Chapters 1 through 6. The color would be shown as green when the future state is fully implemented. If you cannot finish the implemen-

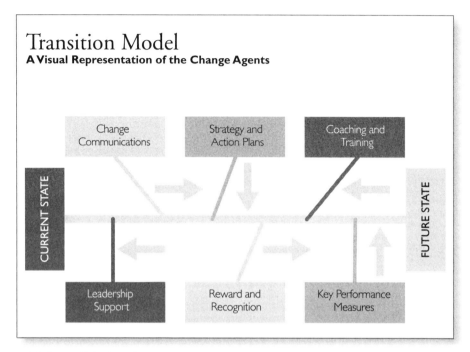

FIGURE 7-1. SIX AGENTS OF CULTURAL CHANGE.
The causes for the transition to the desired state are outlined in the six boxes at the top and bottom.

tation, the box may become yellow at some point in time. Both of these boxes (current state and future state) need not have any further details included in this chart.

The different lines and arrows in the chart should be the same colors as the associated boxes. So a red box indicating a change agent currently working against you would have a red line pointing back toward current state and a red arrow pointing backward. If the change agent is neutral, neither helping nor hindering progress, its color would be yellow. Its line would be yellow with a vertical orientation, and the arrow is yellow, pointing toward the center. If the change agent has become a significant help to achieving change, the box would be green, the line would be green and angled toward the future state end, and the arrow would be green, pointing to the right.

The six boxes representing the agents of change are always the same in title, but they vary considerably in content from company to company or from profit center to profit center inside one company. The six are described as follows:

1. *Change Communications*. Here we describe how the change should be presented. The elements are as follows:

   ◇ *Branding*. The new process should have a name—a brand, so to speak—that is simple and catchy, one word or an acronym.

   ◇ *Channels of Communication*. The venues or publications to be used should be described. There are usually four to six; they include a letter from the CEO, a sticky bun meeting, a newsletter, an e-mail blast, an employee meeting, or perhaps a retreat.

   ◇ *Messages*. The key messages should be outlined. Again, there are usually four to six. These include goals to be achieved, strategy, people sought for inclusion, methods, and/or benefits to individuals, customers, or shareholders.

2. *Strategy and Action Plans*. The critical factors or changes in approach are described in this change-agent box:

   ◇ List three to four major strategies in the box.

   ◇ Do your thinking and boil the strategy down to key phrases that depict action.

   ◇ Start each of the four statements with a verb.

3. *Coaching and Training*. Describe specific guided participatory education activities you will use to accentuate the process, behavior, and vision changes:

   ◇ Include formal education programs, with specific titles and content described in another document.

   ◇ For coaching, involve conducting pilots, proofing new processes, and developing real-world examples.

   ◇ Describe the organizational depth of the expected training.

4. *Leadership Support.* Provide for passionate leaders at various levels:

    ◇ Certainly, CEO support is required.

    ◇ List your approach to gaining ownership among leaders in traditional change-resistant organizations.

    ◇ Give thought to the choice of leaders and who or what organizations should be given responsibility.

5. *Reward and Recognition.* Money and certificates motivate in powerful ways:

    ◇ Describe the specific compensation changes required to gain planning and execution alignment, as opposed to the normal performance incentives.

    ◇ Emphasize team certification or recognition (not individual), such as having implemented a set of processes that score above a nine out of ten in audits.

6. *Key Performance Measures.* Both internally and externally measured metrics should be included:

    ◇ Emphasize the quantitative goal of the overall change process. Again, team metrics are important.

    ◇ Metrics should include process metrics such as forecast accuracy, performance metrics such as free cash flow goals, and customer metrics.

Transition Model in Practice

This chart in Figure 7-1 is used initially to communicate, at a high level of abstraction, the essence of the implementation effort or cultural change requirements. Management will gain a good understanding and a useful overview of the essential facts of the work to be done.

The chart is also used as an introductory or overview chart in each monthly progress meeting. The colors of the boxes and their associated lines and arrows should change as progress is being made. Boxes that stay persistently red should attract most of the attention in monthly meetings. The green boxes may be the lead-ins during your meetings, as you should lead with the positives. The content of the boxes, as we describe later, should not change; if it is necessary to change the contents, a significant explanation is required. The transition plan can be reset and should be periodically, but not at every update meeting. Changing the plan should be an event with appropriate emphasis and approvals given by senior management.

The transition model should be developed for the implementation steps in your journey toward a market-savvy S&OP. The model can be used for many different types of cultural change efforts. As an example, consider a company trying to engage the whole organization in committing to a set of shared values. Shared values are often listed in a mission statement developed in the office of the chair or by an executive committee. These shared values are most often not embraced or put into action down through the organization. However, they are critical and should be part of the culture.

We have a client whose shared values are as follows:

- Teamwork
- Creativity
- Passion
- Accountability
- Integrity

The company had a good chance of gaining acceptance and conformance to these shared values because senior management worked through the leadership to develop the list in the first place. Senior management held an off-site meeting about corporate strategy. The impetus was a particularly challenging financial situation being faced in the coming years. A new strategy was required. Shared values were considered a key part of the strategy, as they should be.

The transition model was used to accomplish the change in the culture.

- Communication had a 4x4 plan:

    - Four venues: A Web conference, newsletter, town meeting, and visual display (posters around the office, in restrooms, etc.).

    - Four messages: Why shared values are important, how people would be expected to use them, changes in performance reviews, and new training offerings.

- The idea was to demonstrate how the shared values were required to achieve strategic alignment throughout the organization.

- Coaching and training was to be accomplished with a formal educational program and in daily exercises for ten minutes in each department throughout the company.

- Recognition and reward were treated seriously:

    - A percentage of the bonus was tied to personal demonstration of the shared values.

    - A recognition program was established to point out exemplary demonstration of the shared values.

    - An un-reward was established for behavior inconsistent with shared values.

- A key performance metric was an employee self-assessment on a defined scale of one to five. The assessment was used in the annual reviews.

The transition plan presented to management at the approval session and in each monthly meeting had the content shown in Figure 7-2.

When the transition plan is applied to your market-savvy S&OP, the boxes will have content depicting the plans to move from the current state. The current state would be defined using a guided participatory assessment against criteria, as described in Chapter 5 and Chapter 6, as well as in Parts I and II. In addition, the team may have completed some benchmarking against other companies known to have installed advanced S&OP processes.

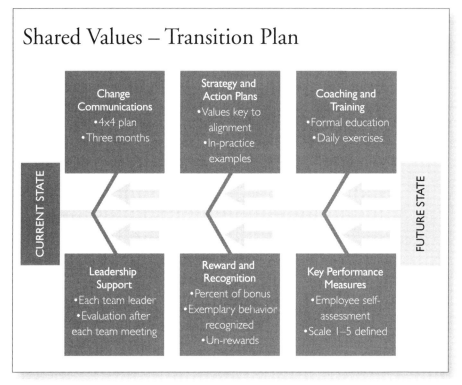

FIGURE 7-2. EXAMPLE OF A TRANSITION PLAN.
Individual boxes contain a very brief synopsis of program details.

The transition plan would then outline communication of the branding of the new process and the key principles. I recommend you have one branding and communication plan for all segment-level S&OPs combined, but an individually tailored transition plan for each segment's customer-facing team to have as a guide. The strategy should consist of the vision from Part I of this book and the behavior changes and analytics from Part II. The coaching and training should include formal guided participatory education of people being added to the design team and then for team members in other geographical areas or profit centers. The leadership support strategy should be based on alignment of management to free cash flow and market-share growth goals of the market-savvy S&OP. Reward and recognition should come from completing the implementation of the new process at a rating above 8, an A rating, as described in Figure 7-3. The key performance measures should be the metrics the team defined in the three categories shown on the high-level S&OP process map (Figure 5-1).

Measuring Transition Progress

A Gantt chart should be developed to document the work steps to accomplish the transition plan. The work plan should show work steps, the lead person, team members, person-day estimates for each team member, timelines, and phase start and stop dates. Each action step will likely go through the following phases to completion:

♦ Design
♦ Proofing and testing
♦ Education
♦ Execution
♦ Rollout and monitoring

In the color version of the transition chart in Figures 7-1 and 7-2, a change from red to green in each of the six change-agent boxes is determined by how progress is made against the transition plan timeline and phase completion schedule. Red, green, and yellow arrows could be shown on the Gantt chart when used in senior management meetings and team meetings.

During the transition plan execution, the design team should be made aware of the eventual audits, the audit criteria, and the process emphasis. Figure 7-3 shows a scoring form for the audit. This form is the same form the external auditor will use to record his or her assessment of the ratings. The process numbers shown on the form are from Figure 5-4—the 26 horizontal planning processes in segment-level S&OP. (The form also includes three globalization processes, which are described later in the chapter.)

Supporting Processes

Process #	Process Title	Rating	Multiplier	Score
1	Strategic Integration		3	
3	Planning in CFCs		3	
4	Rate-Based Planning — Cycle Plans		3	
8	Views of the Forecast		3	
9	Risks/Opportunity Analysis		3	
13	Integrated Financial Projections		3	
14	Annual Operating Plan		3	
20	Monthly Collaboration (segment S&OP)		3	
21	Customer Alignment		3	
23	Meeting Performance Metrics		3	
Total (must be 280 minimum)				Maximum 300

Supporting Processes

Process #	Process Title	Rating	Multiplier	Score
2	Demand Planning		1	
5	Network Design		1	
6	Inventory Simulation		1	
7	Cost to Serve Analysis		1	
10	Contingency Planning		1	
11	Sales-Gap Closure		1	
12	Monthly Financial Reporting		1	
15	Tilt Meetings		1	
16	Demand Sensing		1	
17	Promotional Planning		1	
18	Supplier Alignment		1	
19	Competitor Analysis		1	
22	New Product Planning		1	
24	Generating Free Cash Flow		1	
25	Meeting Customer Metrics		1	
26	Process Governance		1	
Total (must be an 8 rating)				Maximum 160

Globalization Processes

3A	Import and Export Families within CFCs	Rate
8A	Import and Export Views of Forecast	with
20A	Executive S&OP Global, Regional level	number
Grand Total (must be 400 to pass the audit)		**Maximum 460**

FIGURE 7-3. PROCESS RATING AND SCORING CHART.

The fundamental or required processes on the left are given a heavy weighting in the final score calculation.

The team should use the audit list to prioritize its work. The ten fundamental processes shown at the left are the processes you must have performing at a high rating to be recognized by your peers as a company practicing market-savvy S&OP. You must have a rating of 9 or 10 in every one of the fundamental processes and a perfect 10 for at least four of the ten to pass the audit and be rated as having a market-savvy S&OP process. The fundamental processes are the ones that are most important to your achieving competitive advantage and to having strong free cash flow. Meanwhile, there are 16 supporting processes, shown at the right on the form. You can average an 8 on the supporting processes and still pass. None of the processes are easy to install and execute at a high level, but the supporting ones may already exist in part in your organization and be somewhat less time-consuming to complete.

Instituting the Audits and Recognizing the Team Responsible

Both internal and external audits of the new processes are important. Once the transition plan has been nearly fully executed, the team should begin the internal audits of the actual processes being executed.

Preparing the Rating Criteria

You must prepare a chart of the rating criteria for each of the 26 processes. It is best to do this in collaboration with your external auditor to ensure completeness and consistency of thought. Each of the 26 processes should have one page in the audit book containing the pertinent information. Any more than one page would be excessive detail hindering ease of understanding. Figures 7-4 and 7-5 are examples of the assessment criteria for two processes, strategic integration and risks/ opportunity analysis.

The audit criteria should reflect the movement from a Level I S&OP to a Level IV or market-savvy S&OP. The progression is one of becoming centered on customers. The On-Point Group offers an audit

#1 Strategic Integration
(Segment Level)

Goal

A segment-level strategy, forward three to five years, exists and is owned by a customer-facing team. The competitive advantage is clearly detailed, all functional plans are aligned, and performance metrics defined and met.

Rating Scale

1–4 • Does the plan exist in some detail for at least three years forward?
    • Are goals stated and quantified?
    • Are individual team members owners of individual elements?

4–6 • Are there strategic alignment reviews to help each functional organization understand the strategy?
    • Is there a capital expenditure plan tied to the strategy?

7–8 • Are regular meetings held with customer groups to gain inputs on product design?
    • Are the goals of customers reflected in the strategy?

9–10 • Are customer-facing teams meeting with customer management to jointly develop and align strategic plans?
    • Are performance metrics reflective of customer values and measured by the customer?
    • Are the performance metrics met?

Audit Comments

_____
_____
_____
_____

FIGURE 7-4. AUDIT BOOK PAGE FOR PROCESS #1, STRATEGIC INTEGRATION.
The developmental progression is from simply having a plan to having customer alignment and customer metrics in the strategy.

design workbook with suggestions for all 26 segment-level S&OP processes, plus three additional processes required when you expand beyond segment-level S&OP to global concerns.

Process #26—S&OP process governance—is more of a checklist than any of the other processes. I mention #26 here when I am not out-

#9 Risk/Opportunity Analysis
(Segment Level)

Goal

A prioritized list of events that would produce an increase or a decrease to the consensus forecast, coming directly from process #8 (Views of the Forecast), after the impacts on the rate-based plan are understood. Each event would be properly sized and given a probability with the most significant detailed for contingencies.

Rating Scale

1–4 • Is the forecast in the ranges?
- • Can past history point out potential weaknesses with the forecast?
- • Is the field input robust?

4–6 • Are risks across the S&OP identified; inventory, production, product introductions, and supply in addition to forecast?
- • Are commercial and operations management able to cross-identify cause and effect of risks to the forecast?

7–8 • Are risks prioritized in full cross-functional collaboration?
- • Can the cost, investment, revenue, and service impacts be quantified? Are some contingency plans formed?

9–10 • Are customer concerns included in the risk assessment?
- • Is the customer-facing team anticipating opportunities with customers and/or in competitive assessments?
- • Are risk confirmation dates identified and subject to tilt meetings?

Audit Comments

_____
_____
_____
_____

FIGURE 7-5. AUDIT BOOK PAGE FOR PROCESS #9, RISKS/OPPORTUNITY ANALYSIS.
The pattern is the same as in the previous example; the criteria show progress in development, in this case, from looking at ranges in the forecast to having customer-facing teams involved in adding opportunities found from external collaboration.

lining all the processes because the title does not give the reader as much of a clue as to content as the other titles seem to do. The list should include all of the following elements:

1. A calendar of meetings, pre-meetings, and key events or dead-lines maintained by the day for 12 months going forward

2. An S&OP process map

3. A process description book and an audit criteria book, with one page per process

4. A documented list of agenda topics for each meeting and pre-meeting

    a. Actual agenda with expected time allowances

    b. Agendas available 24 hours in advance

5. A record of adherence to the published meeting schedule

6. A record of attendance at the meetings and a plan for encouraging full attendance

7. Documents prepared and available 24 hours ahead (a log should be kept)

8. Meeting minutes taken and distributed within 24 hours

9. Action items documented and a formal follow-up process provided (as discussed in Chapter 5)

10. Documents retained for a rolling 12-month period

The audit rating for process #26 is a count of the checklist items considered fully implemented at a good level of quality and available for audit.

Performing the Internal Audit

In practice, an internal audit is performed using these process-specific rating criteria. The internal audit team should look for evidence the criteria are being met in the actual S&OP documents shared in pre-meetings and S&OP meeting and kept as a permanent record. The external auditor should then be able to readily find the documents in the materials used during the formal audit.

Each company is different in subtle ways, and each segment is different. Where you are different, make sure you have not violated the design criteria in your process design and execution. For the ten fundamental processes, some creativity should be tolerated, but not a violation of the spirit of the design principles.

The process-rating questions in each section of the rating criteria (examples shown as Figures 7-4 and 7-5) are thought-starters. You should not be tied down to a yes or no answer. The processes are supposed to be flowing and interrelated.

The external auditor may not ask all the questions. The external auditor is looking for documentation that the process is being used to manage the business. The assessment will be based upon how decisions are actually made, what information is regularly made available, and the quality of the cross-functional balance being achieved.

Each of the seven guiding principles should be seen in the Level IV process criteria, which is a rating of 9 or 10, as shown in the chart in Figure 7-6. The progression in concept should also be as shown in Figure 7-6.

Performing the External Audit

The external audit is a formal process conducted over several days. The external auditors must have experience with top-performing S&OP companies, or at least they have visited and benchmarked the leading companies. This is no place for a novice or someone with good intentions who is not actually proficient in market-savvy S&OP. The external audit needs to provide specific benchmark information and continuous improvement input into the final audit report. The audit is, in essence, a learning experience, not a final destination.

The auditors should meet with the audit coordinator prior to the formal audit meetings to ensure the materials will be ready and any special circumstances are considered and allowed. They should also discuss the agenda details for approval. Audits normally require three days to complete. The outline is as follows:

Day 1—Business overview, presentations by the profit-center leaders on the following:

	Market In	Segment Level	Mgmt by Analytics	Organize Around Customers	Process Heavy People Light	Rate-Based	Change Culture
0	Process not being used (if this is intended, rate as an 8)						
1	Internal only	No segments	Data gathered	Functional silos	A few informal	No rates, using MRP	Conven'l wisdom
2							
3							
4							
5	Industry level	Product families	Trends recognized	S&OP team	S&OP processes	Some pull processes	Internal metrics
6							
7	Customers recognized	Market/ process	Information shared	Segment teams	Horizontal processes	Customer usage rates	Customer metrics
8							
9	Customer alignment	CFCFs in segments	Metrics are drivers	Customer-facing teams	Strong governance	Production to end-user rates	Customers strategies
10							

FIGURE 7-6. CONCEPTUAL DESIGN OF THE RATING CRITERIA.
Each of the seven guiding principles should be considered in defining the qualifications of the rating levels. The gradients are shown here.

♦ Strategy

♦ AOP

♦ Competitive advantage assessment

Day 2—Inputs to the S&OP meeting, including:

♦ Customer-facing team activity

♦ Views of the forecast

♦ Capacity and RBP activity

Day 3—S&OP meeting and follow-up, including:

♦ Metrics of all three types: process, performance, and customer

♦ Achieving business results

♦ Governance practices

The external auditors should principally be listeners throughout the three-day presentation. They are not permitted to make comments about the specific strategies or decisions being made; those are in the exclusive purview of management. The auditors are concerned only with the process of strategy development and its completeness; the process of decision making and its collaborative quality; and the actual business results achieved as proof of the process execution quality. During the afternoon of the third day, the auditors should take time to discuss their individual findings and reach consensus conclusions supported by specifics. A preliminary report without final rating and scoring should be provided to allow the team to clarify certain points the auditors may have misunderstood.

Shortly following the audit, a formal written report should be prepared by the auditors and reviewed with senior management. A formal review meeting with profit-center management would then be held. If necessary, a corrective action plan should be devised and a follow-up audit schedule roughly defined. As mentioned earlier, the final report should offer suggestions for continuous improvement and a benchmark review from top-performing companies.

Awards and Certifications

Recognition of achieving the top rating should be a priority of the CEO. A formal recognition award ceremony should be held when several profit centers of S&OP teams pass the external audit with a rating of 400 or better. The team should be recognized as *Certified in Advanced Sales and Operations Planning*. (The On-Point Group offers a certification when we are called upon to be the external auditors.) Having a plaque that can be seen near the CEO's office is a good way of reinforcing the recognition. Having a plaque inside the S&OP team room or profit-center headquarters is a good addition.

Moving to a market-savvy S&OP process is a journey that can take one to two years to complete. The business results should herald the accomplishment.

We also recommend annual audits of teams that have completed the process and been recognized. People change, organizations change, customers change, and the external audit conclusions may change. Thus, having an annual touchup is a good idea.

Expanding to Business Units Domestically and Globally

The most successful companies start with one profit center or S&OP team and fully implement a transition plan and final audit before moving on to add further profit centers. The first one should be selected to be a big winner. Start small, or at least with a team having enough passion and commitment to complete the transition. Once you have one good market-savvy S&OP process in actual existence, more can be added, and probably reasonably quickly.

The expansion should start with the guided participatory education and appraisal described in Chapter 5. Certainly, some education can be started before the first S&OP is totally finished.

As more and more teams are established, the need to align them will become apparent.

Alignment Across S&OP Teams Globally

The transition plan and audit plan described is for a segment-level S&OP. Next, you must move to expand to multiple segments within a profit center, to profit centers within regions, and, of course, to multiple regions leading to the total global company S&OP.

Two new processes are required in the pre-meeting activity leading to the segment level S&OP. First, you must define the import and export CFCF families, ideally the subfamilies, to be included in the

RBP process. The import families may include outsourcing alternatives and alternate sources within the company overall. The export families would represent requirements placed on your capacity from another part of the company.

In practice, each capacity resource should be the responsibility of one S&OP team. The assignment of responsibility would be made based on which S&OP team buys most of the capacity. The performance to schedule, inventory, and service metrics are the joint responsibility of the two or more S&OP teams. A team that buys capacity from another team cannot simply throw up its hands and capitulate to whatever performance is achieved.

The second new process is the forecast of requirements from another S&OP team that will used in the development of the overall forecast in the full forecasting process and will be input into the S&OP and RBP cycle plans.

These two processes involved with import and export CFCF families are defined (as shown in Figure 7-3) as 3A and 8A. They do not add to the process count (the 26 horizontal processes), but they are recognized within the pre-meetings associated with those numbered processes.

There is also a third new process, defined as 20A. These are the executive S&OPs, or aggregation of S&OP into the formal management reporting structure. Segments within a profit center roll up to the profit center S&OP, and profit centers roll up in the natural form of the global reporting structure. Certainly, some time is required to accomplish the aggregation; however, the aggregation of the S&OPs should be a natural and readily accomplished task. The requirement is to keep the essential detail in view as the aggregation is accomplished.

One major advantage of using a segment-level S&OP is to preserve the opportunity to aggregate by common segments. Thus, a profit center or regional management team in Europe may have segments that are identical to those in North America and in Asia. The common segments can be aggregated to a global view of performance in the common businesses. Companies such as Goodyear can use this opportunity to roll up, say, all consumer tire businesses or all aviation businesses to a global view, even though regional management is responsible for the profit and loss performance and free cash-flow generation. The segment rollups allow for a good look at worldwide capacity utilization, comparative performance, future trends, and global product development alignment.

Process Clubs

Process clubs are gatherings of people with a passion for one or two processes. The members should come from multiple S&OP teams and global regions. Each process club is responsible for improving the analytics used in S&OP.

Process clubs deal with differences in definition of core analytical values. For example, what is an order when calculating a service performance metric? Some may think an order is one that is entered by the customer, no matter the condition. Some may think an order is one that is accepted by the company after errors in content or policy are corrected. An order for delivery last week would not normally be allowed to be entered as is and have a past-due condition from the outset. What is inventory? Where do you include in-transit between profit centers? The idea is to have metrics and analytics that can be compared across S&OP teams.

The process clubs can have productive discussions about engaging the correct people in the process, overcoming barriers to cultural change, and many other topics.

The process club program is a major continuous improvement element. Process clubs can be used to help an S&OP team move past a stalled installation by sharing experiences and approaches.

We recommend an active schedule of process club meetings at least quarterly. The advent of video conference capabilities in laptop computers has rendered the process club idea a very practical and economical program.

Looking Back

Chapter 7 brings us through the transition to the new culture of market-savvy S&OP. The journey is truly transformational. And, it continues as you develop a change culture that is constantly updating and realigning, primarily due to your own strategic initiatives but also as you sense the competitive forces changing and your customer's strategies changing.

Here are the major lessons of Chapter 7:

♦ A methodical transformational approach is required, not an IT system and not a wish list.

♦ Six agents of change are included in a transition model.

♦ The model provides a quick reference synopsis of the entire transition plan and strategy on one chart used by the team and senior management to enhance participation.

♦ The major phases of each transition work step are to be shown on a transition Gantt chart: design, proof and test, educate, execute, and rollout and monitor.

♦ A process rating and scoring technique should be used to mark progress in the development of the 26 market-savvy S&OP processes.

♦ Formal quarterly audits bring the transition orchestration to points of crescendo where people stop, take note, and realign the transition work.

♦ A three-day external audit is used to bring the transformational journey to a satisfactory conclusion.

♦ Annual external audits of one day each keep the process execution sharp and current.

♦ The segment-level S&OP can be expanded to a profit center and a global process with ease, once the individual segment S&OPs are in place.

♦ Process clubs are used to help individual teams move past sticking points in the transition journey and act as the vehicle of continuous improvement.

Case Study: Medical Technology Company

A publically held medical technology company developed and manu-factured lasers for corrective eye surgery. The company was in the industry from the beginning. Along the way, it decided its products were not being adopted by eye surgery centers fast enough. As a result, the company went into competition with eye surgeons, open-ing and operating its own surgery centers. The plan backfired. The market began to switch loyalty to competitors with comparable prod-ucts. Market share was forfeited, and cash flow turned negative.

A new management team was hired to change the downward spiral and bring the company back into profit and growth. We were hired to assist.

Situation. Cash flow was negative because of high investments in underutilized assets. The lasers had to be produced and then sent to the surgery centers, where they generated revenue only when they were actually used. The company would receive payment for each eye surgery done upon notice over the Internet directly from the machine itself.

The company was valued at the value of its cash reserve. The investors were not placing any value on the future growth or cash-flow potential of the company.

The new management team sought relief from declining market share through acquisition. A new laser technology had been developed by a small startup R&D company in the southeastern United States. The new technology solved one of the biggest complaints about com-plications from the standard surgery.

The manufacturing facility of the new acquisition was attached to its R&D center. Being of an R&D heritage, the culture allowed scientists to stop production for every idea germinating in their fertile brains. The company did not actually ship equipment at anywhere near the pace required to capture enough market share for comfort before com-petition caught on and hit the market with competing products.

Worse, the suppliers to the acquisition's manufacturing facility were the very same small R&D support shops used during product development. The suppliers were good at making one-of-a-kind sub-assemblies and circuit boards, but they had no capability to ramp up to production volumes with high levels of productivity and no automation to help sustain quality and repeatability.

One alternative was to move production from the acquisition's facility in the USA to the company's existing production facility in Europe. The factory in Europe had significant experience in laser manufacturing with similar manufacturing technology as in the acquisition's factory in the USA.

Actions. A cultural change process was undertaken in the European plant to develop a cross-functional management team able to handle high levels of change. The management leads of each functional area were encouraged to share leadership from month to month as a way of gaining respect for each other's particular challenges. The people in production were hired from engineering schools and technical positions. They could thus work with technical specifications of products and create standard work practices, without lengthy industrial engineering programs typical of manufacturing facilities using people who were skilled but less technically educated.

All six agents of the transition model were activated to achieve change in the European plant. The acquisition's manufacturing facility was totally resistant to change from an R&D culture to a production culture.

One of the biggest obstacles to the transition in the European facility came from U.S. manufacturing management, principally from the acquisition's management. The team in Europe was primarily female; only the quality control department was headed by a male. The gender problem actually became a major factor, much to our chagrin. The leadership box would stay red, if we were using a colored transition chart (Figure 7-1, shown in black-and-white only) until we finally had enough performance data to convince the associated leadership of the strength of the shared management approach with females in charge.

The new laser was transferred out of the U.S. plant to the European plant when the change culture in Europe was ready. New high-technology suppliers were identified and contracted to provide lower-cost components.

Business Results Achieved. Shipments of the new laser began to rise quickly. The market-share capture took place before the competition had a chance to finalize their "me-too" product offerings. Cash flow improved significantly. Based on the improved cash flow, the market valuation for the company increased.

A major strategic player became interested in the company and one day announced it wanted to buy the company for nine times its valuation when the new management team took over. The deal was struck and the shares changed hands. The acquiring company management was initially shocked to find a nearly all-female management team steaming along in a European plant with excellent performance metrics. The new management discussed needing to make an immediate "correction." Fortunately, they did nothing for several months. The new management was pleased with the cash flow and eventually became resigned to not fixing what was not broken in Europe.

Time to Start

You may now be wondering: Where do I go from here?

1. Form a team, a cross-functional team.
2. Do the work described in the Wright Medical Technology case study at the end of Chapter 5.

3. Calculate a quantitative goal for cash-flow improvement. This is a big hairy audacious goal.

4. Begin the education.

Market-savvy S&OP will generate profound benefits for your company. The cost of not implementing is probably the loss of the entire business. Most businesses fail because they lose contact with their customers. Businesses grow when they have the cash to fund products and programs to deliver the value the customer desires.

The market-driven supply chain will become a competitive weapon. The competitors who are first to implement will have a significant competitive advantage, similar to being first to market with a new product. So take the challenge and change your culture to a customer-centric one with high growth and strong cash flow. At the end of the day, it is more fun to work in a market-savvy culture and to win.

Index